THE WINES AND WINERIES OF AMERICA'S NORTHWEST

THE WINES AND WINERIES OF AMERICA'S NORTHWEST

The Premium Wines of Oregon, Washington, and Idaho

by Ted Jordan Meredith

map drawings by Cynthia Lenz

Nexus Press
Kirkland, Washington

Library of Congress Catalog Card Number: 86-061599
ISBN 0-936666-03-X

Additional copies of this book may be obtained by sending $12.95 (Washington residents also include sales tax) plus $1.25 for shipping to:

Nexus Press
P.O. Box 911
Kirkland, WA 98083

Bookseller rates available on request.

Printed in the United States of America by Snohomish Publishing, Snohomish, Washington.

Dedicated to Leon D. Adams—

—not only a consummate scholar and chronicler of winegrowing in America, but a catalyst for the American winegrowing industry itself. His landmark work, The Wines of America, *laid the foundation for us later generations of upstart wine writers.*

CONTENTS

AMERICA'S NORTHWEST

OREGON

WASHINGTON

IDAHO

MONTANA

AMERICA'S NORTHWEST

THE NORTHWEST REGION

WINE GRAPE ACREAGE
16,500 acres

MAJOR WINEGROWING REGIONS
OREGON: Willamette Valley, Umpqua Valley
WASHINGTON: Columbia Valley, Yakima Valley
IDAHO: Snake River Valley

MAJOR GRAPE VARIETIES
Riesling, Chardonnay, Chenin Blanc, Pinot Noir,
Cabernet Sauvignon, Sauvignon Blanc

LEADING WINES
Pinot Noir, Cabernet Sauvignon, Chardonnary, Semillon,
Sauvignon Blanc, Merlot, Riesling, Gewuztraminer,
Chenin Blanc, Pinot Gris, Lemberger

Clustered together in America's Northwest, it is easy to think that the wines of the Northwest states, Oregon, Washington, and Idaho, would be similar. There are similarities, but also very great differences. The Northwest's bold and dramatic geology and geography are striking to the eye. Their effects on the Northwest's winegrowing climates are no less bold and striking. America's Northwest winegrowing region is not characterized by a uniform sameness, but by great diversity in land and climate.

Measured in terms of the U. C. Davis climate classification system, Washington state by itself embraces the full climatic range from Region I on the scale through Region V, a range that includes the world's coolest winegrowing climates, typified by Germany's Moselle and France's Champagne district, through the world's warmest, typified by the winegrowing climates of Morocco, Algeria, and the San Joaquin Valley of California.

In the Northwest, nearly all vineyards are on winegrowing sites classified as Region I or II, as are most of the world's premium winegrowing areas. The U. C. Davis system, however, only begins to capture the critical characteristics of premium winegrowing climates. This is no more evident than in the Northwest, where profoundly different winegrowing climates fall into the same Region on the U. C. Davis system.

Parts of the Willamette Valley in Oregon and the Columbia Valley in Washington, for example, are classified as Region I, but the climate and wines from the Willamette Valley, a temperate winegrowing region under the moderating influence of Pacific marine air, are very different from the climate and wines of the near desert Columbia Valley environment.

The Northwest region is divided into two major, and radically different, climates. The towering Cascade Mountain Range, running north to south through Washington and Oregon, divides and defines the two major climates. West of the Cascades, the climate is moderated by marine air from the Pacific Ocean. To the east, the Cascades block the flow of marine air, creating a rain shadow that extends for hundreds of miles. West of the Cascades, the land is lushly vegetated. East of the Cascades, the land is a near desert.

Nearly all of Washington's grapes are grown east of the Cascade Mountain Range. Except for a few growing sites, most of western Washington is too cool, cloudy, and rainy for wine grapes. In Oregon, a low lying range of coastal mountains partially interrupts the flow of marine air, and most of Oregon's grapes are grown west of the Cascade Mountain Range, in the temperate valleys bordered by the Cascade Mountain Range to the east and the Coast Range to the west.

America's Northwest is an exceptional wine producing region in many ways. The Northwest's grape wine industry is based virtually entirely on the *Vitis vinifera* grape species, the species responsible for all the world's greatest wines. The famous French Bordeaux and Burgundy wines are made from vinifera grapes. Cabernet Sauvignon, Chardonnay, Pinot Noir, and Riesling are examples of vinifera varieties. The Northwest produces more premium vinifera grape wines than any other winegrowing region in America, except California. Most other regions rely heavily on native grape species or hybrids, but premium vinifera grape wines are the glory of the Northwest region.

It is important to remember that, although the winegrowing climates in the Northwest region have similarities, the differences are many and quite dramatic. The chapters for each state outline the differences in more detail, but it is well to keep in mind that reference to the Northwest winegrowing region in no way implies a single growing climate or a single style of wine. The differences are great, and so are the opportunities for the wine aficionado.

From Madeleine Angevine to port, from steely dry Rieslings to intensely sweet botrytised Rieslings, from Pinot Noir to Cabernet Sauvignon, from Sauvignon Blanc to Chardonnay, from Pinot Gris to Semillon, and on and on—America's Northwest is rich with wine.

NORTHWEST GEOLOGY— WINEGROWING ALCHEMY ALONG THE PACIFIC RING OF FIRE

America's Northwest is one of the most geologically active regions in the world. The massive explosion of Mount St. Helens on May 18, 1980 symbolizes the powerful dynamics of the region. Equivalent to the force of a 10 megaton hydrogen bomb, the explosion was heard as far as Montana, two states away. The blast propelled powdered rock twelve miles high. For hundreds of miles to the east, the sky darkened, and ash fell like a heavy snow.

Before the eruption blew the mountain apart, Mount St. Helens rose 9,677 feet above sea level, one of several volcanic peaks along the Cascade Mountain Range. Barely touched by erosion, its nearly perfect symmetry prior to the eruption attests to its youthful existence. By far the youngest mountain in America, much of Mount St. Helens is less than 2,000 years old.

Mount St. Helens is one of many active, dormant, or extinct volcanoes embracing the Pacific Ocean along what is known as the Pacific ring of fire. The eruption of Mount St. Helens was awesome, yet it was a relatively small event, the metaphorical tip of a geologic iceberg, an event that speaks of much more powerful events that created it, and indeed, created and shaped the Northwest's landscape and climates—and thus, too, its wines.

The now widely accepted theory of plate tectonics tells us that the earth's crust is composed of about a dozen moving plates. The plates move at different rates in different directions. If the plates slip past each other, they may tear away portions of themselves at their perimeters. California's famed San Andreas Fault is an example of this type of interaction. In the Pacific Ocean Basin, the oceanic plates are pulling away from each other at the crests of ridges along the ocean floor. As the plates separate, molten basalt wells up to fill the rift, pushing the oceanic plate into the continental plate. This type of interaction is taking place off the Oregon and Washington coast, causing the oceanic crust to collide with the North American Continent.

As the ocean floor and the continent collide, the heavier oceanic plate sinks beneath the lighter continental plate, scraping away its topmost sedimentary layers against continent, uplifting the continental perimeter and widening and raising it with the materials from the ocean's crust. The Coast Range Mountains of Oregon were created by this phenomenon, as was the Willamette Valley itself, uplifted out of the sea. In the context of wine, the Coast Range shelters Oregon's Willamette Valley from the cloudy, cool, wet, marine air, creating an ideal climate for winegrowing. Without the Coast Range Mountains, the climate would be too cool and moist to grow wine grapes. We owe our glass of Oregon Pinot Noir to the collision of the ocean floor with the North

American Continent.

As the oceanic crust sinks beneath the continent, it moves deeper and further inland, partially melting as it descends. Approximately 100 miles inland, part of the molten basalt of the ocean floor returns to the surface as a chain of volcanoes paralleling the coastline. The towering Cascade Mountain Range, running north and south through Washington and Oregon, was formed by this fiery phenomenon.

Many of the world's great mountain ranges reach their high elevations from already high beginning points of the surrounding landscape, but the Cascades rise from the coastal lowland, sometimes thrusting more than 10,000 feet into the Northwest sky. The highest volcanic peak, Mount Rainier, rises 14,410 feet above sea level. Even at a great distance, the mountain dominates the skyline. Its active glaciers cover 35 square miles.

The Cascade Mountains shape the Northwest climate. The wall of mountains blocks the flow of marine air, causing heavy precipitation on the western side of the mountains, and a near desert on the eastern side. The vast Columbia Valley, east of the Cascades, is the largest and most productive winegrowing region in the Northwest. The Columbia Valley's winegrowing climate is unique and complex. A discussion of its climate in the Washington section of this book details the climate's characteristics and its effects on the grapes and the wines. For now it is sufficient to say that we owe our glass of Washington Cabernet Sauvignon to the tumultuous volcanic thrustings of the Cascade Mountains, the Northwest's most prominent geologic feature.

We also owe a measure of thanks to the Columbia River. The wall of mountains that divides the Northwest's two major climates is breached only at one point, where the powerful Columbia River cuts through the Cascades on its way to the Pacific Ocean. Just enough marine air flows through this breach to lengthen the growing season east of the Cascade Mountains and moderate the cold, wintertime, inland climate. The Columbia provides drainage for three-quarters of the Northwest region. One of its ma-jor tributaries, the Snake River, cuts a path into Idaho. Even at this far distance, more than 300 miles inland, the Pacific marine influence, courtesy of the Columbia River and its tributaries, makes winegrowing in Idaho's western valleys possible.

The Cascade Mountains were formed in several geologic episodes. About 25 million years ago, the old Cascade volcanoes stopped erupting. Around 15 million years ago, volcanic activity resumed, but further inland. The newer volcanoes were of a different kind. Fissures miles long released floods of basalt lava. The massive quantities of highly fluid lava may have moved as fast as 30 miles an hour across the Northwest landscape. One of the larger flows covered an area of more than 20,000 square miles within a matter of hours. Some flows were more than 200 feet thick. Concentrated in central and eastern Washington and Oregon, the Columbia Plateau lava floods covered nearly 250,000 square miles, reaching into Idaho and northern California, burying the existing landscape of hills and valleys with basalt. In recorded history, there is nothing even remotely comparable.

The Columbia Valley, the Northwest's largest winegrowing region, covering nearly a third the state of Washington, encompasses the northernmost part of the vast Columbia Plateau. Arching across eastern and central Washington, the path of the Columbia River itself was shaped by the floods of basalt lava. The largest volcano in the Columbia Plateau, sometimes called the Grande Ronde Volcano by geologists, was centered in southeastern Washington and northeastern Oregon. Lava from this great volcano flowed over and created what is now the Columbia Valley, pushing the Columbia River's antecedent drainages northward and westward, forcing it to follow the lowest path where the farthest reaches of the gently sloping Grande Ronde Volcano met the Okanogan Highlands to the north and the Cascade Mountains on the west. Washington's prime winegrowing region, the nearly flat 23,000 square mile Columbia Valley, is actually the gently sloping side of an ancient volcano.

Although the eastern part of the Columbia

Valley is almost flat, the western part, where most of the valley's vineyards are located, is contoured with high ridges. Within the last 10 million years, the northward movement of the west coast has caused the basalt lava flows to buckle and form large steep folds. This folding process created and shaped the Yakima Valley, one of Washington's most important winegrowing regions. The Ahtanum Ridge, Rattlesnake Hills, and Horse Heaven Hills, all basalt folds, define the shape of the valley and separate it from the rest of the Columbia Valley from which it was created.

Running in a generally east to west direction, the folded basalt ridges offer shelter from the cold of the north and provide sunny southern slopes for winegrowing. In other parts of the western Columbia Valley, Paterson Ridge, and the Wahluke and Royal Slope, the lower reaches of the Saddle Mountains and Frenchman Hills, are winegrowing sites created by the buckling and arching of old basalt lava flows.

The rivers were not halted by the buckling of the lava plain. As fast as the basalt ridges rose, the rivers cut through them. Nowhere is this more dramatic than along parts of the Columbia River, where towering basalt cliffs plummet vertically to the river below, exposing the angular basalt columns formed by the great lava floods. Along the Idaho and Oregon border, another kind of uplift of the Blue Mountains forced the Snake River to carve a corridor through hard, dense, greenstone rock, creating the aptly named Hell's Canyon, the deepest canyon in North America. Further up river, in Idaho's winegrowing country, the Snake River Lava Plain dips across southern Idaho in a broad crescent.

About 12 million years ago, the great basalt floods subsided, and the volcanic activity along the Cascade Mountains resumed before again slipping into quiescence, marking the last eruptive period for what are now known as the western Cascades. Covered by a succession of lava flows and eroded over many millions of years, the western Cascades consist of a broad chain of high ridges and ravines. Their appearance does not suggest their volcanic origins.

Within the last several million years, however, yet another eruptive period began building a different type of volcano along the Cascade Range. Built on the base of the old western Cascades, the modern high Cascades form a towering chain of volcanic cones. Before destructive eruptions and glacial erosion took their toll, some of the volcanic peaks thrust more than three miles into the Northwest sky. The current peaks, still very young mountains, are only slightly less spectacular. Their height blocks the Pacific marine air and transforms the Columbia Valley climate more dramatically than the lower, older western Cascades ever could. The modern Cascade Mountain Range, more than any other single geologic feature, determines and defines the Northwest winegrowing climate.

Even in western Oregon, where their climatic effect is less obvious, the Cascades shelter the winegrowing environment from inland temperature extremes, lengthening the growing season, and maintaining a temperate climate. The volcanic past leaves its traces—and foundations, throughout the Northwest wine country. The lava floods from the Grande Ronde volcano made their way to the Pacific Ocean, covering parts of Oregon's northern Coast Range and the northern Willamette Valley. Many small volcanic hills dot the western Oregon landscape providing slopes for modern day vineyards. In the northern Willamette Valley, Oregon's largest city, Portland, is flanked by clusters of volcanic hills built on the older basalt from the Columbia Plateau lava floods.

Not only lava flooded the Northwest. During the last ice age, some 16,000 years ago, a massive glacier pushed southward from Canada into Idaho, damming the Clark Fork River. The waters of the Clark Fork backed up into the high mountain valleys of western Montana, forming Glacial Lake Missoula. Two thousand feet deep, the lake contained some 500 cubic miles of water. Inevitably, the rising water floated and broke its glacial dam, instantly releasing a wall of water, and creating one of the world's greatest floods.

The floodwaters raced across the Columbia Valley, scouring away the soil and exposing the hard basalt from the ancient lava floods. All the "normal" flood effects were magnified exponentially. The flood of Glacial Lake Missoula scattered boulders weighing many tons across the Columbia Valley. Ripple marks, like those seen in the sand at the bottom of a stream, still remain today, but these are as much as 30 feet high and hundreds of feet from crest to crest. The moving water created huge gravel bars—made of boulders, miles long and more than a hundred feet high.

After racing across the Columbia Valley, the floodwaters dammed up behind the narrow Wallula Gap near what is today the Tri-Cities area of Pasco, Richland, and Kennewick, creating a temporary lake a thousand feet deep. The briefly stilled floodwaters released much of their sediment in the Pasco Basin, soils for the vines that would follow many millennia later.

The floodwaters then raced through the Columbia Gorge, the narrow breach in the Cascade Mountain Range, reaching a depth of nearly 1,000 feet, scouring away the soil from the underlying bedrock, and ripping away the lower portions of tributary streams, creating precipices and waterfalls. Where the Columbia takes a sharp northward bend before entering the Pacific Ocean, the floodwaters were dammed once again, flooding across Oregon's northern Willamette Valley to a depth of 400 feet. The floodwaters receded, leaving soils and boulders traceable to the mountains of Montana.

This spectacular flood happened not only once, but as many as 40 times, as the massive moving glacier again and again dammed the waters of the Clark Fork River in Montana only to release them in a series of violent torrents. The layers of sediment in some of the Northwest winegrowing valleys correspond to the shoreline markings in the mountains of Montana, modern day traces representing each filling and empty-

The Columbia River, east of the Cascades—from the Washington side looking across into Oregon.

ing of the great glacial lake.

Roughly comparable to the latitudes of France's Burgundy and Bordeaux regions, the northerly latitude of America's Northwest winegrowing region is an important factor in the quality of the region's wines—yet the northerly latitude is far from the whole story. Mooselake, Minnesota, Roundup, Montana, and parts of Mongolia are also at a similar latitude, but little can be said for them as premium winegrowing regions. Clearly, other factors are at work in the winegrowing regions of America's Northwest.

Pacific Ocean marine air, the Coast and Cascade Mountain Ranges, the Columbia River, the great floods of water and molten earth, these elements, and many more, shape the Northwest landscape, shape the Northwest climate, and shape the taste and style of Northwest wine. The wines of America's Northwest are the newly born product of an ancient and powerful alchemy, the great workings of earth, air, fire, and water, antiquity's four primordial elements, distilled in the crucible of America's Northwest. These are the roots of the Northwest vine.

OREGON

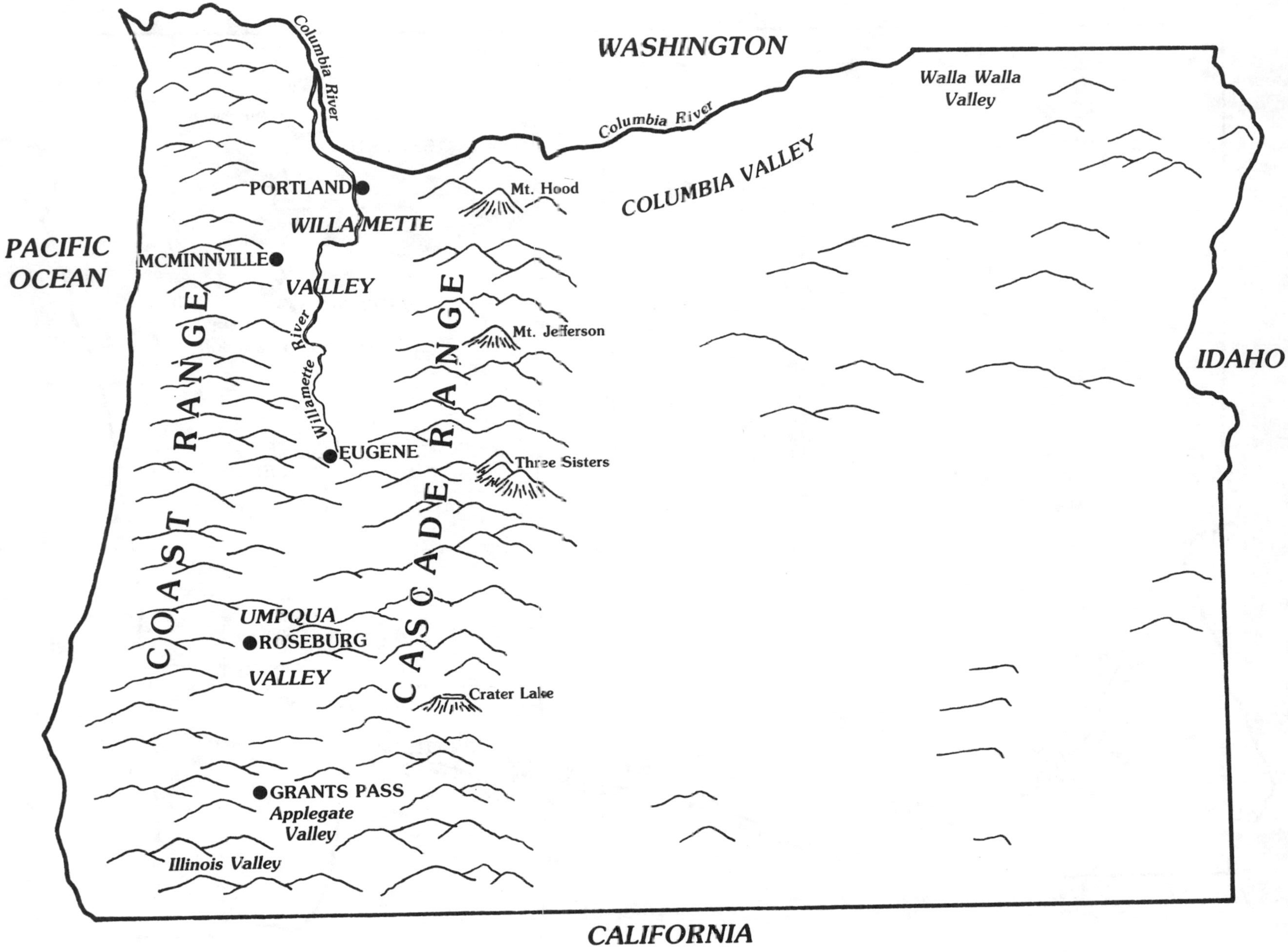

WASHINGTON

IDAHO

CALIFORNIA

PACIFIC OCEAN

Walla Walla Valley

COLUMBIA VALLEY

Columbia River

COLUMBIA VALLEY

Columbia River

Mt. Hood

Mt. Jefferson

Three Sisters

Crater Lake

PORTLAND

WILLAMETTE

VALLEY

Willamette River

EUGENE

CASCADE RANGE

COAST RANGE

McMINNVILLE

UMPQUA

ROSEBURG

VALLEY

GRANTS PASS

Applegate Valley

Illinois Valley

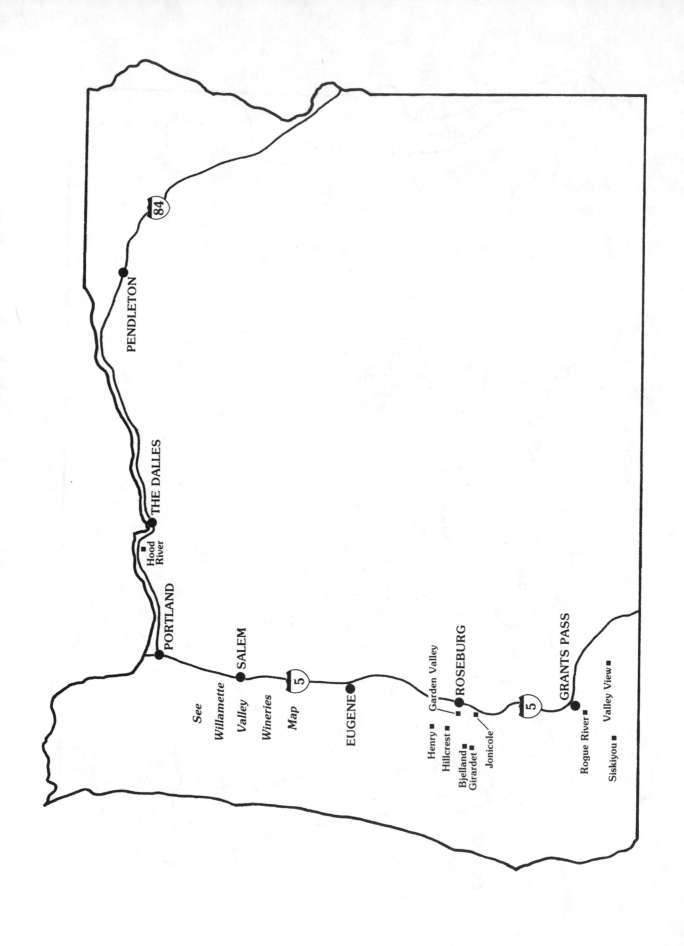

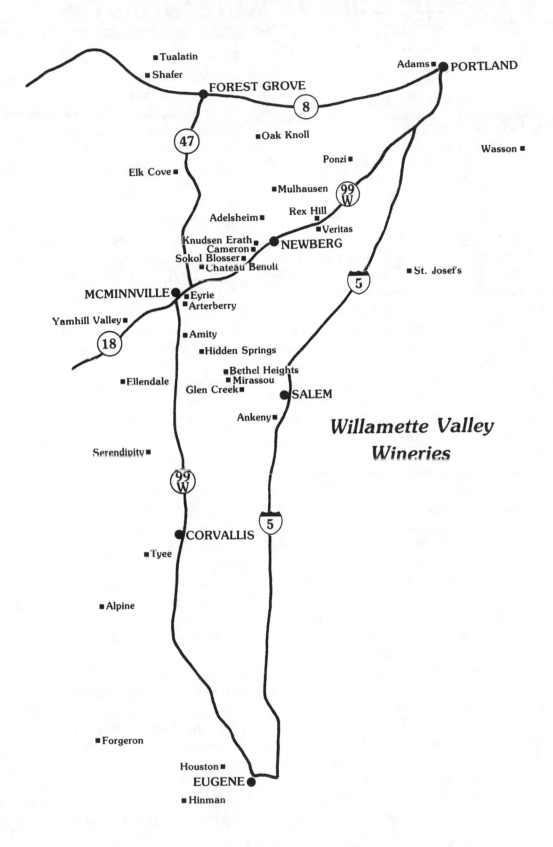

Willamette Valley
Wineries

THE OREGON WINE INDUSTRY

WINE GRAPE ACREAGE
4,500 acres

WINEGROWING REGIONS
*Willamette Valley, Umpqua Valley, Southwest Oregon,
Columbia Gorge, Walla Walla Valley, Columbia Valley*

MAJOR GRAPE VARIETIES
Pinot Noir, Chardonnay, Riesling

LEADING WINES
Pinot Noir, Chardonnay, Riesling, Pinot Gris

Two decades ago, an Oregon State University publication advised that premium vinifera wine grape varieties were not well suited to Oregon climates. The publication recommended *Vitis labrusca* varieties instead. At about the same time, faculty at the University of California at Davis were warning starry-eyed students that the idea of winegrowing in Oregon was worse than foolish. The grapes as well as their high hopes, it was said, would be rotted by endless rains and killed by spring and fall frosts. Two decades, many thousands of acres of premium vinifera wine grapes, and numerous international accolades later, it is reasonably safe to say that the early advice may not have been the best. The stubborn starry-eyed students persevered.

Winemaking and vinifera grape growing came to Oregon more than a century ago. In the 1850s early settlers brought cuttings to Oregon by way of the Oregon Trail, and from California, to southwest Oregon. By the 1880s, Oregon's fledgling wine industry was centered in Jackson County, near the California border, in the far southwestern part of the state. By that time, winegrowing was active in the Willamette Valley as well.

Some of the early varieties were not the best for wine, and Prohibition struck before the wine industry was well developed. At Repeal, a farm winery law encouraged a flurry of small scale wineries. There were 28 such wineries by 1937, most making wines in a sweet style, often from fruits and berries. Demand for this type of wine decreased over time, and by 1960, only four wineries remained. One year later, the Oregon wine industry was reborn.

In 1961, Richard Sommer bought land in the Umpqua Valley, near the town of Roseburg, and planted cuttings from premium vinifera wine grapes he brought from California. Two years later, Sommer bonded his winery, Hillcrest Vineyard. The Oregon wine renaissance had begun. Sommer focused his efforts on Riesling, a grape that still today remains a mainstay of the Oregon wine industry.

In 1965, two years after Hillcrest was bonded, David Lett came to Oregon with the singular intent of finding a climate suitable for the Burgundian grape varieties, and most particularly, a climate for Pinot Noir. Passing by the warmer Roseburg area in southern Oregon, Lett settled in the Willamette Valley, in the Dundee Hills, southwest of Portland, and founded The Eyrie Vineyards. Lett's choice of Pinot Noir proved far-sighted. Today the grape is the glory of Oregon's wine industry.

Dick Erath, of the Knudsen Erath Winery, and a few others followed shortly thereafter in the 1960s. By the end of the 1970s, Oregon's wine industry was growing at a rapid pace, most of the newcomers gravitating to the northern Willamette Valley. A century ago, the wine industry was centered in the southernmost part of western Oregon near the California border. With the wine renaissance, emphasis shifted northward, first to the Umpqua Valley near Roseburg, then to the northern Willamette Valley, still the center of Oregon's wine industry. Now, every winegrowing region in the state is experiencing expansion, including Oregon's sliver of the Columbia Valley, east of the Cascade Mountains.

Growth in the Columbia Valley region may present an image problem for the Oregon wine industry. Oregon winegrowers have been committed to the temperate, cool climate, western Oregon winegrowing regions with near religious fervor. In grape variety and style, Columbia Valley wines have far more in common with their Washington counterparts than with western Oregon wines. Inexpensive land and an agribusiness environment compounds the potential image problem. Oregon's Columbia Valley could rapidly outstrip western Oregon in wine production. Oregon might no longer be singularly synonymous with Pinot Noir and other cool climate western Oregon grape varieties and wines.

To some degree, Oregon has already coped well with a similar image "problem." In the 1970s and early 1980s, Washington had many more grapes than wineries, Oregon many more wineries than grapes. For a time, most Oregon wineries released some wines made solely from Washington's Columbia Valley grapes, identified as "Washington" on the label. Now, with the BATF approved viticultural designation, "Columbia Valley" will play a greater role in the wine's identifying label. The increasing notoriety of Oregon wines may, itself, prove to be the solution for the potential identity problem, as the identity of Oregon's winegrowing regions emerge more clearly. Oregon will have "Willamette Valley Pinot Noir" just as California has "Napa Valley Cabernet Sauvignon."

On average, Oregon's wineries and vineyards are much smaller than those of either Washington or Idaho. Knudsen Erath, Sokol Blosser, and Tualatin are Oregon's largest premium grape wineries, though none produce more than 100,000 gallons a year. The Oregon industry is not dominated by huge vineyards or large agricultural corporations. In contrast with Washington's Columbia Valley, as an example, western Oregon's prime vineyard acreage is expensive, and large tracts of land are not readily available. Roughly three-quarters of Oregon's vineyards are no larger than 20 acres. The existing agricultural environment is not one of expansive agribusiness, but of relatively small orchards and farms in a fairly populous, rural, agricultural community.

Oregon's many, small, estate wineries serve well the pursuit of quality wines with distinctive stylistic signatures, but marketing the wines becomes all the more difficult. Rapid growth in the industry has made it more critical for Oregon to market wines outside the state, but for very good reasons, distributors and wholesalers prefer ample quantities of a few "labels" rather than small quantities of many labels. In this respect, Oregon's many small wineries put the wine industry at a disadvantage.

Some measure of relief has come from national and international press, very favorably comparing Oregon Pinot Noir with much more expensive Burgundies. Small estate wineries with individualistic styles are becoming less of a marketing burden and more of an important selling feature. This image will continue to strengthen as Oregon wines becomes better known.

Still, a much larger winery would help penetrate markets outside the state and create a presence for Oregon wine, much as Chateau Ste. Michelle has done for Washington wine. Fortunately, a much larger Oregon winery is on the horizon, nothing the size of Chateau Ste. Michelle, but much larger than Oregon's currently largest wineries. Montinore Vineyards, in the northern Willamette Valley, will eventually produce about one and a half million bottles of Oregon wine each year.

Most Oregon winegrowers are white collar professionals who have turned to winegrowing out of an interest in fine wines and a rural lifestyle. Few had connections with agriculture prior to winegrowing. Most Oregon wineries are winery estates. The winery and winegrower's residence are adjacent to the vineyards, and the winegrower literally lives with his vines and wines. An urban winery is rare, and even in those rare cases, the urban wineries are associated with their own vineyards.

Oregon's wine labeling regulations are the strictest in the nation. If a grape variety is used in the name of a wine, the wine must be no less than 90 percent of that variety, except Cabernet Sauvignon, which may be blended with up to 25 percent of other Bordeaux grape varieties. Generic names, such as Chablis and Burgundy, are prohibited.

The economics of Oregon winegrowing are

hard. Vines are cane pruned rather than cordon pruned, a method requiring greater skill, attention, and time. Crop yields are small. Some years are too cool. Rain during harvest is not uncommon, and each year's crop faces destruction by unending waves of migrating robins. In most instances, Oregon winegrowers chose the winegrowing enterprise not because it was the easiest way to make money (which in Oregon, it surely is not), but out of an abiding commitment to the enterprise itself, and the profound belief that Oregon is the most qualitatively important winegrowing region in America. Oregon is not the easiest region in America to produce fine wine, but it is easily one of the best.

OREGON WINEGROWING REGIONS

Like Washington, Oregon is divided into two very different climates by the towering Cascade Mountain Range. The Cascades, running north to south through both states, create a barrier to the Pacific marine air. On the eastern side of the Cascades, the climate is very warm and dry, and the land is a near desert. West of the Cascades, the climate is cooler, temperate, and more moist.

Unlike western Washington, western Oregon experiences less of the direct effect of the cool, moist, marine air. Western Oregon's Coast Range forms a continuous partial barrier to the onshore Pacific air flow. Running along the Oregon coast, from the state's northern border southward, the Coast Range partially blocks the marine air. Western Oregon's climate is consequently warmer, drier, and sunnier than western Washington's climate. Enough of the marine effect remains, however, so that western Oregon is ideally suited to well-known cool climate vinifera grape varieties such as Pinot Noir, Chardonnay, and Riesling. Unlike Washington, Oregon's main winegrowing regions are in the western part of the state.

Recently, vineyards have been planted east of the Cascade Mountains on the previously undeveloped Oregon side of the Columbia River Valley. The openness and availability of land and the agribusiness economic environment suggest that a large portion of Oregon's wine production could one day come from grapes grown in the Columbia Valley, a climate greatly different from western Oregon's major winegrowing regions. As yet this has not happened, and Oregon remains firmly identified with the wine grapes and wine styles of the western part of the state.

The Willamette Valley, Oregon's coolest winegrowing region, is the source for most of Oregon's wine grapes. Although the Willamette Valley does not totally dominate the state's wine industry to the same degree that the Columbia Valley dominates Washington winegrowing, the Willamette Valley is by far western Oregon's largest winegrowing region in size, vineyard acreage, and number of wineries.

WILLAMETTE VALLEY

In January 1984, the Bureau of Alcohol Tobacco and Firearms (BATF) formally recognized the Willamette Valley as a designated viticultural area. Approximately 170 miles long and 60 miles wide at its greatest breadth, the Willamette Valley viticultural area covers 5,200 square miles. Forming an elongated "V" narrowing to the south, the Willamette Valley runs from Oregon's northern border on the Columbia River north of Portland to the Calapooya Mountains south of the city of Eugene, half way down the state.

Bordered on the west by the Coast Range Mountains and on the east by the foothills of the Cascade Mountain Range, the Willamette Valley is a mosaic of prairie, open savanna with scattered oak trees, grasslands, and forest and woodlands of Oregon white oak and fir trees. Except for a slight extension into southwest Washington, the Willamette Valley vegetation pattern is unique in the Northwest.

Willamette Valley vineyards are located on wooded hillsides in the western part of the valley, along the foothills of the Coast Range; on the slopes of the valley's volcanic hills; or the many hillsides that have been eroded into the basalt lava plain during the last 20 million years or so.

The Willamette Valley viticultural area generally extends no higher than 1000 feet into the foothills of the surrounding mountain ranges. Willamette Valley winegrowers have found that south facing hillside slopes between 300 feet and 1,000 feet elevation make the best growing sites. Higher slopes are too cool and rainy. Lower slopes risk frost hazards. Nighttime cool air settles in lower elevations, and the vines do not warm as rapidly to the summer sun. Not only does cool air pool on the valley floor, but the heavier moist soils are slow to warm, and delay vine growth in spring. The heavier soils on the valley floor also produce more vegetative growth, delaying grape ripening. The relatively flat valley floor makes up much of the Willamette Valley, but the land is not well suited to grape growing.

In this northerly climate, south facing hillside slopes capture the most energy from the sun. Parts of the Willamette Valley are subject to frequent, morning, low clouds, a reminder that the Pacific Ocean is not far away, and that the Coast Range Mountains only partially block the onshore flow of marine air. Because the clouds tend to dissipate toward afternoon, southwest slopes are considered ideal, taking advantage of the afternoon sun.

Winter freezing is not a problem for the Willamette Valley's temperate climate. Frost is seldom a problem, but in less than ideal growing sites, such as those at very high elevations or on the valley floor, spring frost can strike in unusually cold years. Rain is moderate during the summer months, but increases in fall and winter, and often aggravates the grape harvest.

The Willamette Valley climate is classified as Region I, the coolest of five heat regions in the

The grape harvest.

U. C. Davis classification system. A useful, but very rough guide, the Davis system lumps together a wide range of growing climates under the Region I moniker, and does not capture or address important distinctions that are key to the success of many of the worlds most important grape varieties and winegrowing regions.

In many respects, the Willamette Valley has more direct similarities with notable European winegrowing regions than do other American winegrowing areas. In itself, this does not necessarily mean that the Willamette Valley is inherently superior to other American winegrowing regions, but it begins to explain the interlinkage of the Willamette Valley winegrowing terrain and climate with its grape growing and winemaking practices, style of wine, and the philosophy and outlook of Willamette Valley winegrowers.

The Willamette Valley is a cool, marginal winegrowing climate. In California, as an example, cool climate grapes such as Pinot Noir are grown in the coolest growing sites (such as the Carneros area) of an otherwise very warm winegrowing region. In the Willamette Valley, as in the major European winegrowing regions, winegrowing sites are chosen in the opposite manner, and grapes are grown on the warmest sites of cool, marginal, winegrowing climates.

In Europe's premium winegrowing regions, grape varieties are not planted where they will ripen easily, but where they will ripen best. The

An integral part of the landscape, contouring and terracing are part of the regime for many new Oregon vineyards.

grapes are planted where, in most years, they will just become ripe—but no more than just ripe. European winegrowers expect that in some years the grapes will not fully ripen, a necessary paying of dues for the excellence of other years. Pinot Noir, for example, is not grown in Burgundy rather than Bordeaux simply out of tradition. In Bordeaux, a warmer climate than Burgundy, Pinot Noir would consistently produce "big" wines and ripen easily every year, but the quality would suffer. Pinot Noir ripens more quickly than the Bordeaux varieties, and requires the cooler climate of the Burgundy region. Similarly, the Bordeaux grape varieties (Cabernet Sauvignon, Merlot, etc.) are grown in the warmer Bordeaux region, but not in the even warmer Rhone Valley.

The best wine grapes and the best wines come from winegrowing regions where the grapes are carefully matched to the climate, the climate is marginal for the grape varieties, and the ripening of the grapes coincides with the end of the growing season. A winegrowing climate that ripens the grapes rapidly, early, and easily is also a climate that robs the grapes of their complex flavors, aromatics, and nuance. In Oregon, grape ripening does not come with a rush, but gradually, as summer changes into fall. In most vintages, the Oregon grape harvest occurs in early to mid October, depending on grape variety.

In Oregon, as in Europe's major winegrowing regions, vintages vary considerably from year to year, and in these cool marginal climates, the

vintages that are less good are almost always so because the year was too cool, rarely because the year was too warm or the grapes overripened or ripened too soon. The Willamette Valley is suited to a narrower range of grape varieties than many other American winegrowing regions, but the varieties that "fit" the Willamette Valley climate, such as the highly sensitive and fickle Pinot Noir grape, achieve an excellence of flavors and refinement rarely found elsewhere.

UMPQUA VALLEY

In April of 1984, the BATF formally recognized the Umpqua Valley viticultural area. One of Oregon's oldest grape growing regions, dating back to the 1800s, the Umpqua Valley remained largely dormant in the 1900s, until the early 1960s, when new winegrowing efforts in the Umpqua Valley hailed the rebirth of the Oregon wine industry and its modern day renaissance. Although most Oregon vineyard acreage is now located in the Willamette Valley to the north, the Umpqua Valley remains an important and interesting winegrowing region.

Located south of the Willamette Valley, and entirely within Douglas County in southwest Oregon, the Umpqua Valley covers approximately 1,200 square miles. Running north to south, the Umpqua Valley is approximately 70 miles long and 30 miles at its widest point. Bordered on the north and west by the Coast Range, on the south by the Klamath Mountains, and on the east by the foothills of the Cascade Mountains, the region is not a simple, open basin, but an interconnected series of many small mountains, hillsides, and river drainages. The more restrictive nature of the area lends itself to small or moderate size vineyards and wineries.

Like the Willamette Valley, the Umpqua Valley is classified as Region I on the U. C. Davis scale. The two climates are similar, but the Umpqua Valley is slightly drier and warmer, the growing season is slightly shorter, and summer and winter temperatures are slightly more extreme. None of the individual differences is major, but as a whole, they shape a different climate, particularly toward the southern end of the valley, where the higher mountains to the south and west block more of the Pacific marine air. Pine trees begin to replace the fir trees of the Willamette, and California oak (Quercus kelloggi) intermingles with Oregon oak (Quercus garryana).

The Umpqua Valley viticultural area extends no higher than an elevation of 1,000 feet. Above that elevation, the terrain rapidly becomes very steep and otherwise unsuitable for vineyards. Winter cold is not a problem, but frost, particularly in the spring, can be a threat. Vineyards are situated on the valley floor as well as hillside sites. The selection of grape varieties is quite varied, and has been dependent as much on the individual growing site and preference of the winegrower as any overall climatic imperative. Riesling, Chardonnay, and Pinot Noir predominate. Cabernet Sauvignon, among several other varieties, is grown on some sites, but it is not a major grape variety for the Umpqua Valley.

SOUTHWEST OREGON

Oregon's famed Rogue River begins in the Cascade Mountains east of the southern end of the Umpqua Valley. From there, the Rogue courses south and west along a twisting path to the Pacific Ocean. Passing through the Siskiyou and Klamath Mountains not far from the California border, the Rogue and its tributaries flow through several small valleys. The surrounding mountains shelter the valleys in varying degrees from the cool, moist, Pacific marine air. The valleys nearest the the ocean are the coolest and most moist, getting progressively warmer and drier toward the east.

These differences and distinctions are only relative to each other, however. All Southwest Oregon winegrowing areas have a shorter growing season and are warmer and drier than the winegrowing regions to the north. The Illinois Valley is the coolest of the major southwest

Oregon winegrowing areas, followed by the Applegate Valley, and Bear Creek Valley.

Southwest Oregon is classified as Regions I and II on the U. C. Davis scale. Cabernet Sauvignon, Chardonnay, Gewurztraminer, and Pinot Noir are the principal varieties. Located in more mountainous terrain and sheltered more from the tempering influences of the Pacific Ocean, spring frosts can be severe for southwest Oregon grape growers. Although grape acreage is modest, there are more grapes than the local wineries can handle. Southwest Oregon winegrowing has not yet matured into a stable industry, but its grape growing climates, unique in western Oregon, and its early successes call out for further development.

COLUMBIA GORGE, COLUMBIA VALLEY, AND WALLA WALLA VALLEY

The Columbia River forms most of Oregon's northern border with Washington. As the river passes through the Cascade Mountain Range, it forms an area known as the Columbia River Gorge. Further east, the vast Columbia Valley viticultural area, located almost entirely in Washington, dips across the Columbia River to the Oregon side of the border. The Walla Walla Valley, an easternmost part of the larger Columbia Valley, also extends into Oregon.

The slopes on the Oregon side of the valleys are generally more northerly facing, but otherwise the climate and terrain is very similar to the climate and terrain on the Washington side of the border. Unlike Washington, serious grape growing efforts on Oregon's part of the Columbia Valley are very recent. For more information on the Columbia Gorge, Columbia Valley, and Walla Walla Valley, refer to the entries in the Washington section of this book.

OREGON GRAPE VARIETIES

WESTERN OREGON GRAPE VARIETIES

Beginning with the pioneering days of the 1800s, and again with the rebirth of the wine industry in the 1960s, virtually all Oregon premium wines have been made from grapes grown in western Oregon. Except for miniscule plantings of native American and hybrid grapes, all Oregon wine grapes are vinifera. Oregon vineyards are smaller than those of most of the west coast winegrowing states. Roughly three-quarters of the vineyards in Oregon are 20 acres or less. A third of the vineyards have 5 acres or less, and only about 15 percent are larger than thirty acres. The average size of the vineyards is steadily increasing, however, with the maturation of the state's winegrowing industry.

More than any other Northwest state, Oregon is extensively experimenting with different clones of established grape varieties, as well as less common varieties that might be especially well suited to the growing climate. Virtually all of Oregon's grape vines have their clonal roots in California, issuing from selection programs dedicated to the development of clones best suited to California's much warmer growing climate. The California clones do not always match well with Oregon's cooler climate. Chardonnay is the most prominent case in point.

In 1976, Oregon State University began bringing in cooler climate clones and grape varieties from several European research stations. The time for testing, development, and commercial availability is necessarily lengthy, but the program promises yet further refinement for Oregon grape growing and Oregon wines. Two dozen Pinot Noir clones are under study. True Gamay Noir, true Pinot Blanc, and Auxerrois are among the many grape varieties under evaluation. Gamay Noir, the Gamay grape of Beaujolais (not to be confused with the Gamay clone of Pinot Noir) is generating special interest. Gamay Noir matures early and has a full, flavorful, fruity character and might play a role as a good quality, moderately priced red wine.

Pinot Noir, Riesling, and Chardonnay are the three most widely planted varieties. In the early days of the wine industry, Riesling predominated, but now Oregon's star, Pinot Noir, tops the state in acreage, followed closely by Chardonnay.

CABERNET SAUVIGNON, not a major grape for most of Oregon, does best in the southern part of the state. Some excellent Cabernets have been produced in the northern two-thirds of Oregon in the Umpqua and Willamette valleys, but little is planted, and it does well only on the best sites in the warmest vintages. In the southernmost part of the state near the California border, in areas that include the Illinois and Applegate valleys, Cabernet is the predominant red varietal, and shows excellent promise.

CHARDONNAY, is Oregon's premier white wine grape—and one of the state's most fickle. Of the several clones grown in the state, the "108" is the most prevalent, producing large clusters of relatively high acid grapes. The less prevalent Draper clone has smaller clusters of lower acid, earlier ripening fruit. Oregon Chardonnays are generally more delicate than their Washington and California counterparts, with an elegant completeness of flavors. In structure and profile they generally resemble White Burgundies, though the flavors are their own.

Within the general range, the style of Oregon Chardonnay varies widely. Depending on the vintage, the grapes, and the winemaker, a Chardonnay may be crisp and steely, or undergo a major malolactic fermentation and be soft almost to a fault, or have a ripe fruit intensity, or a complex, Burgundian, leesy character. Unlike most Washington Chardonnays, Oregon Chardonnays are often fermented in small oak barrels rather than stainless steel tanks, go through malolactic fermentation, and sometimes remain in lengthy contact with the lees prior to racking. This style trades some of the fresh fruity flavors of the grape for more complex flavors and a less angular profile.

Oregon grapes yield good Chardonnay at a wide range of sugar levels, but high acidity is a frequent concern, and grapes are often picked more according to acid than sugar. In the vineyard, Chardonnay is susceptible to mildew and bunch rot, and careful vineyard practices are essential. For grape grower and winemaker alike, Chardonnay is a challenge. New clones may reduce the difficulties and further the quality of the wines, but already, the best Oregon Chardonnays, in a range of styles, are outstanding. For those who prefer the taste of aged Chardonnay, the best from Oregon have a long life and improve in the bottle.

CHENIN BLANC, in America, has a reputation for producing huge yields and undistinguished wines. This reputation largely stems from grapes grown in California's warmest growing areas as a primary constituent in many jug wines. In the cool growing areas of France's Loire Valley, however, Chenin Blanc produces interesting, long-lived wines. Some authorities consider Chenin Blanc from the Loire much superior to the Sauvignon Blanc grown in the valley. This is not to say that Chenin Blanc is highly distinctive or exceptionally distinguished, but the grape can offer far more than its American reputation would suggest.

Very little Chenin Blanc is grown in Oregon, but the grape is successful from the northern Willamette Valley to the California border. Although it ripens later than the Willamette Valley's major varieties, Chenin Blanc develops character early and makes a good wine even when picked at low sugar levels. Chenin Blanc will probably never have a major role in western Oregon, but it offers additional diversity and interest in the Oregon wine spectrum.

GEWURZTRAMINER, produced in small quantities by many Oregon wineries, successfully avoids the classic faults of the grape when it is grown outside its Alsatian homeland. Its sometimes heavy, flat, bitter, or "juicy fruit" attributes are minimized or eliminated. As a variety, Gewurztraminer is plagued with erratic berry set, and Oregon's cool, wet springs are not a help. The average yield is low, and the profit margin is slim for winegrowers. Gewurztraminer has devoted followers, but not broad consumer interest. Oregon Gewurztraminers are made in styles ranging from slightly sweet to nearly dry. The best can be excellent, showing well the spicy fruit of the grape.

MERLOT, in Oregon, makes very fine wine. Unfortunately, it makes very few grapes. Unless conditions are just right, Merlot refuses to set berries, and in Oregon, during berry set, conditions are seldom just right. Growers have experienced successive years with no crop at all. Needless to say, very little acreage is devoted to the grape. Growers in southern Oregon experience the problem to a much lesser degree, and Merlot may become a significant grape in that part of the state, perhaps with the aid of refined clonal selection.

MULLER-THURGAU, a cross of Riesling and Sylvaner developed by Prof. Dr. Hermann Muller-Thurgau in 1882, yields high quantities of soft, pleasant, Riesling-like wine. Muller-Thurgau is naturally low in acid, ripens early, produces relatively high yields, and does best in cool growing sites. The common grape of Liebfraumilch, Muller-Thurgau can have a more distinguished character if grown in suitable locations and cropped to more moderate yields.

In Oregon's cool vintages, when Riesling is sometimes excessively acidic, Muller-Thurgau can be blended in to temper the acidity, although the degree of blending is limited by Oregon's rigorous labeling laws. Muller-Thurgau offers winegrowers a relatively high producing, reliable, cash-flow wine. For consumers, Muller-Thurgau offers a good, fruity, Riesling-like wine at a moderate price.

MUSCAT OTTONEL, is grown only in miniscule quantities. Contrary to its reputation elsewhere, the grape does not produce consistent yields in Oregon. The grape ripens early in the season, and acquires its distinctive flavors at the early stages of ripeness. It is one of the most refined members of the Muscat family, but because of small and irregular yields and the lack of name familiarity in the marketplace, it is highly unlikely that it will ever be widely planted.

PINOT GRIS, a genetic relative of Pinot Noir, may someday become one of Oregon's more important white wine grapes. As yet, the grape is planted only in miniscule quantities. At its worst, Pinot Gris can be heavy, flat, and dull, but given the right growing climate, and Oregon's Willamette Valley is such a climate, Pinot Gris can be a crisp, full-bodied, full-flavored wine of distinction.

Occasionally, Pinot Gris is finished in a fruity style with some residual sweetness, but its subtle, textural flavors suggest that it is at its best as a dry wine to accompany food, and this is the main style of Oregon Pinot Gris. Within this style, there are as many variations as winemakers making the wine. Some have oak, most do not. Some are crisp and austere, others are put through malolactic fermentation and are fuller and more rounded. Unlike some dry white wines which can taste a bit hollow without oak, Pinot Gris seems complete even when the wine sees only stainless steel. Like Chardonnay, Pinot Gris has distinctive flavors, but they are subtle and complex rather than singular and insistent.

In Oregon, Pinot Gris ripens well and produces reliably. Commercially, without a well-known name like Chardonnay or Riesling, Pinot Gris has much to overcome, but the strength of Oregon's wine industry is its ability to produce wines that few other growing regions can produce successfully. Pinot Gris may join its cousin Pinot Noir as one of Oregon's special grape varieties.

PINOT NOIR, without question, is Oregon's stellar wine grape. More acreage is devoted to Pinot Noir than any other variety. Produced in all of western Oregon's growing regions, it is the special star of the Willamette Valley where it dominates the wine scene. One of the world's noble grape varieties, Pinot Noir rarely does well outside of its French homeland in Burgundy, making Oregon's exceptional success with this difficult but rewarding grape all the more remarkable.

This is not to say that Oregon Pinot Noir tastes just like French Burgundy. Burgundies themselves range widely in style and flavor, and though the styles of Oregon Pinot Noir and French Burgundy intersect, Oregon Pinot Noir, especially when young, typically displays more forward spicy fruit, but less of the pleasant earthy dankness characteristic of many Burgundies.

American wine aficionados have long had California Cabernet and the reasonably priced (relatively speaking), consistently high quality Bordeaux wines as solid taste references for Cabernet Sauvignon. Pinot Noir is not so lucky. Especially until recently, most California Pinot Noirs were either indifferent, or simply tasted bad. The quality of French Burgundies is inconsistent, and the wines are often exorbitantly expensive.

Unlike Cabernet Sauvignon, Pinot Noir does not have a pronounced varietal profile, but rather a subtle textural weaving of scents and flavors. The American consumer has a good idea of what to look for in Cabernet Sauvignon, but America's collective palate has had little experience tasting and assessing top quality Pinot Noir, especially knowing what to expect of the wine when it is young, and how to judge its potential development as it ages. We have a vague idea that Pinot Noir should be silky, and rich, and full-bodied—but those vague conceptions do not always guide us with sufficient clarity.

Absolute emulation of French Burgundy is not necessarily desirable, but quality Burgundies provide a beginning point for understanding. French Burgundy is usually considerably higher in acid than most Oregon Pinot Noir. Regrettably, many Oregon winemakers choose to release Pinot Noir with relatively modest acidity. There is the conception, even among many American wine judges, that newly released Pinots should have a silky, full-bodied softness. This usually translates into wines that are low acid, high pH, and possibly overly alcoholic. Such wines may have a certain charm when first released, but quickly brown with only a few years in the cellar, lose fruit, and fail to gain in complexity.

Adequate acid and concentrated varietal fruit are keys to longevity and greatness in Pinot Noir. Of necessity, the very best Pinot Noirs from any region will have a certain angularity in their youth. As befitting the nature of the grape, young Pinot Noirs do not have the unrelenting hardness of young Cabernet, and often show a certain suppleness even when first released, but an overly soft or silky young Pinot Noir is a sure sign of a short declining life in the bottle. Sometimes such Pinot Noirs are released with fairly high alcohol and a heavy tannic overlay for "bigness," but the ability of the wine to age and develop in the bottle is not furthered.

As a variety, Pinot Noir has fewer red coloring pigments (anthocyanins) than any other major red vinifera grape variety, and Pinot Noir wines are inherently less darkly colored. Pinot Noirs from the best vintages are often more darkly colored than those from lesser vintages, but not always. Winemaking methods can turn overcropped grapes from a mediocre vintage into a darkly colored wine. Depth of color is not a reliable measure of fruit intensity. Taste and smell are.

More than any other grape variety, Pinot Noir is sensitive to crop levels. A rule of thumb in Oregon for good quality Pinot Noir is a yield of no more than three tons an acre. Also more than most varieties, vine age is a significant factor in quality Pinot Noir. The older the vines the better.

Pinot Noir is a highly mutable grape variety. There are over 200 known clones of the grape, and over time, individual vines seem to change and adapt to their growing site. Pommard and Wadenswil are the two major clones grown in the state. Pommard is considered to produce darker, bigger wines. Wadenswil is said to be more delicate, providing better fruit flavors and a more scented nose. This exaggerates the differences, however, and the vineyard climate and the age of the vines as well as winemaking methods can easily override any clonal differences.

A third clone, Gamay, has fallen out of favor, and vineyard acreage is actually decreasing. The Gamay clone has a reputation for high yields of acidic, modestly flavored fruit. The reputation may not be deserved, however. Older Gamay vines on good growing sites, cropped to lower yields, offer important acid structure and good fruit intensity. Some winemakers actively seek quality grapes from the Gamay clone as an important constituent in their Pinot Noir wines. Winemakers sometimes blend two or more clones with the idea of achieving a more complex wine.

Pinot Noir is one of the main grapes in the state's premium sparkling wines. White Pinot Noir, a wine sometimes made with a slight blush of color, and usually finished with crisp acidity and slight residual sweetness, is made from grapes that are not ripe enough to make a good red wine. A popular wine, wineries sometimes make white Pinot Noir from fully ripe grapes to satisfy market demand.

Oregon Pinot Noirs are an excellent value relative to French Burgundies, and as important national and international judgings have shown, the very best Oregon Pinot Noirs can compete with some of the best from Burgundy. Unlike the earliest days of the wine industry, even the average Oregon Pinot Noir is very good, and the standard is continually increasing as growers and winemakers alike come to a deeper understanding of this temperamental but highly rewarding grape. At their finest, Oregon Pinot Noirs are already outstanding, and the best is still to come.

RIESLING, also known as White Riesling and Johannisberg Riesling, is the third most widely planted variety in the state. Usually made in a style with some residual sweetness, Oregon Riesling is flavorful, crisp, and piquant. As a variety, Riesling develops its distinctive flavors even when it is not fully ripe. Ironically, even though Riesling does its best in marginal, cool climates, the variety requires a relatively long growing season. As in Germany, Oregon Riesling is often picked when marginally ripe.

Generally, Oregon Rieslings more closely

resemble their German counterparts than do the riper Rieslings of Washington and Idaho. Though infrequent, excellent ice wines and sweet botrytised wines are occasionally made. The very best Oregon Rieslings achieve that elusive balance of ripeness, refinement, crisp acidity, and complex flavors and scents that is the hallmark of the finer Rieslings from Germany. Like their counterparts from Idaho and Washington, however, Oregon Rieslings, on average, are simply very good, if not particularly exciting wines.

Riesling can be cropped higher than Pinot Noir and Chardonnay (as examples). Often bottled, sold, and consumed within a year of the harvest, Oregon Riesling provides wineries with quick cash flow and consumers with a pleasant drink. In Washington and Idaho, and now the Columbia Valley of eastern Oregon, however, Riesling ripens more easily, and can be cropped higher still. The Northwest already has an overbalance of Riesling, and economics suggest that less emphasis on the variety may be warranted. Riesling will continue to be one of western Oregon's three major grape varieties for the foreseeable future, however.

SAUVIGNON BLANC, also called Fume Blanc, is grown in small quantities from the California border to the northern Willamette Valley. On the warmer growing sites, the Willamette produces very good Sauvignon Blanc in most vintages, although the climate is marginal for this variety. Southern Oregon offers a more reliable climate for the grape, and production there should increase in future years. The cool Oregon growing climate emphasizes the herbaceous qualities of the grape.

SEMILLON, is similar to Sauvignon Blanc, but it is a more refined variety with less of Sauvignon Blanc's sledge hammer herbaceousness. Semillon does well in southern Oregon, and acreage, though small, is increasing. Semillon ripens slightly later than Sauvignon Blanc, but is otherwise probably the superior grape variety for western Oregon. Because of its lesser reputation relative to Sauvignon Blanc in California's warmer growing climates, however, Semillon has largely been ignored by American winegrowers (though not in Bordeaux where it is considered superior to Sauvignon Blanc for "serious" long-lived wines).

SYLVANER is planted only in very minor quantities. A German variety, Sylvaner crops higher and ripens earlier than Riesling. The wines are somewhat similar to Riesling, with a slightly coarse earthiness.

COLUMBIA VALLEY AND COLUMBIA GORGE GRAPE VARIETIES

Winegrowing efforts in Oregon's Columbia Valley are relatively recent, but quantitatively may rapidly become very significant. The openness of the land and agribusiness environment make large scale expansion possible. Located on the southern side of the Columbia River, the slopes on the nearly flat landscape are generally more north facing than on the Washington side of the river.

Part of the larger Columbia Valley, the Walla Walla Valley also extends into Oregon along the northeastern part of the state. Very few vineyards are developed in the Walla Walla Valley, but Cabernet Sauvignon shows excellent promise.

The Columbia Gorge area is not a part of the Columbia Valley appellation. Cutting through the Cascade Mountain Range, the gorge is a unique growing climate with limited area for expansion. As on the Washington side of the gorge, grape growing is qualitatively important, though limited in acreage.

Refer to the the entries on Columbia Valley grape varieties in the Washington section of this book for detailed discussion of specific grape varieties.

OREGON WINE NOTES

The winegrowing climate and wines of western Oregon are fundamentally different from those of other Northwest or west coast winegrowing regions. Western Oregon winegrowing, particularly in the Willamette and Umpqua Valleys, follows a pattern associated with some of Europe's major winegrowing regions.

Like Europe's most important winegrowing regions, grapes are grown on the warmest sites of a generally cool winegrowing climate. For most varieties in most years, grape ripening takes place in October, in moderating fall temperatures. Like the European pattern, grape sugars at harvest are usually moderate. The major winegrowing regions of Washington and Idaho also have similarities with European winegrowing, but their unusual climates, with intense sun, and wide daily and seasonal temperature fluctuations, follow the traditional European pattern less closely than western Oregon.

Grapes grown in cool climates, such as the Willamette Valley in Oregon, and Burgundy in France, become ripe at lower sugar levels. This is neither wishful thinking nor speculative opinion on the part of cool climate winegrowers. Throughout the grape berry's development from the spring flowering and formation of the individual berries throughout the growing season, specific physiological changes take place in the berry, including, as examples, maturation of the pips (grape seeds) and veraison (coloration of the grapes).

In cool grape growing climates, such physiological changes occur at lower grape sugars, and the grapes are literally ripe, and develop their best flavors, at lower sugar levels than grapes grown in warmer climates. In the earlier years, this was not always well understood, and still, today, this remains a psychological barrier for many Oregon winegrowers.

As recently as the 1960s, Oregon State University was recommending *Vitis labrusca* grapes as the only viable varieties for the Oregon climate. Premium *Vitis vinifera* wine grapes were not recommended. U. C. Davis professors were advising that Oregon's Willamette Valley, now the state's major winegrowing region, was too frosty, too cold, and too rainy. In sum, the idea of premium winegrowing in western Oregon was considered quite foolish.

The doubters were soon proved very wrong, yet in the earlier years of Willamette Valley winegrowing, young grape vines and less than optimum grape growing and winemaking practices meant that wine quality was inconsistent. In warmer years, when the grapes were higher in sugar, good wines were easier to achieve. The legacy of disdain for even trying to grow grapes in Oregon, the early experience that the warmest years and highest grape sugars more often and more easily made the best wine, and a mind set shaped by California criteria for relatively high sugar levels at "ripeness" led not a few Willamette Valley winegrowers to a preoccupation with very warm vintages and high grape sugars.

As if to prove absolutely that the doubters were wrong, chaptalization, the addition of sugar to the must, was shunned at all cost, at least with Pinot Noir, the very soul of the Oregon wine industry. This legacy and mind set did not serve the industry well. In cool years, wines did not have the benefit of chaptalization. In warm years, Pinot Noir grapes were allowed to become over-ripe, losing flavors, aromatics, and acidity.

Unconsciously, California, at least partially, remained the winemaking model. Europe would have served better. Europe, in fact, especially Burgundy, was the chosen model for many Oregon winegrowers from the beginning, and would became more fully and genuinely so as winegrowers increasingly set aside inappropriate California practices in favor of those more suitable to Oregon's climates.

In France's Burgundy district, winegrowers are legally permitted to add either sugar or acid to their must. In most years, at least some sugar is added to the red Burgundy grape must. Stated another way, chaptalization is standard practice, and not adding sugar to the must is an exception to the rule. By law, Burgundians cannot add both sugar and acid to the grape must. In reality, even the most conscientious and dedicated Burgundian winemakers add both sugar and acid to the grape must in some years.

The Willamette Valley routinely achieves higher sugar levels than Burgundy, and chaptalization is less frequently needed. It should be noted that chaptalization is not simply a Burgundian aberration. The practice is relatively common in Bordeaux as well. In sum, chaptalization is not inherently a dirty word. In cool vintages, chaptalization in moderation benefits the wine. The physiological ripeness of the grape at harvest determines wine quality, not the sugar level of the grape.

In warm years, particularly with Pinot Noir, Willamette Valley winegrowers still have a tendency to pick grapes too ripe and release the wines with relatively low acid levels, but the unusually hot 1978 vintage offered a valuable lesson. Following the cool, rainy, 1977 vintage, some winegrowers were eager to achieve the highest possible sugars. For others there was no choice in that highly unusual vintage. The year was simply too hot.

Many Pinot Noirs produced in 1978 had plenty of body, alcohol, and "bigness," but the grape acids, flavors, and aromatics were burned away in the summer sun, and with few exceptions, the wines did not age well. Said one Willamette Valley winegrower countering the initial enthusiasm for the vintage, "If I wanted to make wines like this, I would have stayed in California."

Adequately high acidity and concentrated varietal fruit, not alcohol and tannin, are key elements in wines that compliment food and develop rich, textural, flavor complexities with bottle age. Already outstanding, many Oregon Pinot Noirs from better vintages call out for bottle aging, but without sufficiently high acidity, the wines have no chance of reaching their potential. The best Oregon Pinot Noirs need acid and pH levels closer those typical of Burgundies. This is not to say that Oregon should slavishly imitate Burgundy—but there are lessons worth learning.

Ironically, there is a disincentive for Oregon winemakers to produce truly great Pinot Noir. Most Oregon Pinot Noirs are released within two to three years of the vintage. At this age, lower acid, higher pH Pinot Noirs are seductively attractive, but Pinot Noirs with the higher acids and structure for aging often seem unyielding and ungenerous. Inevitably, these wines are less popular with consumers and wine judges. In two or three more years, the better structured wines begin to open up and reveal the complex textures and flavors that can only come with bottle age. By that time, the Pinots that were so seductive just a few years before will have already begun to brown, their fruit and initial charm quickly fading.

Winemakers producing outstanding Pinot Noir may be vindicated several years after a vintage is released, but retrospective vindication does not help sell the current release of wines, and does not help the winemaker get deserved recognition in wine judgings.

In America, we have developed a reasonably good appreciation of Cabernet Sauvignon and its aging characteristics, but we have had very little experience with Pinot Noir, a very different grape, and a very different wine. Oregon is offering us a great opportunity. Our knowledge and appreciation of these wines is evolving in concert with the evolution of Oregon Pinot Noir winegrowing and winemaking. Already outstanding, and more than deserving of the recent, and long overdue, accolades, Oregon Pinot Noir has not yet been pushed to the limits of its potential. The impressive successes thus far merely announce the beginning of future greatness.

OREGON WINERIES

1985
OREGON
SAUVIGNON BLANC
Willamette Valley

PRODUCED AND BOTTLED BY
ADAMS VINEYARD, PORTLAND, OREGON, USA
BW—OR—100, ALCOHOL 13.2% BY VOLUME

ADAMS VINEYARD WINERY

1922 N.W. Pettygrove Street
Portland, Oregon 97209
(503) 294-0606

Wine Production
3,000 cases

Vineyards
13 acres

Year First Planted
1976

First Vintage
1981

Leading Wines
Pinot Noir, Chardonnay, Sauvignon Blanc

Washington has many urban wineries, some dating back to the beginning of state's wine renaissance, but Oregon's first urban winery, Adams Vineyard, did not begin operations until 1985. Unlike many urban Washington wineries, Adams is closely tied to its vineyards. Owned and operated by Carol and Peter Adams, the Adams' vineyard is located southwest of Portland, in the hills near the town of Newberg. Before opening their winery in Portland, the first vintages were custom crushed at the Adelsheim winery near the Adams' vineyard.

Peter Adams is president of a construction materials firm. Carol Adams writes a cooking column for a weekly newspaper. The two owned a retail wine store in the early 1970s before deciding that a vineyard and winery was a more interesting venture.

By now, the phrase "food wines" is heavily overworked, stated glibly with equal fervor by the newly converted as well as those long dedicated to the cause, but the Adams practice this ethic in their selection of grape varieties as well as their wine style. Nearly every Oregon winery makes Chardonnay, Pinot Noir, and Riesling, Oregon's three major grape varieties. The Adams' vineyard is devoted to two varieties, Chardonnay and Pinot Noir. They do not grow, purchase, or make Riesling.

For their third variety, the Adams purchase Oregon Sauvignon Blanc grapes. Sauvignon Blanc requires a fairly warm climate. Because the variety has a difficult time in the Willamette Valley's cooler vintages, relatively few acres of the grape are planted in the valley. Carol Adams likes the inherently crisp nature of Oregon Sauvignon Blanc, a "third variety" that compliments food much better than Riesling.

ADELSHEIM VINEYARD

22150 N.E. Quarter Mile Lane
Newberg, Oregon 97132
(503) 538-3652

Wine Production
13,000 cases

Vineyards
18 acres

Year First Planted
1972

First Vintage
1978

Leading Wines
Chardonnay, Pinot Noir, Pinot Gris

David and Ginny Adelsheim are the owners and operators of one of Oregon's more innovative wineries. To prepare for the wine business, David Adelsheim worked with David Lett during one of Eyrie's crushes, researched French and German viticulture and winemaking texts to gain a broader perspective than that offered by the teachings of the University of California at Davis, and studied and worked in France at the Lycee Viticole in Beaune.

An ardent and studied advocate of western Oregon's exceptional winegrowing climate, Adelsheim speaks not only of the future of his own winery, but of the future and destiny of the Oregon wine industry. On behalf of the Oregon Winegrowers Association, Adelsheim researched and successfully petitioned the Bureau of Alcohol Tobacco and Firearms (BATF) for "viti-

cultural area" designations for Oregon's Umpqua and Willamette Valleys.

Adelsheim authored the strict Oregon wine labeling regulations, and is an advisor to Oregon State University on the importation of grape varieties and clones. His research writings include the publication of a paper in the Proceedings of The International Symposium on Cool Climate Viticulture and Enology, and his comprehensive benchmark work on training and trellising methods for western Oregon vineyards published in the *Oregon Winegrape Growers Guide*.

In many respects, Adelsheim epitomizes the spirit of Oregon winegrowers—not idle hobbiests, not agribusinessmen growing grapes because its the new cash crop, and not armchair investors who like the idea of owning a winery (if not the mental and physical effort), but deeply dedicated individuals committed to the belief that western Oregon is one of the world's finest winegrowing regions.

Oregon, Adelsheim believes, will increasingly become one of America's most important premium wine producing regions as consumers are better educated to the higher acidity and more delicate and complex flavors of European and Oregon wines. The process of understanding and acceptance will be gradual. Adelsheim makes his own Chardonnays in a fairly ripe, rich style, yet they manage to maintain the delicate nuances of the grape. Adelsheim's Pinot Noirs have very moderate tannins, and emphasize spicy fruit and a supple character.

Pinot Noir, the glory of Oregon's Willamette Valley, does not have a clear frame of reference for the average American palate. French Burgundy has become so costly and unreliable that few Americans are familiar with the taste of good Pinot Noir. Adelsheim points out that Cabernet Sauvignon, the American standard of reference for red wines, is a much different kind of wine. Cabernet is strongly and distinctively flavored, using high tannins as part of the balance of the wine, and striking the palate immediately with a highly defined taste.

Pinot Noir, on the other hand, does not have such a readily recognizable taste, but rather un-

The Adelsheims.

folds on the palate in manifold nuances. In Adelsheim's view, an important aspect of wine tasting often ignored by Americans is the feel of a wine in the mouth. Fine Pinot Noir, at least fine aged Pinot Noir, has a distinctive velvety feel—it is what Adelsheim calls a textural wine.

For several years a broker for French oak barrels, Adelsheim has experimented with the effects of six different French oaks on the flavors of Pinot Noir and Chardonnay. For Pinot Noir, Adelsheim uses a combination of three oaks, Allier for complexity and backbone, Troncais for spicy flavor and accents, and Nevers for body.

For Chardonnay, Adelsheim prefers Limousin and Nevers. In his experience, Limousin accentuates the wine's acidity, offering pleasant, lemony qualities, though at the expense of some tendency toward bitter flavors. Nevers, on the other hand, brings out the softer, rounder qualities of the wine, while playing down the acidity and any bitter tendencies.

In addition to the standard Oregon grape varieties, Pinot Noir, Chardonnay, and Riesling, Adelsheim is also working with Pinot Gris, Sauvignon Blanc, and more recently, the true Gamay grape of Beaujolais, a variety very different from the misnamed Gamay Beaujolais clone of Pinot Noir—and very different from California's Napa Gamay which is now believed to be the Rhone variety, Valdiguie. A counterpoint to his Chardonnay, Adelsheim's Pinot Gris

is made in a crisp style, fermented at cool temperatures in stainless steel, and released without any oak aging.

When the Adelsheims started making wine, Oregon grapes were in short supply, so they purchased Merlot and Semillon, two varieties that are not well suited to the Willamette Valley, from Washington's Columbia Valley. The Adelsheims continue to use the Columbia Valley grapes, but increasingly they will look to Oregon's Umpqua Valley and southwestern Oregon for their Merlot and Semillon.

The Adelsheim home and winery is a single, beautifully integrated structure. The view from the living room window is of the lush vineyard and the expansive valley below. An artist, Ginny's work graces the Adelsheim home as well as the labels for their wine.

ESTATE BOTTLED
Willamette Valley
WHITE RIESLING
1985
alcohol 11.2% by volume
produced and bottled by Alpine Vineyards, Alpine, Oregon
BW-OR-79

ALPINE VINEYARDS

25904 Green Peak Road
Monroe, Oregon 97456
(503) 424-5851

Wine Production
4,000 cases

Vineyards
20 acres

Year First Planted
1976

First Vintage
1980

Leading Wines
Riesling, Chardonnay, Pinot Noir

High on a sunny hillside, the modern, "passive solar" home of Dan and Christine Jepsen overlooks their lush vineyards and the expansive valley below. The hillside site faces due south, above the cooling temperature inversions and fogs of the valley floor. The grassy slopes and scattered oak trees confirm that the site is warmer, sunnier, and drier than the surrounding norm — sunny and warm enough for a solar home, and sunny and warm enough to crow Cabernet Sauvignon as well as the more typical Willamette Valley varieties, Pinot Noir, Riesling, and Chardonnay.

Good as it is, the growing site is still marginal for Cabernet Sauvignon, and Jepsen does not expect to produce a great Cabernet every year. As in Bordeaux, the most famous region for Cabernet Sauvignon, cooler years yield lighter wines, but the experience of several vintages shows that good wine can be made even in less desirable vintages, an affirmation of Jepsen's decision to plant a a portion of his vineyard to Cabernet Sauvignon. Alpine's Cabernets are typically harvested in mid-November, fermented in stainless steel, and aged in French oak.

The Cabernet Sauvignon and Pinot Noir are fermented at 70 to 75 degrees, a moderately cool fermentation temperature for red wines. Although higher fermentation temperatures are sometimes thought to extract more from the grape, Alpine's fermentation is quite lengthy, lasting about two weeks. Each day for the first week, more grapes are harvested and added to the tank, thereby perpetuating the fermentation and prolonging the length of time the grapes are in contact with the skins. The Pinot Noir is inoculated for malolactic fermentation during the final stages of the primary fermentation, and then racked into four different

Christine and Dan Jepsen.

41

kinds of French oak, Allier, Nevers, Vosges, and Limousin, for aging.

Unlike most Oregon winemakers, Jepsen does not automatically put Chardonnay and every red wine through malolactic fermentation. Although his Pinot Noir goes through a malolactic fermentation, his Cabernet Sauvignon does not. Jepsen's Cabernet grapes already have moderate acidity. Preferring a higher acid level for his Cabernet wines, Jepsen avoids a malolactic fermentation that would further reduce the wine's acidity. Alpine's Chardonnay is fermented in small stainless steel tanks at around 65 degrees, then aged in a combination of Allier and Never oak barrels. It, too, is usually not put through a malolactic fermentation.

Alpine's Riesling is fermented at a cool 45 degrees for six to eight weeks to preserve the delicate fruit esters of the grape. Jepsen often bottles the Riesling at a cold temperature, so when it is later opened, the trapped carbon dioxide is released to give the wine a slight spritziness.

Alpine's grapes grow on their own rootstocks, but Jepsen has planted a patch of phylloxera resistant, native American rootstocks for grafting, in case the dreaded root louse should ever invade Oregon. The vineyard soil is a Jory clay loam running fifty feet to rock, interrupted only by occasional stretches of shallow Bellpine. The vineyard is not irrigated.

All of Alpine's wine is made from the grapes of the adjacent estate vineyard. Alpine is one of the few Oregon wineries that does not purchase grapes from other growers. Jepsen believes that 80 percent of a wine's quality comes from the vineyard. Growing all his own grapes insures control over that 80 percent.

Although the mailing address indicates Monroe, the winery's location is actually in the nearby town of Alpine. The Alpine winery also operates a tasting room on the Oregon coast. Located in The Wood Gallery at 818 S.W. Bay Boulevard in Newport, the tasting room is open daily, noon to 5 PM.

AMITY VINEYARDS

18150 Amity Vineyards Road S.E.
Amity, Oregon 97101-9603
(503) 835-2362

Oregon Winetasting Room
at the Lawrence Gallery, Bellevue, Oregon,
9 miles southwest of McMinnville on Highway 18.
(503) 843-3787
Daily, 11:30 AM to 5:30 PM.

Wine Production
7,500 cases

Vineyards
12 ½ acres

Year First Planted
1970

First Vintage
1976

Leading Wines
Pinot Noir, Chardonnay, Gewurztraminer, Riesling

Myron Redford, Amity's winemaker, and one of the principal owners, did not set out to be an Oregon winegrower. First attracted to winemaking through part-time work at Washington's Associated Vintners winery, Redford wanted to build a winery in western Washington near Port Townsend, and make wine from grapes grown in Washington's Columbia Valley. While planning his winery, Redford learned of a vineyard for sale near Amity, Oregon, 45 miles southwest of Portland. Redford abandoned his plans for the

Washington winery, and in 1974, formed a partnership and purchased the Oregon vineyard.

In the early years, Amity became best known for a carbonic maceration Pinot Noir Nouveau. Initially made from the earlier ripening grapes from Washington's Columbia Valley, the Nouveau grapes now come from Oregon. Patterned after the French Beaujolais Nouveau, the wine is released in the fall, less than two months after the beginning of the vintage. Dry Riesling and Gewurztraminer also became Amity trademarks, but none of these wines reflected the driving interest of Amity's winemaker.

From the beginning, Redford wanted Amity to be known for its Pinot Noir, not the "nouveau," but oak aged Pinot Noir from Oregon grapes. It was his interest in this wine that caused him to radically alter his plans and come to Oregon. In 1977, a very poor year for Oregon Pinot Noir, Redford succeeded in making fine Pinot Noir, including the excellent 1977 "Wadenswil," a wine that was available in such a miniscule quantity, 302 bottles, that it was scarcely available commercially. The following year, Redford made more Pinot Noir, but held most of it back for four years before release.

Widespread recognition of Amity Pinot Noir was late in coming, but come it did. In a tasting of 180 American Pinot Noirs sponsored by a national wine magazine, Amity's 1978 Winemaker's Reserve was one of only eleven given an outstanding rating.

Redford buys grapes from other vineyards to supplement production from his own vineyard. Every clonal and vineyard lot is fermented and aged separately. Redford believes that selecting blends from the separate lots is an important winemaking consideration. He and his tasting panel first test blends comprised of lots from his own estate. Secondly, blends that include grapes from other Oregon vineyards are evaluated, and lastly, though rarely, Redford may blend Washington and Oregon Pinot Noir.

From each vintage, Redford releases at least two, and sometimes more, barrel aged Pinot Noirs. Usually one of the Pinots is intended for more current consumption, and one intended for,

and often needing, longer aging. Because he releases different styles of Pinot Noir, Amity's "house style" encompasses a wide range, but Redford's preferences are best reflected in the wines intended for longer aging—fairly tannic, aromatic, full-bodied wines with a sturdy acid structure.

In addition to his winemaking skills, Redford has a keen eye for grapes. Some of his best Pinot Noirs have been made in what are generally less good vintages. Redford's 1977 "Wadenswil" release from Pinot Noir grapes of that clone was a benchmark wine in that cool and poor vintage. Conversely, 1978 was an inordinately hot vintage, and most Oregon Pinot Noir did not fair well. For his excellent 1978 "Winemaker's Reserve," Redford blended in grapes from older Gamay vines.

The Pommard and Wadenswil Pinot Noir clones predominate in Oregon vineyards. The Gamay clone was planted in the earlier years of the Oregon wine industry, but rapidly fell out of

Myron Redford.

43

favor. In spite of rapid vineyard expansion, acreage of the Gamay clone is actually declining. The Gamay clone is the most distinctive of the three principal clones, both in the growing habit of the vine and in the character of the grapes. A naturally higher acid clone, the Gamay was often cropped heavily on poor growing sites, and developed a reputation as a clone to avoid. In retrospect, some of Oregon's best and longest lived Pinot Noirs have included Gamay grapes in their blend.

Gamay is still not in wide favor, but Redford is among the clone's most ardent supporters. Seemingly light and delicate in its youth, Redford's 1977 Oregon Gamay clone Pinot Noir is still going strong a decade later, and has developed a Burgundian character with age. Beginning with the 1978 vintage, the Gamay clone has often been a key element in Redford's Winemaker's Reserve releases.

The best of Redford's Pinot Noirs are higher in acid and tannin than the average Oregon Pinot Noir. These characteristics, combined with good varietal fruit, make Amity's Pinot Noirs good candidates for cellar aging. Similarly, Amity's Winemaker's Reserve Chardonnays are released with traditional Burgundian levels of acidity for longevity and development in the cellar.

For the wine traveler unable to visit all the wineries, Amity operates the Oregon Wine Tasting Room at in the Lawrence Art Gallery in Bellevue, Oregon, nine miles south of McMinnville, on Highway 18, a major route to the Oregon coast. Staffed by Patric McElliott, the tasting room was the first of its kind in Oregon, featuring wines from wineries throughout the state for tasting and purchase, as well as knowledgeable discussions for the serious wine aficionado. The tasting room is open daily, from 11:30 AM to 5:30 PM.

ANKENY VINEYARDS

2565 Riverside Road South
Salem, Oregon 97306
(503) 378-1498

Wine Production
350 cases

Vineyards
10 acres

Year First Planted
1982

First Vintage
1985

Leading Wines
Chardonnay

Named for the nearby Ankeny Federal Wildlife Refuge, home for masses of wild geese, Ankeny vineyards is situated in a relatively new grape growing area along the southernmost part of the Salem Hills. Ankeny Vineyards is a partnership of Joe Olexa, Loyd Henion, Bob Harris, Karl Remmy, and Don Jackson, five grape growers located within a five mile radius of each other.

The estate vineyard is situated on one of the Willamette Valley's earliest homesteads, Federal

Land Claim Number 38, dated 1846. On a corner of the property, an early pioneer cemetery dates to 1849. Looking out across the broad sweep of the Willamette Valley toward Eugene, Ankeny's land has been in continuous cultivation since the original claim. The land has supported many crops since the settler's era, including walnuts, prunes, wheat, and now wine grapes.

Most Willamette Valley vineyards are planted on sloping hillsides along the western side of the valley. Ankeny is situated near the center of the valley, only 50 feet from the valley floor. Frost, often a problem for vineyards near the valley floor, has not troubled Ankeny. Olexa reports that not only is frost not a problem, but the site is in a particularly warm localized climate with early bud break in the spring and a longer fall season.

The vineyards are not far from the Willamette River, and the soil is a deep, heavy, clay loam. Vine growth is vigorous, and Olexa reports that the site supports heavier crop loads than the Oregon norm, with good sugar and acid balance.

Instead of the Willamette Valley's usual cane pruning, the vines are trained in bilateral cordons. Cordon trained vines are easier and less expensive to maintain, but the critical basal buds are not always reliably fruitful in the Oregon climate. Most of the vines are very young, but, so far, cordon pruning works well on Ankeny's growing sites.

Although produced only in small quantities, Cabernet Sauvignon is an Ankeny specialty. Pinot Noir is made into a white wine, Pinot Noir Blanc. Chardonnay, Ankeny's main focus, is barrel fermented and left on the lees for several months. If the vintage is favorable, the Chardonnay grapes are picked at high sugars for a ripe, full-bodied wine. Ankeny is also working with Pinot Gris, one of the state's more interesting new wine grapes.

ARTERBERRY WINERY

905 E. 10th Street
P.O. Box 772
McMinnville, Oregon 97128
(503) 472-1587

Grape Wine Production
3,000 cases

Sparkling Cider Production
700 cases

Vineyards
none

First Vintage
1979

Leading Wines
Red Hills Brut, Sparkling Riesling,

McMinnville, a small college town in the heart of Oregon's northern Willamette Valley winegrowing region, is home for two wineries. Located within a block of The Eyrie Vineyards, the first winery in Oregon dedicated to Pinot Noir, Fred Arterberry's Arterberry Winery earns another first by producing the state's first sparkling wine from traditional Champagne grape varieties. The first cuvee, in 1979, was made entirely from Chardonnay. Subsequent cuvees have included Pinot Noir, and Arterberry's expanded line of sparkling wines now includes Riesling.

Focusing on sparkling beverages, a low alcohol sparkling cider comprised most of Arterberry's production in the first years. Sparkling Cider filled a gap while awaiting the release of Arterberry's bottle fermented sparkling wine.

A high quality, labor intensive process, bottle fermented sparkling wine is made by adding sugar and yeast to the base wine after it has finished fermentation. The wine is then bottled with temporary closures, and a second fermentation takes place within the bottle. This second fermentation, and the subsequent resting of the wine on the yeast is responsible for the natural carbonation and distinctive character.

After the secondary fermentation and aging, the wines are riddled, repeatedly turning and bumping the bottles until they are vertical and the remnants of the yeast rests on the bottle closure. The wine is then carefully disgorged by discharging the yeast, then topping up the bottle and sealing it with a permanent Champagne cork closure. Arterberry's first sparkling wine rested two years on the yeast. Clearly, bottle fermented sparkling wine is not a bankers idea of a cash flow wine.

Arterberry, like all sparkling beverage producers, is forced to contend with absurd taxation laws. Still wine is taxed at the rate of 17 cents a gallon, but sparkling wine, classified as a luxury item, is taxed at twenty times that rate, at $3.40 a gallon. Even Arterberry's inexpensive cider is taxed at $2.40 a gallon. As sparkling wine moves through the distribution channels, the tax's impact on the eventual price to the consumer is magnified even further.

An enology graduate of U. C. Davis, Arterberry believes that Oregon's Willamette Valley is ideal for sparkling wine. If grapes are too high in sugar, the base wine will be too high in alcohol, and the second fermentation cannot take place. Grapes for sparkling wine must be picked at lower sugar levels, but in warmer climates, grapes become physiologically ripe at higher sugar levels. In a warmer growing climate, picking the grapes early lets the winemakers make sparkling wine, but the underripe grapes do little for wine quality. In Oregon's cooler climate, grapes fully ripen at lower sugars, an important criterion for premium sparkling wines. Arterberry prefers grapes at 19 degrees Brix, a sugar level that produces a base wine with an alcohol content of about 11 percent.

In 1982, to augment his sparkling wine production, Arterberry made his first table wines for release under the Arterberry label, Chardonnay, Pinot Noir, and Rose of Pinot Noir. A major portion of Arterberry's grapes come from the Red Hills Vineyard near the town of Dundee, a vineyard known for producing ripe, richly flavored Pinot Noir.

Oregon is destined to become a qualitatively important sparkling wine producing region. Other winemakers soon followed Arterberry and began producing bottle fermented sparkling wine from Pinot Noir and Chardonnay, but Arterberry retains the distinction of being the first.

BETHEL HEIGHTS VINEYARD

OREGON CHARDONNAY

WILLAMETTE VALLEY

1984

GROWN, PRODUCED AND BOTTLED BY
BETHEL HEIGHTS VINEYARD, INC., SALEM, OREGON BW-OR-98
ALCOHOL 12% BY VOLUME

BETHEL HEIGHTS VINEYARD

6060 Bethel Heights Road N. W.
Salem, Oregon 97304
(503) 581-2262

Wine Production
4,000 cases

Vineyards
51 acres

Year First Planted
1977

First Vintage
1984

Leading Wines
Pinot Noir, Chardonnay, Chenin Blanc

Geologic remnants of a volcanic past are evident throughout America's Northwest. The massive crater formed by the violent 1980 eruption of Mount St. Helens is the newest monument to the northwest's geologic history. In the Eola Hills of the Willamette Valley, the Bethel Heights vineyard has its roots in a far more ancient volcanic crater. The vines are planted on a south facing slope along the crater's rim. The crater and the remnants of the volcano have merged into the landscape with the passing of many millennia, but the distinctive bowl-shaped valley remains.

Bethel Heights Vineyard is a family owned corporation operated by brothers, Ted and Terry Casteel, and their wives, Pat Dudley and Marilyn Webb. In the late 1970s, both families left their former occupations, purchased the vineyard, and moved to Oregon. Ted Casteel is the vineyard manager, Terry the winemaker. Webb edited the *Oregon Winegrape Growers Guide* for the Oregon Winegrowers Association. The book is a classic practical reference on Oregon winegrowing.

Befitting its volcanic origins, the vineyard's shallow soil is high in minerals, but is otherwise agriculturally poor—except for wine grapes, which seem to produce the best wines from the least rich soils. The soil is classified as a Nekia, silty, clay loam, and averages a depth of three feet, overlying a bedrock of fractured basalt. The land was once owned by Vic Winquist who had planned his own winery for the site. Winquist had recommended drip irrigation for the vineyard, and it remains one of the few irrigated vineyards in the Willamette Valley.

Although costly, the irrigation helped pay for itself by allowing vine cuttings to be planted directly in the vineyard and brought into production more rapidly. Because of the shallow soils, vineyard irrigation, especially in the hotter years, keeps the vines from becoming overstressed. The vines are deeply irrigated twice each summer, the last time in August to carry the vines through ripening. The yield from the vineyard is moderate, averaging two to three tons an acre for Pinot Noir and Chardonnay, but moderate yields, particularly for varieties like Pinot Noir, are a factor in producing grapes with balance and concentrated varietal fruit.

Until recently, many of Oregon's vineyards were planted at wide California style spacings, eight feet between the vines, ten feet between the rows. In retrospect, a denser spacing is desirable for the Oregon climate. Some growers have interplanted their vineyards for a denser spacing, but new vine pruning and training methods are an alternative, and can offer other advantages as well. Bethel Heights is one of the vineyards working with the Geneva Double Curtain system, a technique originally developed in New York for Concord grapes, but receiving attention in Europe and other winegrowing areas for vinifera grapes. With this system, the grapes and next year's buds are better exposed to the sun. In the sections of the vineyards that have been converted to the system, Ted Casteel reports increased and more reliable yields without a reduction in sugar levels, and better color in Pinot Noir.

Emerging as a distinctive growing area, the Eola Hills rise up from the Willamette River near Salem and run northward along the river for a brief distance. Bethel Heights is positioned in the path of coastal breezes that flow through a low lying gap in the Coast Range. The breezes flow through in late afternoon, tempering the climate, and cooling the evening temperatures. Cool nights help preserve the acids and fruit flavors. According to the Casteels, the vineyard is cooler than other vineyard sites in hot years, and warmer in cool years.

Pinot Noir and Chardonnay are the winery's major focus, but Bethel Heights also produces limited quantities of Chenin Blanc, a grape seldom planted in Oregon. In California Chenin Blanc is grown in warm growing areas and has a reputation for producing large quantities of indifferent wine. In Europe, however, Chenin Blanc is grown in cooler climates, and in the Loire, has a reputation that exceeds Sauvignon Blanc. Bethel Heights Chenin Blanc is made in a crisp style with some residual sweetness, and offers a change of pace from Oregon's ubiquitous Rieslings.

Bethel Height's wines are 100 percent estate grown and bottled. "The vineyard is especially important to us," says Terry Casteel, "We really want our wines to be an expression of this particular piece of land. We came out of our former lives to this piece of earth, and this is where we have our roots."

Ted and Terry Casteel.

BJELLAND VINEYARDS

Bjelland Vineyards Lane
Roseburg, Oregon 97470
(503) 679-6950

Grape Wine Production
500 cases

Fruit And Berry Wine Production
500 cases

Vineyards
19 acres

Year First Planted
1967

First Vintage
1969

Leading Wines
various berry wines, Riesling, Semillon

Located not far from Wildlife Safari, a popular tourist attraction, Bjelland Vineyards is just off Highway 42, one of the main routes from Interstate 5 to the Oregon coast. The winery and vineyards are at the base of Bjelland Rock, the highest mountain in the area, and one of the more distinctive landmarks in Oregon's wine country.

After many years in Los Angeles working in the public relations field, Bjelland sought a complete reversal in lifestyle, and eventually came to settle in this rural area of Oregon near Roseburg with his wife Mary. His striped bib overalls have become a trademark, and bespeak the way of life he had sought, and now lives. After more than a decade, Bjelland still believes that it is the best life. In Paul Bjelland, the romance of winemaking has grown deep roots.

One of the new era pioneers, Bjelland's first decade of winemaking in Oregon was spent not only establishing the viability of his own winery, but as a corollary, the viability of the Oregon wine industry itself. The first years at Bjelland were devoted to breaking new ground—both figuratively and literally. In 1968, Bjelland founded the Oregon Winegrowers Association, and two years later, the first Oregon wine festival.

Bjelland wines are characterized by a light, easily palatable style. In addition to the traditional vinifera grape bottlings, Bjelland makes a woodruff flavored May Wine and several fruit and berry wines. In 1982, the Bjellands began giving additional emphasis to dry and semi-dry berry wines. In all, the Bjellands make fifteen different wines. All the wines, including the berry wines, are aged, at least in part, in American oak, though the older barrels Bjelland uses for aging do not impart a pronounced oak character.

At Bjelland, vine rows are 12 feet apart, and within the rows, vines are planted every eight feet. Although standard Oregon practice dictates much closer spacing to achieve the best grape quality and consistent crop yields, Bjelland believes that his wider spacing is best, reducing moisture and mildew problems, and easing tractor work.

The Bjellands and Bjelland winery epitomize rural country living. Raising poultry and livestock for their own consumption, butchering, sausage making, and other traditional self-sufficient pursuits share equal importance with winegrowing.

CAMERON WINERY

P. O. Box 27
Dundee, Oregon 97115
(503) 538-0336

Wine Production
2,000 cases

Vineyards
3 acre test plot of Pinot Noir clones

Year First Planted
1986

First Vintage
1984

Leading Wines
Pinot Noir, Chardonnay

Cameron owner and winemaker, John Paul, a PhD marine biochemist, still does consulting work for a San Francisco firm, exploring antibiotic compounds extracted from seaweeds. Before coming to Oregon, Paul was assistant winemaker for California's Konocti and Carneros Creek wineries. But of all the wines he drank, Paul most loved those from Burgundy. In pursuit of his interest, Paul travelled to France to learn more about Burgundian wines and winegrowing.

After his trip to Burgundy, Paul made an exploratory trip to New Zealand, a cool climate winegrowing area, and one of the few in the world capable of producing fine Pinot Noir. Paul found that New Zealand had great potential, but lacked a discerning consumer market for fine wines. Without such a market, the quality of the wines was much less than it could have been. Instead

of New Zealand, Paul opted for one of the few other locations outside of Burgundy capable of producing fine Pinot Noir—Oregon's Willamette Valley.

But why come to Oregon at all? Paul already had vineyard and winemaking experience in California's Carneros region, a region touted as having a cool climate particularly suited to the Burgundian grape varieties, Chardonnay, and, especially, Pinot Noir.

"Carneros does produce good Pinot Noirs," says Paul. "but I really love the wines of Burgundy, and neither the Carneros climate nor its wines have much in common with Burgundy. It is a misconception that Carneros is cool. It is cool only relative to other California growing climates, but it is still a warm climate. I don't mean to say that Oregon's Willamette Valley is exactly like Burgundy, but the climate and wines are very similar. Even the vegetation, which is a good indicator of climate, is very reminiscent of Burgundy."

Unique in Oregon, Paul built 1000 gallon stainless steel fermenters for his Pinot Noir. Similar in size to the fermenters he saw in Burgundy, the ratio of volume to surface area allows the wine to reach a high 95 degree peak fermentation temperature for good color and fruit extraction.

Much emphasis is put on winemaking technique, but Paul believes that deciding when to pick the fruit is one of the most important parts of winemaking. In the very warm 1985 vintage, Paul picked his grapes earlier than most, so that the fruit would not be overripe, and the acids and flavors would not be burned away in the heat.

In Paul's view, Oregon Pinot Noirs, especially in the past, have been released with too little acidity. Paul favors the higher acid levels of Burgundies. "Acidity is important for a wine's longevity," says Paul. "If a wine tastes about right when its goes into the bottle, it will probably taste too flat after it has some bottle age. With a little higher acidity, wines taste better with food, and they are better able to develop in the bottle."

And about Chardonnays, "California Chardonnays are great as aperitifs, good to drink on their own, but with food, I much prefer the acid balance and delicate fruit of Oregon Chardonnays," says Paul. "I also enjoy them more as a winemaker. California Chardonnays pretty much make themselves, but Oregon Chardonnays are very responsive to slight changes in winemaking technique. They are winemakers' wines."

Most wineries produce a line of several wines, including at least one cash flow wine, such as Riesling, that can be released soon after the vintage. But Paul came to Oregon with the sole purpose of making Pinot Noir and Chardonnay in the Burgundian tradition. With the exception of tiny experimental batches of wine, the Cameron winery produces Pinot Noir and Chardonnay exclusively.

CHATEAU BENOIT WINERY

*6580 N.E. Mineral Springs Road
Carlton, Oregon 97111
(503) 864-2991 or 864-3666*

Wine Production
10,000 cases

Vineyards
42 acres

Year First Planted
1972

First Vintage
1979

Leading Wines
Sauvignon Blanc, Brut Sparkling Wine, Muller-Thurgau

In 1972, Fred and Mary Benoit planted 10 acres of grapes near Veneta, a small community just west of the city of Eugene, in the southern Willamette Valley. What began as an investment and hobby, a diversion from Fred Benoit's medical practice, evolved into a major enterprise.

The northern Willamette Valley is the center of Oregon's winegrowing industry. When the time came for expansion, the Benoits found the land, and the community of winegrowers and winegrowing traditions they were seeking, near McMinnville in the northern Willamette. Now, the winery and half of the vineyards are at the

McMinnville site.

Although the general climatic conditions are similar in the Eugene and McMinnville areas, individual vineyard climates can vary widely. The Benoits' Veneta site is a benchland, and the soil is a rich, deep, silty loam called Salkum. It is a cool vineyard climate, subject to ground frost in the spring that can be particularly damaging to young vines. In cool years, the vineyard may receive only 1,700 to 1,800 heat units. The site near McMinnville is quite different. The soil is Willakenzie, and its climate is one of the warmest and sunniest in the McMinnville area, receiving 2,500 to 2,700 heat units in warmer years, according to Benoit. Situated on a hillside, air movement is good, and spring frost is not a problem.

Benoit prefers the cooler Veneta site for his Pinot Noir. The new vineyards near McMinnville are all planted to white varieties, including twelve acres of Muller-Thurgau, Oregon's largest single planting of this variety. Muller-Thurgau produces a soft, Riesling-like wine much in the style of the popular and ubiquitous Liebfraumilch from Germany.

Interest in Muller-Thurgau evolved during the tenure of Chateau Benoit's first winemaker, Max Zellweger, a native Swiss and a graduate of the College of Technology, Viticulture, and Horticulture in Wadenswil, Switzerland. Zellweger later took the winemaking position with the F.W. Langguth Winery, a large Washington winery with ties to its parent corporation in Germany.

The Benoit's son, Mark, graduated from Fresno State in viticulture, and now runs a vineyard management consulting service in the Willamette Valley, managing, among his accounts, Chateau Benoit's vineyards. Oregon grape growers are working with many new vine training ideas and methods. For the Benoit vineyards, Mark Benoit is pruning the vines to four canes per vine instead of the more conventional two. With this method, Benoit is hoping to gain some of the cropping and ripening advantages of a denser vine planting without the expense of planting and maintaining additional vines.

The majority of the winery's wines, and all the wines under the Chateau Benoit label, are made from Oregon grapes. From Washington grapes, Chateau Benoit also produces a line of wines under the Nisqually Ridge label, including Sauvignon Blanc and Riesling. The Nisqually Ridge Riesling is made in a sweeter, fuller style than the Riesling from Oregon grapes.

In 1981, a cool and rainy year, Benoit's Chardonnay did not ripen well enough to make a quality table wine, so Benoit decided to try a sparkling wine from the grapes. The Blanc de Blanc sparkling wine succeeded, and led Benoit to refine the cuvee in subsequent vintages. The Brut cuvee is predominantly Pinot Noir with lesser portions of Chardonnay and Pinot Blanc. The wine rests on the yeast for a year prior to disgorging. Less yeasty, but similar in structure to a racy French Champagne, Chateau Benoit Brut exemplifies the potential of the Oregon sparkling wine industry.

ELK COVE VINEYARDS

Route 3, Box 23
Gaston, Oregon 97119
(503) 985-7760

Wine Production
12,000 cases

Vineyards
27 acres

Year First Planted
1974

First Vintage
1977

Leading Wines
Pinot Noir, Chardonnay, Riesling

At the outskirts of the small town of Gaston, a paved road winds its way up the hillside. A turn-off just beyond its crest is the entryway to Elk Cove, a vineyard and winery named for the Roosevelt Elk that migrate through the area in the spring. Solely owned and operated by the Campbell family, Pat and Joe Campbell, wife and husband, share winemaking and vineyard management duties. On the crest of a hill on the 136 acre estate, the winery and tasting room offer a sweeping view of the Elk Cove vineyard. Elk Cove has grown considerably since its early years, but still retains a personal and personable flavor that makes it a pleasure to visit.

Many premium American wineries are, to a degree, moving away from strict adherence to the methodologies and mind set of the University of California at Davis, and looking again toward European winegrowing practices. Because Oregon's climate is similar to some of Europe's premium growing regions, the state has more to gain in the new world's return to its viticultural roots. The look back, however, is not a return to unscientific practices. Europe has a long tradition of rigorous and comprehensive inquiry into the science and art of grape growing and winemaking in cooler climates. In Oregon, Elk Cove is among those wineries most oriented toward European methods.

This is not to say that the teachings of U.C. Davis are ignored or rejected out of hand. Pat Campbell regards the short courses she attended at U.C. Davis as a valuable source of winemaking information, but the California school is, understandably, directed more toward the problems and interests of California winemaking, problems and interests that frequently differ from those of Oregon winemakers.

In Europe, vines are often planted much more densely than is common in California. Many believe that increasing the number of vines per acre insures more consistent yields at favorable sugar and acid levels. Elk Cove's vines are planted six feet apart, in rows seven feet apart, a density of 1,054 vines per acre. Domestic farm machinery cannot cope with these narrow rows, and the Campbells are forced to put up with the scarcity of parts and repair service for their 48 inch wide Italian tractor. Because each vine must be pruned, trained, and cared for, the expense of this higher density planting is considerably greater.

It is commonly believed that increasing the vine's foliage increases its capacity to produce and ripen grapes, but as European studies show, this is only partially true. After approximately the fourteenth leaf on the main shoots and the fourth leaf on the lateral shoots, nutrient production merely supports foliage and no longer benefits the grapes. Elk Cove and other Oregon growers have taken to a practice called hedging, trimming vine shoots to benefit grape production and ripening, a time consuming procedure, and an added expense.

Traditional methods are applied in the winery as well as the vineyard. The Chardonnay is fermented in French oak barrels and kept on the lees (yeast cells and other sediment) without racking for four to seven months. During this time period, the lees are stirred. These practices contribute to the wine's flavor complexity. During one of their earlier vintages, the Campbells did not have enough cooperage to ferment all their Chardonnay in oak, and some of the wine was fermented in stainless steel barrels. After two weeks, when fermentation was completed, both the oak fermented and stainless steel fermented wines were put into oak barrels for aging. After nine months, the Campbells report that the wines were distinctly different. Although the oak fermented wine did not have a stronger oak flavor, it was fuller and more complex. This firsthand comparative experience made the Campbells strong advocates of oak barrel fermentation.

Pat Campbell—the winemaking begins.

Before pressing and fermentation begin, Elk Cove's Chardonnay is left on its skins and stems for 12 to 18 hours. The Campbells ferment their Chardonnay with the Montrachet strain of yeast, a strain that has a reputation for producing fuller, richer wines, but at increased risk of the undesirable byproduct, hydrogen sulfide. To avoid the problem of hydrogen sulfide, the Campbells treat their grapes with little or no sulfur, and their Chardonnay benefits from the Montrachet yeast without suffering its undesirable byproduct.

The hard realities of economic necessity weigh heavily on the winegrower. Winegrowers need a grape that produces a reliable crop, and can be turned into wine and released soon after the vintage, in short, a cash flow wine to keep the home fires burning and the bankers happy. In Oregon, for this purpose, Riesling is the grape of choice. Not only is Riesling a good "safety grape," it also produces good wine. The ultimate Rieslings, however, are made from botrytised grapes, grapes that have been infected with the *Botrytis cinerea* mold in such a way that the grape essences are more concentrated. But if conditions are not ideal, the botrytis becomes gray rot, and the crop can be damaged or lost. Oregon's frequently rainy falls make botrytised wines a very risky business, and few winegrowers are willing to subject their "safety wine" to such a risk.

Elk Cove is an exception. In years when conditions are favorable, the vines are left unsprayed, and the botrytis is allowed to develop. In the best years, in German fashion, a Riesling is made from individually selected clusters of the most botrytised grapes. These wines are expensive to produce. In addition to the risk, twice the picking time is needed, and the grapes, shriveled from the botrytis, yield much less juice. Toward the end of harvest, after many nights of little sleep, winegrowers do not look forward to additional risk, worry, and time consuming tasks, but the Campbell's botrytised Rieslings have rewarded them well, and have become benchmarks in the exploration of Riesling's potential in Oregon.

Pinot Noir, Elk Cove's premier wine, is cropped to a moderate 2½ tons an acre in most years. The wine is fermented in 200 gallon bins, and the cap of pulp and skins is punched down three to four times a day. According to the year, varying amounts of stems are included during fermentation. In less ripe years, the stems are green and fewer are used. After fermentation is completed, the pulp, skins, and stems are left to macerate in the must for five days. The wine is then pressed, and racked into Allier and Nevers oak barrels.

Grapes are highly sensitive to small changes in growing environment. The grapes Elk Cove purchases from other growers in the northern Willamette Valley are fermented and bottled separately. Differences in soil, climate, and growing methods are brought more clearly into focus when these different grapes are made into wine by the same winemaker. Comparison of Elk Cove Pinot Noirs from their own estate, and from the Wind Hill Vineyard in the Forest Grove area west of Portland is a case in point. Both vineyards were planted the same year, to the same clone of Pinot Noir, obtained from the same source. The Wind Hill Vineyard is planted in a clay shot soil, the Elk Cove Vineyard in a sandier soil called Willakenzie Silty Loam. The Wind Hill Vineyard has had lighter yields. The site is warmer, and ripens one to two weeks ahead of Elk Cove's vineyard. The Wind Hill Pinot Noirs tend to be more tannic and display a more forward fruit intensity. The estate grown Pinot Noirs tend to be rounder and earthier.

Low acid and high pH were a common fault with earlier Oregon Pinot Noirs, and the problem, thankfully to a lesser degree, continues today. Low acid, high pH Pinot Noirs brown within a few short years and fail to develop the grape's manifold flavor complexities with age. The Campbells learned these lessons well in their first vintages, but regrettably, because low acid, high pH Pinot Noirs have a softer, silkier allure when first released, consumers and wine judges alike are often lead astray, motivating some Oregon winemakers to continue the style. The best Pinot Noirs are often harder and less yielding in their youth, developing the textural elements with age, along with the flavor complexities. Cellaring Elk Cove's Pinot Noirs for a few years readily affirms the wisdom of the higher acid wine style.

ELLENDALE VINEYARDS

300 Reuben Boise Road
Dallas, Oregon 97338
(503) 623-5617

Grape Wine Production
2,000 cases

Fruit And Berry Wine And Mead Production
500 cases

Vineyards
15 acres

Year First Planted
1979

First Vintage
1982

Leading Wines
Gewurztraminer, White Pinot Noir

While waiting for their own vineyards to mature, Robert and Ella Mae Hudson took advantage of an abundance of Oregon fruits, berries, and honey to satisfy local consumer demand for wines made from those products. By the mid 1980s, local consumer interest was shifting toward grape wines, a transition that coincided with the maturation of Ellendale's estate vineyard. Now, more than three-fourths of Ellendale's wines are made from grapes.

Mead, made in three degrees of sweetness, is still an Ellendale specialty. The Hudsons make a completely dry mead from mild honey, a slightly sweet mead with 1 ½ percent residual sugar from flavorful crimson clover honey, and a sweet mead with four percent residual sugar from intensely flavored wildflower honey.

Making mead is different than making grape wines, or any other fruit or berry wines. Grapes and other fruits have ample nutrients for the yeast. Honey does not naturally have the nutrients, so they are added during fermentation. Fruit wines require the addition of sugar, but for mead, acid is added to give the right balance. No sugar is added to any of Ellendale's meads, only honey at bottling for the two meads with residual sweetness. Aged in oak, the Hudsons make their meads in a relatively drier style than most, emphasizing the flavors of the honey.

Most of the Ellendale vineyard is planted to conventional Oregon grape varieties, but some of the acreage is planted to less usual varieties. Aurora, a white French-American hybrid, ripens successfully in a very cool spot of the vineyard. The Hudsons grow two Bordeaux grape varieties, Cabernet Franc and Cabernet Sauvignon. In ideal vintages, the Willamette Valley can produce fine wines from these varieties. In cooler vintages, the Hudsons are quite content to make rose and "blanc" wines from the grapes, wines that are very popular with consumers.

A landscape artist as well as winemaker, Robert Hudson's works are on display and for sale in the winery tasting room. Hudson specializes in scenes of Oregon and the Oregon Trail.

THE EYRIE VINEYARDS

P.O. Box 204
Dundee, Oregon 97115
935 East 10th Avenue
McMinnville, Oregon 97128
(503) 472-6315 or 864-2410

Wine Production
6,000 cases

Vineyards
26 acres

Year First Planted
1966

First Vintage
1970

Leading Wines
Pinot Noir, Pinot Gris, Chardonnay, Muscat Ottonel

David Lett is one of the true pioneers of Oregon's wine industry. Although he came to Oregon in 1965, four years after Hillcrest's Richard Sommer had settled in the Roseburg area, Lett was the first winemaker in recent times to grow vinifera grapes in the Willamette Valley area near Portland, and moreover, the first Oregon winemaker choosing to focus his efforts on a red wine—Pinot Noir.

With a degree in viticulture from the University of California at Davis, and some practical

56

California winemaking experience, Lett began looking for an area to grow the Burgundian grape varieties, Pinot Noir and Chardonnay. Then as now, successful California Pinot Noirs were rare, and although Chardonnay is now perhaps California's best wine, in the 1960s, California Chardonnays were picked too early, saw little or no oak, and were for the most part unexceptional. With this frame of reference, Lett came to Oregon. He passed by the Roseburg area believing it too warm for Pinot Noir, and chose the Willamette Valley's Dundee Hills as the site for his vineyards.

In selecting this site, Lett was not only singular in his conviction, but virtually solitary. Oregon State University was then recommending *Vitis labrusca* as the only commercially viable species. Everyone from Lett's U. C. Davis professors to local farmers advised against his enterprise. Said one of his professors, "You'll be frosted out in the spring and fall, rained on all summer, and you'll get athlete's foot up to your knees." Fortunately, Lett ignored the advice, but years would pass before his beliefs could be validated.

Lett's interest in Pinot Noir proved farsighted. Pinot Noir, a grape that rarely does well outside of Burgundy, is Oregon's stellar wine grape, a fact confirmed by the now famous tastings published in the french food and wine magazine, *Gault/ Millau, Le Nouveau Guide*. In 1979, the magazine sponsored an "Olympics of the Wines of the World," pitting the 330 best of 586 original entries from 33 of the world's wine producing regions.

To the disappointment of many, including Robert J. Drouhin of the well-known Burgundian wine firm Joseph Drouhin, the French wines did not do as well as had been expected. Drouhin contended that the tasting had been unbalanced, and that less than the best Burgundies had been chosen to compete against the very best "foreign" wines. Drouhin proposed a rematch, pitting the top-scoring foreign Pinot Noirs against Burgundies selected from the Drouhin cellars.

On January 8, 1980, under the supervision of M. Jacques Puisais, President of the International Union of Enologists, twenty French, English, and American wine judges of con-

siderable repute conducted a formal tasting of the wines. Drouhin's 1959 Chambolle-Musigny was the first place wine. In third place was his 1961 Chambertin Clos-de-Beze. The second place wine, two tenths of a point out of first, was the 1975 Eyrie Vineyards South Block Reserve from Oregon.

After fifteen years of pioneer adversity, the results of the *Gault/Millau* tasting were sweet indeed. This landmark tasting not only brought Eyrie instant recognition, it helped bring well-deserved and long overdue attention to the Oregon wine industry.

Lett believes that more than any other variety, Pinot Noir is a winegrower's, and above all, a winemaker's grape. Cabernet Sauvignon has a strong and immediate varietal profile, but Pinot Noir is delicate, elusive, and subtle. Grown in less than ideal conditions, the varietal character disappears completely, yet this subtle quality makes the grape highly responsive to slight changes in grow-

David Lett.

57

ing conditions and winemaking methods. More than any other variety, Pinot Noir reflects the winemaker's style, the winemaker's art.

Eyrie Pinot Noirs are reflective of Lett's preferences and predilections. Of Burgundies Lett tends to prefer those with perfumed finesse rather than the bigger, and, to his taste, sometimes more clumsy wines of the northernmost Cote de Nuits.

Eyrie's Pinot Noir is fermented without the stems in small, four-foot-square bins. Temperatures reach the high 80s. At the height of fermentation, Lett sleeps in the winery, and punches down the fermenting cap of skins and pulp every two hours around the clock. Lett believes that frequent and vigorous punching-down extracts the most and best flavors from the grape. Lett's Pinot Noir goes through malolactic fermentation, and is bottled after 14 to 23 months in French oak. Some special reserve Pinot Noirs may spend as long as 30 months in oak.

Most of Eyrie's Pinot Noir is the Wadenswil clone. Lett concedes that clonal differences exist, but emphasizes that other factors are far more significant. Distinctive character tends to show itself as vines grow older. With age, the vines, and so too their grapes, are subject to transformation. It is in keeping with the elusive nature of Pinot Noir that attempts to capture clonal differences with definitive statements is a tenuous proposition at best.

Eyrie Pinot Noirs are not darkly colored wines. Lett decries the American, and particularly the West Coast, prejudice that high tannin, high alcohol, and inky color somehow equate with quality or aging potential. Lett believes that good acidity and concentrated varietal fruit are the keys to longevity and fine Pinot Noir.

Lett's wines give credence to his views. Often seemingly light and delicate when first released, Lett's Pinot Noirs have earned a justifiable reputation for developing fine, complex flavors—and continuing to age in the bottle long after the inky, high tannin, high alcohol, low acid Pinot Noirs have faded.

Lett produces Chardonnay, another Burgundian grape variety, and a mainstay of the Oregon wine industry, but eschews Oregon's traditional third major variety, Riesling. Many feel that Riesling does not make a very good dry wine, but is at its best with some residual sugar. Lett prefers dry wines to go with food, and has budded over his Riesling vines to another grape variety, Pinot Gris, a little-known white wine grape.

For years, Lett produced miniscule quantities of Pinot Gris from a few experimental vines. Lett became enamored with the grape variety and its wines. A direct relative of Pinot Noir, Pinot Gris is a viable alternative to Riesling. Riesling is popular with winegrowers because it produces palatable wines even in poor years, requires no oak and no aging, and can be released soon after the vintage, providing much needed cash flow for the winegrower. Pinot Gris has these same attributes, but it is an excellent food wine as well.

Except for Chardonnay, virtually all white grape varieties grown in the Willamette Valley on a commercial scale are Germanic in style, Riesling or Riesling-like, floral in character, and best suited to a slightly sweet style. Pinot Gris is different. At its worst, Pinot Gris can be slightly heavy and flat, with some bitterness in the finish. As its best, it is a crisp, full-bodied, flavorful wine of distinction.

A color mutation of Pinot Noir, Pinot Gris is similar to its red cousin in that it does not have a high varietal profile as does, for example, Cabernet Sauvignon or Sauvignon Blanc, but instead communicates its merit through a subtle interplay of flavors. Unlike Oregon Chardonnay, Pinot Gris is not temperamental, but ripens easily, reliably produces good crops, and is relatively easy to turn into good wine.

Lett does not intend Pinot Gris as a replacement for Chardonnay. In his rendition, Pinot Gris is fermented in stainless steel, put through a malolactic fermentation, bottled without oak aging, and released soon after the vintage.

Without oak aging, Chardonnay usually seems incomplete, but Pinot Gris makes a complete wine even without oak. The texture and fullness of Pinot Gris often conveys the sensation that the wine has been in oak, even when it has not. Pinot Gris is the dry wine drinker's answer to Riesling, and in many ways, it is preferable to all but the better Oregon Chardonnays.

In very small quantities, Lett makes a dry Muscat Ottonel, a refined and uncommon member of the Muscat family. To avoid confusion among buyers expecting a sweet wine in the manner of most Muscats, Lett is now bottling his Muscat Ottonel in a Chardonnay-style bottle, a shape more readily associated with dry wines.

Two decades ago, Lett assumed considerable risk, and pioneered Pinot Noir in Oregon's Willamette Valley. Two decades later, Lett again subscribed to risk and committed himself to Pinot Gris, a direct relative of Pinot Noir. In partnership with an adjacent grower, John Schetky, Lett is committing half of his yearly wine production to this unknown and unrecognized grape.

To a marketing consultant, Lett's large commitment to Pinot Gris would seem unwise at best, but two decades ago, his commitment to Oregon Pinot Noir was similarly foolish. If Pinot Gris does not become one of Oregon's major grape varieties, it will not be for lack of merit, and it will not be for lack of pioneering commitment.

FORGERON VINEYARD

89697 Sheffler Road
Elmira, Oregon 97437
(503) 935-1117

Wine Production
6,000 cases

Vineyards
20 acres

Year First Planted
1972

First Vintage
1978

Leading Wines
Riesling, White Pinot Noir, Pinot Noir

Climate measurements at the city of Eugene suggest that this southern portion of the Willamette Valley is nearly identical to the northern Willamette near Portland. Such is not the case. The climates surrounding Eugene vary considerably, and some are warmer and otherwise differ significantly in character from the growing areas of the northern Willamette. Forgeron vineyard is one such climate.

The choice of Forgeron's vineyard location

was no accident. In the late 1960's, the Federal Government conducted an environmental impact study to evaluate the feasibility of a nuclear power plant near Eugene. The power plant was never built, but its latent legacy was a highly comprehensive source of climatological information. Taking advantage of this data, Lee and Linda Smith selected their vineyard site, and in 1972, planted their first grapes.

According to Smith, Forgeron has 55 more days of sunshine than Eugene, and seven to ten inches less rainfall. Although the days are warm, the nights are quite cool, a condition Smith feels is a key factor in the quality of his Pinot Noir and Cabernet Sauvignon, and also an important element in encouraging the growth of *Botrytis cinerea*, a mold that, under the right conditions, is responsible for special, sweet, white wines of exceptional quality. Oregon vintages, like vintages of European winegrowing climates, vary much more than those of California. Smith reports that heat summation measurements in his vineyard

have ranged from 2,000 to over 3,000, though "typical" years average 2,400 to 2,500.

In part because of this warmer climate, Forgeron is one of the few Oregon wineries pursuing Cabernet Sauvignon. Forgeron produces much more Pinot Noir than Cabernet Sauvignon, but the Cabernet is Smith's personal favorite. He reports that his Cabernet Sauvignon ripens well nearly every year. This is no great trick with small experimental plots producing low, non-commercial yields, but Smith's vines are generously cropped to a commercially viable four to five tons an acre.

Forgeron's Pinot Noir is planted half to the Wadenswil clone and half to the Pommard. Smith, preferring a blend of the two clones, believes that Pommard has a more typically Burgundian character, but that Wadenswil contributes more aromatics. Having lived and traveled in the winegrowing regions of France, Smith very much believes that important flavor characteristics in wines come from the soil. Burgundy's limestone soils are legendary. Forgeron's vineyard is not a limestone soil per se, but a soil interestingly different from other Oregon vineyard soils. The topsoil is Bellpine, but at 18 inches, is a layer with bits of a sandstone-limestone mix. At 30 inches, the soil changes to a permeable sandstone-limestone layer. Smith saw a beneficial change in the character of his Pinot Noir beginning with the 1981 vintage, a change Smith attributes to the vine's penetration of the major sandstone-limestone layer.

Riesling is Forgeron's major grape variety. Smith ferments the Riesling at very low temperatures, about 40 to 45 degrees, to preserve the delicate fruit esters of the grape. He has found that the standard strains of dried yeast do not work well at these temperatures, and now imports live yeast cultures from France to do the job.

Smith believes that most Chardonnay planted in Oregon is a high acid clone poorly suited to the Oregon climate. Forgeron is focusing efforts on the less widely planted Chardonnay vine known as the Draper clone. Other white varieties include small amounts of Chenin Blanc and Pinot Gris. Although Chenin Blanc barely ripens in most

Lee Smith.

60

years, it lends itself well to the beneficial botrytis mold. The Pinot Gris is made in both a dry and an unusual semi-dry style.

Several experiments with vine training and vine pruning are underway. One of the more interesting methods is the "Italian T." Four fruiting canes are allowed to grow vertically until they bend over into the rows from their own weight. Pruning is easy. Each season, the vines are clipped off at the top of their training wires. The remaining cane becomes a cordon, a permanent portion of the vine from which new canes grow each season. Not only does this method increase sun exposure, but the vines can be mechanically harvested. No Oregon winegrowers are mechanically harvesting now, nor is there any immediate need for mechanical harvesting, but if hand harvesting became too expensive or there were a labor shortage, the mechanical harvesting option would be desirable. The "Italian T," with the canes and grapes hanging into the rows, is suited to the type of machinery that could be practical in Oregon—not the mechanical monsters that straddle entire vine rows, but smaller, less expensive machinery, harvesting one side of a row at a time, and capable of operating in hillier terrain.

GARDEN VALLEY WINERY

251 Camino Francisco
Roseburg, Oregon 97470
(503) 673-3010

Wine Production
6,000 cases

Vineyards
25 acres

Year First Planted
1973

First Vintage
1984

Leading Wines
Gewurztraminer, Riesling, White Pinot Noir

Most Oregon wineries look to France, primarily Burgundy, for their approach to winemaking, but Garden Valley Winery embraces Germanic winemaking methods and philosophies. The Germanic point of view comes from winemaker Richard Mansfield. While completing his studies in viticultural and enological engineering at Geisenheim, West Germany, Mansfield, an Oregon native, returned to make Garden Valley's first vintage.

Ray Higgins and Frank Guido are the principal owners of Garden Valley Winery. Half the winery's grapes come from the Umpqua Valley, the other half come from Ray Higgins' vineyard in the southeastern Willamette Valley. Although the winemaking approach is different, the grape varieties are traditionally Oregon's.

Mansfield's Chardonnay reflects a Germanic influence. The varietal character of the grape is not masked by an insistent overlay of oak, and the wine is not put through malolactic fermentation. Mansfield believes that malolactic fermentation destroys the fruitiness of the wine. In years when a reduction in acidity is necessary, Mansfield employs alternate methods to reduce the acidity.

Mansfield's Riesling and Gewurztraminer have a clean character and fresh fruitiness. The Gewurztraminer is made in both dry and late harvest, slightly sweet styles. If conditions are right, Mansfield makes special Rieslings from heavily botrytised grapes. The grapes for his first, intensely sweet Riesling were harvested over a period of 14 days. The grapes, shriveled by the botrytis, yielded a mere 100 gallons of juice at an exceptionally high sugar reading of 36 degrees Brix. High acidity, measuring 1.4 grams per liter, balances the intense sweetness. The finished wine is highly concentrated and intensely sweet, with 16.6 percent residual sugar.

Mansfield makes a traditionally styled Pinot Noir, putting the wine through malolactic fermentation and aging it in oak, but he also makes a Germanic style Pinot Noir with low tannin, no wood aging, no malolactic fermentation, and slight residual sweetness. Garden Valley's alternate approach to winemaking adds another dimension to Oregon's wine scene.

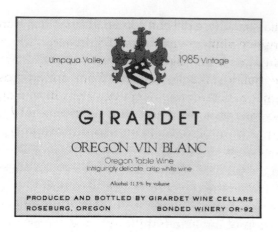

GIRARDET WINE CELLARS

895 Reston Road
Roseburg, OR 97470
(503) 679-7252

Wine Production
4,000 cases

Vineyards
18 acres

Year First Planted
1972

First Vintage
1983

Leading Wines
Vin Blanc, Riesling

Working as a design engineer at the California Institute of Technology, Swiss born Philippe Girardet met his wife Bonnie, and soon after, the two opted for a change in careers and lifestyle, moving to Oregon's Umpqua Valley near Roseburg.

Girardet's Swiss background led him to a belief in high quality, moderately priced, everyday wines to serve with food. This perspective, and the nature of the Girardets' vineyard site prompted them to explore French-American hybrids, crosses between vinifera and native American varieties.

Parts of the Girardets' vineyard are prone to frosts, and the soils are very shallow, with underlying shale. The hybrid varieties are much more

62

suitable to these difficult conditions than the more sensitive vinifera varieties. Additionally, hybrids suffer less from mildew than vinifera vines, and the hybrids readily recover from spring frost damage. Girardet's vinifera vines produce about two tons an acre. The hybrids produce four to five tons an acre, ripening early at good sugar levels.

One of the few winegrowers in the Northwest working with hybrid varieties, the Girardets like the hybrids not only for their performance in the vineyard, but for their ability to produce good quality, moderately priced wines—a fundamental tenet of the Girardet philosophy. None of the two dozen hybrids in the vineyard is released as a single bottling. All are blended into Girardet's principal wines, Vin Blanc and Vin Rouge. The Vin Blanc is comprised of 75 percent Chardonnay and usually five hybrid varieties, mainly Verdelet and Aurora. The Vin Rouge is usually about 55 percent Pinot Noir, blended with small amounts of other vinifera varieties, including Zinfandel and Merlot, as well as hybrid varieties, Baco Noir, DeChaunac, Chancellor, and others.

The Girardets also release single variety vinifera wines, including Riesling, Gewurztraminer, and Chardonnay. The Chardonnay is made in a fruitier, lighter oaked style than the norm for this variety. Among the blended wines, the Vin Rouge is fermented and aged in stainless steel to emphasize the wine's fruity characteristics. Riesling is Girardet's most the popular wine, but the Vin Blanc may be considered Girardet's principal wine, embodying the philosophy of blended wine, hybrid grapes, and good, moderately priced, easily approachable wine to serve with food.

GLEN CREEK WINERY

6057 Orchard Heights Road N.W.
Salem, Oregon 97304
(503) 371-WINE

Wine Production
5,000 cases

Vineyards
10 acres

Year First Planted
1983

First Vintage
1982

Leading Wines
Sauvignon Blanc, Chardonnay, Pinot Noir

Founder of a leading southern California wine shop, Thomas Dumm was among the first few in the state to stock Northwest wines. In 1976, Dumm and his family left California for a better life style in Oregon. Settling in a rural area near Salem, Dumm planted a few grape vines and continued with his interest in home winemaking, a hobby that would soon to grow into a commercial enterprise.

Dumm prepared for winemaking on a commercial scale by attending a series of courses at the University of California at Davis. In 1982, Glen Creek had its first crush, 6,000 gallons of wine from Washington grapes. Glen Creek now produces all its wines from Oregon grapes. Most of Glen Creek's grapes are grown in the Eola Hills where the winery is located.

An emerging winegrowing subregion of the Willamette Valley, the Eola Hills rise up from the Willamette River near Salem, and run northward along the river for a short distance. Situated in the middle of the wide Willamette Valley, the Eola Hills offer a slightly different winegrowing climate from most Willamette Valley vineyards which are situated along the western edge of the valley.

In 1983, Dumm planted ten acres of an unusual Oregon grape variety, Cabernet Franc, one of the Bordeaux grapes. The vines are cordon pruned, a practice predominant in California, but rare in Oregon where vines are almost always cane pruned. With cordon pruning, the vines are left with permanent lateral arms called cordons. In the spring, new growth emerges from these cordons. Although this vine training method is in-frequent in cooler climates, cordon pruned vines are more easily maintained, and require less skilled labor and attention.

Dumm built Glen Creek's tasting room in the aging cellar so that visitors would not be isolated from the sights and smells of the winery. Just outside, tall, temperature controlled tanks glisten in the sun, and an arbor covered picnic area offers a tranquil setting for visitors. During the grape crush, a raised viewing deck affords a good view of winery operations.

Sylvia and Thomas Dumm.

HENRY WINERY

P.O. Box 26, Highway 6
Umpqua, Oregon 97486
(503) 459-5120 or 459-3614

Wine Production
10,000 cases

Vineyards
31 acres

Year First Planted
1972

First Vintage
1978

Leading Wines
Pinot Noir, Chardonnay, Gewurztraminer

The Henry Winery is a paradox, a winery firmly rooted in Oregon's rural, pioneering, winegrowing traditions, yet contrasting with, and contradicting, many of those same traditions. Scott Henry, the winery's founder, became interested in wine from his close friend and colleague, the late Gino Zepponi. Both worked for the same California engineering firm. Zepponi became the "Z" in California's ZD winery, and later vice president of the large California sparkling wine producer, Domaine Chandon.

In 1971, Henry and Zepponi came to Oregon to look at the prospects for winegrowing. In 1972, Henry left California and the engineering firm, moved to Oregon, and planted 12 acres of wine grapes in Oregon's Umpqua Valley.

Many of Oregon's winegrowers have come to the state from California, but Henry is not a newcomer. The Henry family has lived and ranched in the Umpqua Valley for over a hundred years. The family ranch and orchards are on bottomland near the Umpqua River, and it is there that Henry planted his grapes, thus immediately violating Oregon winegrowing traditions, and the fundamental tenet that Oregon vineyards should be planted on southerly slopes above the valley floor.

The soil is a Roseburg Sandy Loam, running fifteen feet to gravel. Skeptics believed that the flatland vineyards would not have enough air movement to dispel destructive spring frosts, would not be sunny or warm enough to ripen the grapes, and would produce mostly vegetation instead of grapes. All these predictions proved wrong.

The nearby Umpqua River protects the vines from frost. As the temperature approaches freezing, the moist, river air fogs up, protecting the vines from frost much in the same way that overhead sprinkler systems are used to create a moist heating-freezing shield around the vines. The vineyard site has had an average of 2,200 heat units a year. During the growing season, a cut in the Coast Range Mountains corresponds with the position of the setting sun, thus increasing the effective day length. Adequate grape sugars have not been a problem.

The Henrys' decorative grape arbor consistently produced grapes every year, and Henry had little doubt that his vineyard would have a commercially viable grape yield. This proved more than true. In Oregon, three tons an acre is considered a good average yield for most grape varieties. Scott Henry's vineyards yield six to eight tons of Chardonnay and Pinot Noir per acre.

Most feel that higher yields tend to dilute a wine's quality, particularly with respect to Pinot Noir, but Henry maintains that after experimenting with a wide range of yields, six to eight tons results in the best wine for his growing site.

Scott Henry.

Henry accepted the advice, and the wines have proven both successful and controversial. The pronounced American oak character quickly polarizes wine tasters. Henry prefers a riper, fuller style of wine, a style that best suits the American oak, and is achieved most fully in Oregon's warmer vintages. Because of these stylistic predilections, some critics have suggested Henry's wines more closely resemble the wines of California than the wines of Oregon. Others praise them highly, especially the fuller bodied wines from the warmest vintages.

Because Henry's vineyards produce more than twice as much wine per acre as most Oregon vineyards, the sometimes hard financial realities of Oregon winegrowing do not impact Henry so severely.

The type of wines the Henry Winery produces, however, presents an extra expense. Most Oregon wineries produce substantial quantities of a cash flow wine, usually Riesling. Rieslings can be released within six months of the harvest, offering immediate income, and clearing out storage and fermentation tanks for the next vintage. Henry produces no Riesling, and only small amounts of Gewurztraminer. Virtually all of Henry's production is in Chardonnay and Pinot Noir. The Henry winery, in fact, is one of the state's larger producers of these wines, although many wineries have greater total wine production.

These factors dovetail into another unconventionality. Both Pinot Noir and Chardonnay are customarily aged in small oak barrels, and are not released for one to two or more years after the vintage. This requires an immense investment in cooperage. With rare exception, Oregon wineries use only the more expensive French oaks for aging. At several times the price of American oak, this seemed prohibitively expensive to Henry. His friend and consultant, Zepponi, had urged Henry to use American oak cooperage, a widespread practice in California. Zepponi suggested that consumer acceptance and awards in wine judgings would be no different than if French oak were used.

1983

Hidden Springs

Oregon
Pinot Noir

PRODUCED AND BOTTLED BY
HIDDEN SPRINGS WINERY, INC.
AMITY, OREGON, U.S.A.
BW-OR-81

Alcohol 12.5% by Volume

HIDDEN SPRINGS WINERY

9360 S.E. Eola Hills Road
Amity, Oregon 97101
(503) 835-2782

Wine Production
3,500 cases

Vineyards
20 acres

Year First Planted
1973

First Vintage
1980

Leading Wines
Pinot Noir, Chardonnay

Hidden Springs Winery is a corporation owned by two families, Don and Carolyn Byard and Al and Jo Alexanderson. The Byards own their own vineyard and sell grapes to the corporation. The Byard vineyard, in the Eola Hills between Amity and Hopewell, is a former cherry and prune orchard. The remaining prune trees supplement the income from the Byards' grape crop. The nearby prune drying building was converted into the Hidden Springs winery.

Most of Oregon's climatological information comes from data gathered at airport weather stations, but since airports are usually in valleys, and vineyards are usually at higher elevations, on hillsides with southerly exposures, winegrowers have not had the benefit of reliable basic information, much less information on important subtleties, comparing, for example, the implications of a southwesterly exposure versus a southeasterly exposure, the effects of cloud cover at different times during the growing season, and so on. Byard is participating in an experimental program with Oregon State University to gather more accurate and useful data. Thermographs have been placed at several vineyard locations in the Willamette Valley, including Byard's. Thermographs measure, automatically and continuously, temperature, humidity, and the intensity of the sunlight.

When conversation turns to clonal selection, Pinot Noir is the grape that comes first to mind, but other varieties have clonal variants as well,

Al Alexanderson and Don Byard.

though not to the same degree as Pinot Noir. As part of another experimental program, three different clones of Riesling are planted at the Eola site.

Oregon's principal grape varieties, Riesling, Chardonnay, and Pinot Noir, comprise most of Hidden Spring's production, but other less usual varieties are produced as well. Sauvignon Blanc has proven particularly successful, and is the basis for the winery's blended white wine. In warmer years, Cabernet Sauvignon is made. Land near the winery building does not have the best exposure to the sun, but Muller-Thurgau, a Riesling-like variety, does well on cooler, less sunny sites, and some may be planted.

Hidden Springs also operates a tasting room in the Schubert Gallery, at 103 Main Street S. E. in Albany. Artwork from the gallery is featured each month in the winery's tasting room.

HILLCREST VINEYARD

240 Vineyard Lane
Roseburg, Oregon 97470
(503) 673-3709

Wine Production
8,000 cases

Vineyards
35 acres

Year First Planted
1961

First Vintage
1963

Leading Wines
Riesling, Pinot Noir, Cabernet Sauvignon

In 1961, Richard Sommer bought acreage and planted wine grapes in Oregon's Umpqua Valley near Roseburg, and with that, became the proverbial father and founder of Oregon's wine industry.

Sommer studied agronomy and viticulture at the University of California at Davis, and after an intervening period, came to Oregon in search of a cooler winegrowing climate. Sampling some of the few vinifera grapes that were then growing in Oregon, Sommer was satisfied he had found the proper climate. Although remnants of earlier winegrowing efforts remained, when Sommer came to Oregon, no prior precedent gave adequate assurance of success.

For the winegrowers that followed, Sommer not only provided direct assistance, but perhaps even more importantly, served as an example that commercial, premium, vinifera winegrowing in Oregon was not only possible, but viable. More than two decades have passed since Sommer came to Oregon. Although the state's wine industry has grown tremendously, and many wineries are vying for attention and recognition, for many years, Sommer's Hillcrest Vineyard and premium Oregon wine were virtually synonymous.

The trip from the town of Roseburg to the Hillcrest winery is a convoluted journey, well marked, but entailing many turns and side roads. At 850 feet above sea level, the Hillcrest vineyard is higher and slightly cooler than any other estate vineyard in the Roseburg area, but well suited to Riesling. Fully two thirds of Hillcrest's 35 acre vineyard are planted to the grape, and Hillcrest's reputation is based on Riesling wines. Oregon is now known for several grape varieties, but when Sommer pioneered this cooler grape growing region, Riesling, a well known, premium, cool climate grape, was the most logical choice, and today, Riesling is still a mainstay of the Oregon wine industry.

Nearly every Oregon winery releases Riesling soon after the vintage as a cash flow wine to keep the bankers away from the door. Most Oregon Riesling is purchased and consumed within a year of the vintage. Although a tasty wine when young, Riesling is a better wine with some bottle age, though few Rieslings are stored long enough to show their best. Hillcrest Rieslings are given a better chance. Sommer does not release them until about two years after the vintage, fully ready to drink, though still receptive to longer aging.

Hillcrest's Rieslings are fermented at a temperature of 50 degrees in stainless steel tanks. The fermentation is stopped when the desired level of sweetness remains. In recent years, the Riesling has been selectively harvested. Pickers make several passes through the vineyard at different times, harvesting only the ripest grapes. Sommer has also made Riesling ice wine. The grapes are picked frozen on the vine and quickly crushed before they thaw. The sweetest berries freeze the least, and in the first pressing, only the

juice from the ripest berries is released. True ice wines are much more concentrated than their regularly picked brethren.

Best known for his Rieslings, Sommer has also made a mark with his red wines, produced in small quantities. All the red wines are aged in a combination of French and American oak. Pinot Noir has been successful, and in warmer years, Cabernet Sauvignon ripens well and is a wine for laying down. In 1974, Sommer set aside a Cabernet made from his oldest vines. A wine for long aging, Sommer did not release it for sale until eight years after the vintage.

Zinfandel, a long season grape, seldom ripens properly in Oregon, but in choice years, when the grape does ripen, the wine can be very good. Hillcrest, in very small quantities, is one of the few Northwest wineries producing a Zinfandel, and in those rare good years, it is a most worthy wine.

Richard Sommer, founder of Oregon's first premium grape winery in the modern era, bonded winery 44.

To achieve high yield, good ripening, and well defined varietal character, Oregon vines need more leaf area exposed to the sun than warmer climate vines. To this end, Sommer has trained most of his vines into a tall double curtain. When viewed down the vine row, the vines are shaped like a "U." Open in the center, each vine's double canopy form the sides of the "U." Developed independently, Sommer's vine training method closely parallels the "Open-Lyre" or "U" system developed by Carbonneau in France, a system that has garnered much attention even in tradition-bound France.

Most winegrowers are anxious to show off their winery or wines. Sommer steers an inquisitive visitor to his vineyard. A man of the seasons and the soil, after more than two decades, Sommer's life is deeply rooted in his Hillcrest vineyard—so, too, the Oregon wine industry.

HINMAN VINEYARDS

27012 Briggs Hill Road
Eugene, Oregon 97405
(503) 345-1945

Wine Production
15,000 cases

Vineyards
10 acres

Year First Planted
1972

First Vintage
1979

Leading Wines
White Pinot Noir, Tior, Gewurztraminer

Now more than two decades old, the Oregon wine industry is entering an era of maturing stability. Pinot Noir, Chardonnay, and Riesling are Oregon's three principal grape varieties. Winemaking methods vary, but generally follow a similar stylistic theme. The industry, however, is far from stagnant. Interest continues in new growing sites, new varieties, improved grape growing practices, and alternate winemaking styles.

Doyle Hinman and David Smith.

Hinman Vineyards, a partnership of Doyle Hinman and David Smith, varies from the established norm more than most. Doyle Hinman has worked and studied at the Geisenheim Institute in Germany. While most Oregon winegrowers look primarily to France's Burgundy district for perspective on their own winemaking methods and styles, Hinman's Geisenheim experience significantly influences his own approach to winemaking.

Among its activities, the Geisenheim Institute develops new vinifera grape crosses for Germany's cool winegrowing climates. During his study, Hinman helped make wine from the experimental grape varieties. German wines, whether experimental or not, can generally be characterized as flavorful but delicate, low in alcohol, and fairly high in acid. The white wines are almost always made with some residual sugar, which in combination with the higher acidity, gives German wines their characteristic piquancy.

Hinman's Riesling, like most produced in Oregon, are made in the Germanic style. A wine with residual sugar can be made either by stopping fermentation before all the sugar has fermented, or by fermenting the wine to dryness, then adding unfermented grape juice to the wine. This latter practice, called the "sweet reserve" method, is prevalent in Germany, and it is the method Hinman uses for his wines.

One of Hinman's specialties is Tior, a pro-prietary name that means "deer" in Old High German. The wine is an unconventional blend of Riesling and Chardonnay.

Many Oregon wineries make a white wine from Pinot Noir grapes, usually finishing it with a slight amount of residual sweetness. Often wineries make this kind of wine when a vintage is too cool for a good red wine, or when the skins and pulp are needed to add to other Pinot Noir to make a sturdier, more darkly colored red wine, or, if the market calls for more white wine. Unlike most Oregon wineries, Hinman's White Pinot Noir is a special mainstay of the winery. The White Pinot Noir is Hinman's most popular wine.

Hinman's devotion to Germanic wine styles is not confined only to winemaking methods. The vineyard includes small plots of Limberger and Ehrenfelser, two German grape varieties uncommon to Oregon. Limberger, also spelled Lemberger, is grown principally in Germany's Wurttemberg region where it produces a fruity red wine. Ehrenfelser, a grape developed at the

The Hinman winery.

Geisenheim Institute, is one of the more successful crosses of Riesling and Sylvaner. The variety ripens earlier than Riesling, and the quality of the fruit is excellent. If the grapes from the experimental plots are successful, Hinman will plant more acreage to them.

To preserve the fruitiness of his Chardonnay, Hinman ferments the wine in stainless steel at a cool fermentation temperature of 45 to 50 degrees. The Chardonnay is then aged in large 1,500 gallon French oak tanks before bottling.

Hinman is offering Riesling, White Pinot Noir, and Chardonnay in 18 liter bag-in-a-box packages for restaurants. Unlike most bag-in-a-box wines which are, at best, indifferent "jug" wines, Hinman's bag-in-a-box offerings are made from premium varietals. The Chardonnay is finished in a completely dry style, a welcome relief for those who want a glass of dry white wine at a restaurant, but are inevitably served a wine with noticeable residual sweetness.

The Hinman winery is not just a production facility. Its grounds and buildings are attractively designed with visitors in mind. Picnicking is encouraged, and during the summer months, jazz and classical music festivals are held in an outdoor amphitheater.

HOOD RIVER VINEYARDS

4693 Westwood Drive
Hood River, Oregon 97031
(503) 386-3772

Grape Wine Production
2,000 cases

Fruit And Berry Wine Production
600 cases

Vineyards
12 acres

Year First Planted
1974

First Vintage
1981

Leading Wines
Chardonnay, Gewurztraminer, Riesling

Hood River Vineyards is the first Oregon vinifera grape winery in the modern era to be located somewhere other than west of the Cascade Mountain Range—but that is not to say Hood River is east of the Cascades. The winery and vineyards are nestled in a unique growing climate at the intersection of the Cascade Range and the Columbia River.

At this intersection, the opposite climates of eastern and western Oregon collide to form a climatic habitat quite different than either. The summers are warmer and the winters colder than those of western Oregon's Willamette Valley, and rainfall is less. The unirrigated vines are cane pruned as in western Oregon. Hood River's estate vineyards are on shallow two-foot soils with an underlying layer of friable volcanic basalt. A constant wind blows through the Columbia Gorge, bending the vines and modifying the climate.

Owned and operated by Cliff and Eileen Blanchette, the Blanchettes started making fruit wine from some of the eight acres of pears on their farm. Becoming enthused with Oregon's grape wines, the Blanchettes planted an experimental acre of Riesling in 1974, and increased their grape acreage to the present twelve. Additional grapes are purchased from other growers along the Columbia Gorge.

The Hood River area is warmer than the Willamette Valley, and Cabernet Sauvignon is a more viable variety, especially in warmer years.

Cliff Blanchette.

Chardonnay is perhaps Hood River's leading wine, but the Gewurztraminer is also especially noteworthy. Blanchette's grandfather was born in the Alsace region of France, and Blanchette makes his Gewurztraminer in the traditional dry Alsatian style.

If Blanchette were to make his Gewurztraminer in the more prevalent style, with modest character and some residual sweetness to mask any bitterness, his task would be much easier. A fine dry Gewurztraminer is more difficult to grow and make, but the end result is more rewarding. The Hood River area has proven ideal for Gewurztraminer. Blanchette ferments his at a temperature of about 62 degrees to achieve a balance of fruit and complexity.

Hood River continues to make small quantities of fruit wines, including Perry, a pear wine, and an intensely flavored raspberry wine made with very minimal water amelioration. Grape wines, however, are now the major focus. Because of limited acreage, the Columbia Gorge will never be a large grape growing region, but Blanchette is successfully exploring the potential of this unique growing climate.

Hood River Vineyards also operates a tasting and sales room at 4040 Westcliff Drive in Hood River, just off I-84 at exit 62.

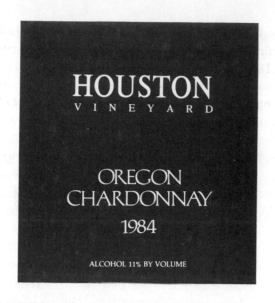

HOUSTON VINEYARDS

86187 Hoya Lane
Eugene, Oregon 97405
(503) 747-4681

Wine Production
1,000 cases

Vineyards
5 acres

Year First Planted
1981

First Vintage
1983

Leading Wines
Chardonnay

A fifth generation grape grower with a degree in viticulture from U.C. Davis, Steve Houston, and his wife, Jewelee, came to Oregon in 1979 to find a vineyard site and grow grapes. Before coming to Oregon, Houston worked with his father, growing grapes near Lodi, California.

The Houstons do not actually have a winery. Their grapes are made into wine, in accordance with their specifications, at another Oregon winery. The Houstons set out to be grape growers, but the maturing of their vineyard coincided with an oversupply of Oregon grapes. "We thought we should get Napa Valley prices for our grapes," says Jewelee Houston. "Since we didn't, we decided to sell our grapes another way—as wine."

The Houstons have enough land for a 34 acre vineyard. Unusual for Oregon, their vineyard site is not on a hillside, but on river bottom. The valley floor site makes frosts more likely, but river irrigation water is readily available for frost protection.

The Houstons' Chardonnay is very different from the usual Oregon Chardonnay. Made in a style similar to Riesling, the wine is intended for immediate sale and consumption. It is light and fruity, with no oak, a little spritz, and two percent residual sugar.

Before Houston got into the grape growing business, his grandfather, during a lengthy conversation, told him, "Grape growing is a young man's game that takes an old man's money." Houston's grandfather was a grape grower of 40 years—but he gave it up for gold mining.

What if grape prices go up? Will the Houstons stop selling wine? "We won't go back," says Houston. "If anything, we'll get a winery facility of our own."

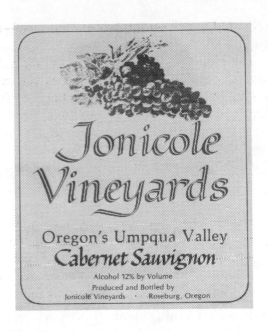

JONICOLE VINEYARDS

491 Winery Lane
Roseburg, Oregon
(503) 679-5771

Wine Production
3,000 cases

Vineyards
5 acres

Year First Planted
1968

First Vintage
1975

Leading Wines
Cabernet Sauvignon, Cabernet Rose

In the early 1970s, three friends and assoc iates came to Oregon from the Napa Valley looking for vineyard land and a place to start a winery. On their first trip to Oregon, the three found a small vineyard already bearing grapes, in the Umpqua Valley near Roseburg. Along with their wives, the three formed a partnership and built a winery. Two of the couples continued to live outside the state most of the year. The third couple, Jon and Laurie Marker, moved to Oregon to manage the daily operations of the vineyard and winery. The name Jonicole is a derivation of the first names of the three original partners.

Inevitably, the partnership fell apart, and Jonicole slipped into a period of inactivity, but in 1984, a reborn Jonicole Vineyards began crushing grapes again. Jon and Laurie Marker formed a small public corporation and bought out the other partners. New financing allowed Marker to build a much needed road for better visitor access to the winery.

Since its inception, Cabernet Sauvignon has been Jonicole's main focus. In the warmer years, the Roseburg area produces fine Cabernet fruit, as the Jonicole wines that survived the vagaries of the partnership demonstrated. Chardonnay is the main white grape.

In addition to the single varietal wines, Marker makes blended wines from several of the tiny, but immaculately maintained vineyards in the Umpqua valley, from grapes that might not otherwise find a home because the tiny vineyards yield only two dozen or so boxes of grapes, a harvest too small for the larger wineries to purchase.

KNUDSEN
ERATH

VINTAGE SELECT
1985
OREGON
WHITE RIESLING
ESTATE BOTTLED

WILLAMETTE VALLEY

PRODUCED AND BOTTLED BY
KNUDSEN ERATH WINERY, DUNDEE, OR., USA   BW-OR-52
ALC. 10% BY VOL.

KNUDSEN ERATH WINERY

Route 1, Box 368
Dundee, Oregon 97115
(503) 538-3318

Wine Production
30,000 cases

Vineyards
118 acres

Year First Planted
1969

First Vintage
1972

Leading Wines
Pinot Noir, Riesling, Sparkling Brut, Chardonnay,

Dick Erath is another of the genuine pioneers of the Oregon wine industry, one of the early few who came to Oregon in the 1960s to make wine. A home winegrower and electronics engineer from California, Erath became interested in starting a commercial winery. On a trip through Oregon in 1967, Erath bought some grapes and made them into wine. Impressed with the quality, Erath and his family purchased vineyard acreage in the Chehalem foothills in Oregon's northern Willamette Valley and moved from California to start their new winery.

Later, in 1972, Erath developed a vineyard

for Cal Knudsen in the picturesque Red Hills, near the town of Dundee. Erath and Knudsen each wanted to have their own separate wineries, but share the cost and use of expensive winemaking equipment. Legal restrictions prevented them from carrying out their plans, and, instead, the two men joined in partnership in 1975 and formed the Knudsen Erath Winery. For a time, the wines were sold under separate as well as joint labels, but beginning in 1980, Knudsen Erath adopted a single uniform label for all their wines.

In a state where small wineries are the rule, Knudsen Erath is one of Oregon's largest, one of the state's few wineries with yearly production at the 30,000 case mark. The winery, tasting room, and Knudsen's vineyard are just a few miles outside the town of Dundee. Erath's vineyard is situated five miles north of the winery.

Pinot Noir is Knudsen Erath's best wine. In the late 60s, when Riesling was still the "safe" grape to grow in this new and uncertain winegrowing region, Dick Erath was among the

Dick Erath.

first to emphasize Pinot Noir, and in the early and mid 70s, when Oregon Pinot Noir was not yet consistently good, Erath developed a reputation for producing some of the best. Knudsen Erath Pinots are full-bodied and full-flavored, sometimes fairly tannic, but often with an almost sweet character. The Pinots with higher acidity, from good years, age well.

Knudsen Erath's Pinot Noir is primarily the Pommard clone. Erath believes that Pommard may offer a bit more on the palate than other clones, though perhaps with less nose than the Wadenswil clone, but he emphasizes that microclimate, viticultural and winemaking practices, and year to year variation have far more effect than any clonal differences. Erath excepts the Gamay clone from this view. The Gamay has bigger berries and clusters and a higher acid to sugar ratio. Erath does not care for Gamay, and blends the little he has into a generic red.

Erath ferments his Pinot Noir in closed, 3,000 gallon stainless steel tanks, and macerates the rising cap of skins and pulp by pumping the must over and through it under high pressure. Erath believes that the closed tank keeps the volatile flavor constituents from escaping, condensing them back into the must. Erath inoculates the must to undergo malolactic fermentation concurrently with the alcohol fermentation. It has been Erath's experience that the troublesome haze sometimes associated with malolactic fermentation is not present when the fermentations are run concurrently. A further advantage, the winemaker need not delay adding sulfur dioxide while waiting for the bacterial malolactic fermentation, thereby insuring more immediate stability against contamination.

Erath allows the must to reach 90 degrees, and at the height of fermentation, pumps the must over the cap every two hours. Fermentation is usually completed in five days. At seven days, the wine cools to about 65 degrees, the cap is nearly sunk, malolactic fermentation is complete, and the wine is pressed and racked into French oak where it ages for a minimum of 11 months. Twenty percent of the barrels are renewed each year.

Erath explains how the vines are hedged between the rows to remove excess foliage.

In 1980, for the first time in nine vintages, Erath chaptalized Pinot Noir. Part was moderately chaptalized to raise the sugar content of the grape must from 21 ½ degrees Brix to 22 ½ degrees Brix. The remainder was left unchaptalized. The chaptalized wine became the basis for Knudsen Erath's 1980 "Vintage Select" Pinot Noir, a wine that won national acclaim in a comparative Pinot Noir tasting. French Burgundies are usually chaptalized almost every year. Success with the 1980 Pinot Noir convinced Erath that chaptalizing can help produce fine wine in a difficult vintage.

Chardonnay, Riesling, and Pinot Noir are Knudsen Erath's major wines. Smaller quantities of other varieties are also produced, including, in some years, Oregon Cabernet Sauvignon. The best wines from the best years are given the designation "Vintage Select."

Bottle fermented sparkling wine is a growing trend in Oregon winemaking. Erath's early experiments with small batches of sparkling wine led to a full scale commercial commitment to the wine. Knudsen Erath planted new vineyard acres on cooler slopes for a steady supply of suitable grapes, and in cooler vintages, Erath sets aside less ripe grapes for the sparkling wine. The cuvee is 75 percent Chardonnay and 25 percent Pinot Noir.

Knudsen Erath also operates two tasting and sales rooms, one in the town of Dundee at 1st Street and Highway 99W, and the other at the Blue Heron Cheese Factory in Tillamook.

PELLIER

1985

OREGON
GEWÜRZTRAMINER

Willamette Valley

PRODUCED & BOTTLED BY MIRASSOU CELLARS OF OREGON
SALEM, OREGON • BW - OR - 105   alcohol 12% by volume

MIRASSOU CELLARS OF OREGON

6785 Spring Valley Road N.W.
Salem, Oregon 97304
(503) 371-3001

Wine Production
8,000 cases

Vineyards
45 acres

Year First Planted
1982

First Vintage
1985

Leading Wines
Riesling, Chardonnay, Pinot Noir

Pellier may not be a familiar wine name, but Mirassou probably is. Mitch Mirassou is the fifth generation of American winemaking Mirassous. California's Mirassou Vineyards is the family's most visible presence, but other branches of the family are in the business as well.

In 1854, in California's Santa Clara Valley, Mitch Mirassou's great great grandfather, Pierre Pellier, planted vine cuttings he brought from France. Pellier's oldest daughter, Henrietta, married a neighboring winemaker, Pierre Mirassou, and the three sons from that marriage carried on the family's winemaking business—and the Mirassou name.

The Mirassou winery survived phylloxera, Prohibition, and urban encroachment, but the lean years, and the increasing size of the family, spread the newer generations into other wineries and businesses. A California grape grower and winemaker, Mitch Mirassou traded some of his California land for 90 acres in Oregon's Willamette Valley. In 1981, Mirassou and his family moved to their land in the Willamette Valley's Eola Hills and planted wine grapes.

Mirassou is trying one of the newer training systems for his vines, a version of the Carbonneau or "open lyre" system. Looking from the end of a vine row, the vine trunks and canes form a "U" shape. The Carbonneau trellising system is expensive, but potentially it can produce higher yields of good quality grapes. Mirassou's vines are still young, but so far, he is very pleased with the system.

Except for a few Riesling grapes, all of Mirassou's wines are made from grapes grown in the Eola Hills, one of the Willamette Valley's emerging new winegrowing areas. A fifth generation American winegrower, Mitch Mirassou begins a new generational cycle of Oregon winegrowers.

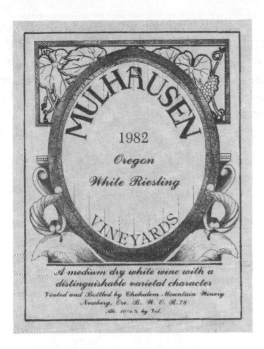

MULHAUSEN VINEYARDS

Route 1, Box 99C
Newberg, Oregon 9713
(503) 628-2417

Wine Production
5,000 cases

Vineyards
30 acres

Year First Planted
1973

First Vintage
1979

Leading Wines
Riesling, Pinot Noir Blanc, Pinot Noir

Zane Mulhausen developed an interest in wine while in Europe in the 1950's. Returning to his native Oregon, he held in his mind the idea that the Willamette Valley ought to be a good place to grow grapes and make fine wines. In 1969, Mulhausen purchased land that would become his vineyard site. In 1973, he planted grapes, and in 1979, he bonded the winery. A mechanical engineer by profession, Mulhausen turned to work in the construction industry in the boom years of the 1970's. In 1980, he retired to work full time in the vineyard and winery.

The vineyard soil is a deep Chehalem Mountain Jory, running eighty feet to rock. Six inches down, the soil is red. It is a shot soil, containing hard, relatively insoluble nodules of clay the size of a B-B, making the soil more permeable and providing good drainage. Typically, Oregon vineyards are planted on the southernmost sides of mountain ranges on slopes with southern exposures. Somewhat unusually, the Mulhausen vineyard is planted on the northern side of the Chehalem Mountains, though on a slope with a southeastern exposure.

As with most Oregon growers, Mulhausen is plagued with robins. The local robins are less offensive, learning more readily about shotguns and noise cannons. The massive Canadian migrations, however, present a continuing problem as wave after wave move through the Willamette Valley. Mulhausen reports that robins provide a good indication of grape ripening. Before sugar levels reach 17 degrees Brix, robins show little interest in the grapes. At 17 degrees Brix, robins begin coming into the vineyard, and by 18 degrees Brix, their interest is intense. A pair of Mulhausen's hunting dogs work the vineyard rows, helping to frighten the robins. As the vineyard's size increases, Mulhausen will turn to netting to protect the grapes. At harvest, the grapes are picked into five gallon buckets, then dumped into 1,000 pound totes for the trip to the crusher.

Only French oak is used to age Mulhausen's wines. In Oregon, it is frequent practice to ferment as well as age Chardonnay in small oak barrels, but believing that fermenting in stainless steel better insures cleanliness, Mulhausen shuns oak for fermentation in favor of stainless steel tanks and barrels, fermentation containers that are also more suited to his preference for preserving more of the fruity quality of the grape in the wine. Fermenting white wines at cooler temperatures also emphasizes this quality. Mulhausen's first wines were fermented with Montrachet yeast, but Montrachet is not the best performing strain at lower temperatures, and having had problems with fermentations that were reluctant to carry through to completion, Mulhausen now uses Champagne and Steinberg strains.

Mulhausen buys Sylvaner grapes from a Washington County grower, and produces the only varietally labeled release of this wine in Oregon. An unusual wine, Sylvaner is both Riesling-like and earthy. Like Gewurztraminer, it is not for everyone's taste, but those who enjoy the wine can find it nowhere else in Oregon. Supply is limited, and Mulhausen has planted some vines of his own to satisfy the demand.

Besides Sylvaner, Mulhausen produces Riesling, Chardonnay, Pinot Noir, and Gewurztraminer. In his own vineyard, Pinot Noir is planted half to the Wadenswil clone and half to Pommard in alternate rows. In cooler years, a sparkling wine will be made from a cuvee of Chardonnay and Pinot Noir.

The tasting room, run by Zane's wife Pat, is in a converted portion of the Mulhausens' large and massively constructed home. Designed and built by Mulhausen from four kinds of custom cut wood, the structure makes modern "spec homes" seem utterly fragile in comparison. The tasting room feels as if it is still an integral part of the home, and is adjoined by a comfortable sitting area with a picture window view. Wines for tasting are served on an antique seventeenth century table.

OAK KNOLL WINERY

Burkhalter Road
Route 6, Box 184
Hillsboro, Oregon 97123
(503) 648-8198

Grape Wine Production
28,000 cases

Fruit And Berry Wine Production
6,000 cases

Vineyards
none

First Vintage
1971

Leading Wines
Pinot Noir, Riesling, Chardonnay

Each year, on the third weekend in May, Oak Knoll hosts the "Bacchus Goes Bluegrass Wine Festival," an event that draws nearly 20,000 visitors to a rural setting that was once the site of a dairy farm. Ron and Marjorie Vuylsteke, natives of Oregon, have seen their winery grow from one gallon of homemade blackberry wine to an annual production of more than 30,000 cases of fruit, berry, and grape wine.

An electronics engineer, Vuylsteke quit his job at Tektronix to start a commercial winery. In 1970, the Vuylsteke family moved to the Willamette Valley countryside and produced their first commercial vintage, 1,500 cases of fruit and berry wine. In 1978, Oak Knoll was producing a third of all Oregon wine sold within the state. Still relatively small by most standards, Oak Knoll remains one of Oregon's larger wineries.

Oak Knoll began as a fruit and berry winery, but has shifted its emphasis to premium grape wines. Grape wines now comprise more than 75 percent of Oak Knoll's production. The old dairy barn that in 1970 seemed much too large for the Oak Knoll winery, became much too small, and the Vuylstekes built a second building to house the tasting room, office, and bottling and storage facilities.

The Vuylstekes own no vinifera vineyards of their own, relying on independent growers for their grapes. This arrangement offers less direct control over the grapes, and less assurance of continuity from year to year, but there are also advantages. Less capital is tied up in land and vines, more grapes can be purchased in better years and fewer in less favorable years, and Oak Knoll is not tied to a single growing area or a fixed range of grape varieties. In recent years, the ample supply of Oregon grapes has worked favorably for Oak Knoll.

Some of the winemaking philosophies developed with the fruit and berry wines are carried over to grape winemaking. The Vuylstekes believe that the fruity qualities of the grape should be preserved and emphasized. Oregon Pinot Noir is often fermented in open top containers, but the Vuylstekes prefer closed stainless steel fermenters. In their view, the closed fermenters trap volatile flavor constituents that would normally escape into the air, and condense them back into the wine.

After fermentation the white wines are centrifuged and pumped into barrels or tanks. At one time, the red wines were also centrifuged, but the Vuylstekes found that some of the flavoring constituents were stripped away, and the practice was discontinued.

Oak Knoll's wines are by no means outside of the mainstream of winemaking styles and tastes, but they do carry the signature of an individual's winemaking philosophy. At one time, Oak Knoll's red wines were prevented from go-

The wines.

ing through a malolactic fermentation. Malolactic fermentations reduce acidity and contribute added complexity to a wine, but they also reduce its fruity quality. In 1979, the Vuylstekes bought French oak barrels that originally came from Chateau Lafite. The barrels retained the malolactic organism, and now all Oak Knoll's red wines automatically go through a malolactic fermentation. Oak Knoll's Chardonnay is inoculated with a malolactic from Oregon State University.

Oak Knoll's Pinot Noir earned the acclaim of André Tchelsitcheff, America's most distinguished winemaker. Of Oak Knoll's 1980 vintage select Pinot Noir, Tchelistcheff told the Vuylstekes, "I have spent the last fifty years of my life searching for the world's finest Pinot Noirs, and yours is among the greatest I have ever tasted."

Oak Knoll's fruit and berry wines, made in a slightly sweet to moderately sweet style, are exceptionally good, and vinifera wine drinkers should not totally dismiss them out of hand. Gooseberry and rhubarb may find most favor for those with a vinifera wine palate, although some of the other berry wines offer a fresh taste and change of pace.

For visitors to the Oregon beach, Oak Knoll has a second tasting room overlooking the Pacific Ocean, Shipwreck Cellars, at 3521 S.W. Highway 101, in Lincoln City, Oregon.

OREGON PINOT GRIS

WILLAMETTE VALLEY · TABLE WINE

PONZI

PRODUCED AND BOTTLED BY PONZI VINEYARDS
BEAVERTON, OR.   BW-OR-56

PONZI VINEYARDS

Route 1, Box 842
Beaverton, Oregon 97005
(503) 628-1227

Wine Production
6,000 cases

Vineyards
12 acres

Year First Planted
1970

First Vintage
1974

Leading Wines
Pinot Noir, Riesling, Pinot Gris, Chardonnay

Approached from the many back roads that interlace the northern Willamette Valley, a new visitor would never imagine that Ponzi Vineyards' idyllic rural setting is only a short distance from Portland's suburban sprawl. Located in protected farmlands 15 miles southwest of Portland, and only a few miles from one of the northwest's largest shopping centers, Ponzi Vineyards remains well shielded from the urban milieu.

The vineyard's microclimate and soil are different from others in the Willamette Valley. Though most vineyards are planted up to a 1,000 feet above sea level on sloping hillsides, the Ponzi vineyard is planted in sandy benchland at an elevation of 250 feet. Nearby soil is quite claylike and less well suited to grape growing because of its poorer drainage characteristics. Ponzi's sandier soil may be attributable to geologic changes in the course of the nearby Tualatin River.

Although the vineyard has a slight southerly slope, the land is generally level. Concerns that insufficient air drainage would cause frost problems proved unfounded. Air movement has been more than adequate, flowing through the vineyard and dropping over the bench into the valley.

A family owned winery, Dick and Nancy Ponzi have made their home on the 17 acre estate for nearly two decades. Supplementing their own grapes, the Ponzis purchase grapes on long-term contracts from two other vineyards, Five Mountain Vineyard near Hillsboro and Medici Vineyard near Newberg, both within ten miles of the winery.

The Ponzi estate vineyard is divided equally among Chardonnay, Pinot Noir, Riesling, and Pinot Gris. Ponzi was among the first Oregon wineries to work with Pinot Gris, a grape variety with origins in Alsace and northern Italy. As yet, very little Pinot Gris is planted in Oregon, but the grape, a genetic relative of Pinot Noir, promises to play a significant role in the state's wine industry. Ideally suited to the Willamette Valley growing climate, Pinot Gris produces a premium white table wine, and offers yet another choice for matching food and wine.

Ponzi's Pinot Noir vines consist of two clones—Pommard, and a clone obtained from California's Mirassou winery. According to Ponzi, the Mirassou clone is easier to train and produces a darker wine, but also ripens later than the Pommard clone. Ponzi's Pinot Noir is fermented in small open containers. At first, Ponzi limited fermentation temperatures to 70 degrees or lower, but temperatures are now allowed to reach 80 degrees for better character and color extraction. After fermentation, the Pinot Noir is put into French oak barrels to age. Except for a light egg white fining in some vintages, the wine is neither fined nor filtered.

Richard Ponzi.

patina that changes color with the weather. Heavy timber, and stone from a nearby quarry complete the solid, rustic appearance. A spacious lawn provides a setting for informal picnics, festivals, and a summer jazz concert series.

Ponzi's Pinot Noirs are typically tightly structured wines that are relatively closed-in in their youth, showing their best with bottle age. Unlike some Oregon Pinots that are opulent in youth only to fade after a few years in the bottle, Ponzi's Pinot Noirs are capable of lengthy aging, offering the complex flavors and scents that can only come with time in the bottle.

Ponzi, an advocate of oak barrel fermentation for Chardonnay, prefers Allier oak to Limousin. Limousin, he feels, gives a less desirable lemon flavor to the wine. Comparing his own experiences, Ponzi indicates that oak fermented wines begin malolactic fermentation more easily and continue it more smoothly and consistently. Although the oak barrel fermented wines do not necessarily have a stronger oak taste, they display a rounder, fuller character. Ponzi ferments his Chardonnay at very cool temperatures, and the wine may require as much as two months for the fermentation to finish.

Most Riesling is made with some residual sweetness, but Ponzi's is made in a completely dry style to accompany food. Fermented at about 50 degrees, the wine sometimes requires up to four months to complete fermentation.

The attractive winery building successfully marries modern and traditional building materials. The roof is made of an expensive, highly durable material designed to oxidize with exposure to the elements, forming a protective barrier, and a rustic

REX HILL VINEYARDS

30835 North Highway 99W
Newberg, OR 97132
(503) 538-0666

Wine Production
9,000 cases

Vineyards
10 acres

Year First Planted
1982

First Vintage
1983

Leading Wines
Pinot Noir, Chardonnay

"If I had my choice," states Paul Hart, owner of Rex Hill Vineyards, "I would make nothing but Pinot Noir." Fortuitously, Hart chose 1983, the best of all possible years to to start his winery and to pursue his commitment to Pinot Noir.

Although the 1983 vintage was Oregon's best ever for Pinot Noir, yielding low tonnages of intensely flavored berries, Hart had little trouble purchasing choice Pinot Noir grapes. Oregon's grape production was beginning to exceed the crush capacity of the state's wineries, and America was in the midst of a white wine boom. Grapes from several well-established vineyards became available, and Rex Hill produced 1,800 cases of Pinot Noir, releasing separate bottlings from five different vineyards.

An insurance actuary by profession, Hart sold his business in 1981 to start the winery. Raised on a farm, Hart wanted to return to his agricultural roots. Hart established a winery and small vineyard on Rex Hill, a foothill of the Chehalem Mountains. The majority of the winery's grapes come from independent grape growers. David Reiner Wirtz, a winery consultant associated with the Oregon wine industry for many years is Rex Hill's winemaker.

Rex Hill is situated on the site of an old prune and nut drying building. Hart virtually rebuilt the old building, but retained much of its character, including the original wooden beams and decking. The modified drying tunnels are now barrel aging tunnels and vaults for Rex Hill's wine library. Rustic yet refined, Alsatian wallpaper and intricate wood carving by a local artist help set the tone for the winery.

Paul Hart.

Of the white wines, Chardonnay, another Burgundian variety, is Rex Hill's specialty. Both the Pinot Noir and Chardonnay are packed in wooden cases. In Burgundian tradition, the Chardonnay receives lees contact for added complexity. Approximately half of Rex Hill's production is devoted to red wine, a higher percentage than most Oregon wineries, reflecting Hart's commitment to Pinot Noir.

The Pinot Noir is fermented in 400 gallon bins. For added tannin and character, a portion of the stems are included during fermentation. Rex Hill is experimenting with three different French oaks and three levels of charring for barrel aging. Lightly charred Nevers and Allier oak barrels are proving the favorites for aging Pinot Noir. The mixture of oaks and chars contributing added complexity to the wine.

Rex Hill is one of the closest wineries to the Portland metropolitan area. Located along Highway 99 West, a major route to the Oregon beaches, Rex Hill is a popular stop for the wine traveller.

ROGUE RIVER VINEYARDS

3145 Helms Road
Grants Pass, Oregon 97527
(503) 476-1051

Wine Production
10,000 cases

Vineyards
5 acres

Year First Planted
1981

First Vintage
1983

Leading Wines
Chardonnay, Cabernet Sauvignon

Rogue River Vineyards is a partnership of four families, all former employees of a large winery in California's San Joaquin Valley. For several years, the group worked weekends to build their small Oregon winery, returning during the week to their jobs at the California winery. By 1986, all four families had moved to southern Oregon.

Under the Rogue River Vineyards label, the winery releases a line of wines that includes Cabernet Sauvignon, but emphasizes light, fruity wines such as Pinot Noir Blanc, Cabernet Blanc, Riesling, Gewurztraminer, and Merlot Nouveau.

Oriented toward creating new markets with new product concepts, Rogue River releases a second line of wines called Lumiere Vineyards. For these wines, the winery buys white wine from California and flavors it with fruit essences. The first in this line are Apri Blanc and Strawberry Blanc. In the words of Gail Tanabe, marketing manager, "These are not fruit wines, but basically "chablis" with a fruit accent. They are everyday wines to go with food for people who are just learning the pleasures of wine." Rogue River is continuing development of other types of wines, including berry flavored cordials.

ST. JOSEF'S WEINKELLER

28836 South Barlow Road
Canby, Oregon 97013
(503) 651-3190

Wine Production
5,000 cases

Vineyards
10 acres

Year First Planted
1981

First Vintage
1983

Leading Wines
Riesling, Cabernet Sauvignon

In 1980, Josef and Lilli Fleischmann planted a small vineyard near Canby, in Oregon's northern Willamette Valley. The winery and vineyard are situated on benchland between the Molalla and Pudding Rivers. A visit to St Josef's Weinkeller can include a picturesque Willamette River crossing via the Canby Ferry.

A baker by profession, Fleischmann retired from his former occupation and turned to wine—another product of yeast. For wine, Fleischmann often shuns commercial yeasts in favor of the naturally occurring yeasts harvested with the grapes. A Hungarian, raised in Germany before emigrating to America, Fleischmann is returning to the winemaking craft practiced by his forebears.

The winery, complete with a Gothic script rendering of the winery name, suggests a Germanic flavor. Riesling is one of St. Josef's Weinkeller's principal wines, but some of the other wines are often quite different from a Germanic style. Fleischmann makes a Cabernet Sauvignon from Oregon grapes, and a late harvest Zinfandel from California grapes, a wine that tips the scale at more than 15 percent alcohol.

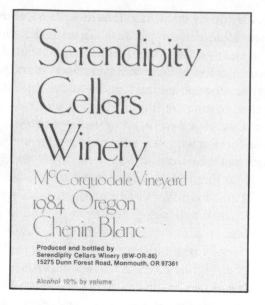

SERENDIPITY CELLARS WINERY

15275 Dunn Forest Road
Monmouth, Oregon 97361
(503) 838-4284

Wine Production
1,000 cases

Vineyards
3 acres

Year First Planted
1980

First Vintage
1981

Leading Wines
Chenin Blanc, Marechal Foch

Except for a small experimental vineyard, owners Glen and Cheryl Longshore purchase all their grapes under long-term contracts from other growers in Oregon's Umpqua and Willamette Valleys. In addition to conventional Oregon wine varieties, the Longshores produce several that are relatively uncommon. "Because we are small," says Cheryl Longshore, "it is advantageous for us to feature wines that are somewhat unique, and we make a conscious effort to do so."

Muller-Thurgau and Marechal Foch are Serendipity's main wines. The Muller-Thurgau, a Riesling-like wine, is released with about two percent residual sweetness. French-American hybrid wines, like Marechal Foch, are prevalent in eastern and midwestern America, but uncommon on the west coast. Serendipity's Marechal Foch is one of the few French-American hybrid wines in the Northwest. The early ripening Marechal Foch is made into a red wine every vintage, but other red wine grape varieties, Pinot Noir, Cabernet Sauvignon, and Zinfandel, are made into red wines only in the best vintages. In other years, the Longshores make roses or the popular "blanc" wines out of the grapes.

In California, Chenin Blanc is grown in hot growing climates, and cropped heavily to make indifferent, inexpensive jug wines. Serendipity is one of the few producers of Oregon Chenin Blanc. Made only in small quantities, Serendipity's Chenin Blanc shows that the grape is capable of interesting wines in Oregon's cooler growing climate.

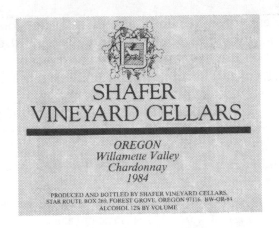

SHAFER VINEYARD CELLARS

Star Route, Box 269
Forest Grove, Oregon 97116
(503) 357-6604

Wine Production
6,000 cases

Vineyards
20 acres

Year First Planted
1973

First Vintage
1978

Leading Wines
Chardonnay, Pinot Noir, Sauvignon Blanc

In 1973, Shafer Vineyards planted their first vines. For a time, Shafer supplied other Oregon wineries with grapes, but the Shafers' desire to make their own wine from the fruit of their land became overwhelming. Harvey Shafer believes that 80 percent of a wine's quality comes from the vineyard. As winemaker, Shafer now furnishes the other 20 percent.

Nearly all the grapes for Shafer's wines come from the Shafer estate, located in the narrow Gales Creek Valley, at an average elevation of 450 feet. Shafer speaks of localized climates and vineyard interrelationships, emphasizing the importance of grape growing to winemaking. Across the narrow valley, the exposures are more northerly and the hillsides often shrouded in fog.

Even sites with southern exposures on the "good side" of the Gales Creek and Tualatin River Valleys can vary markedly. Vineyards within six miles of each other ripen as much as three weeks apart.

A winemaker must have a close relationship with the vineyards. Citing an example of this, Shafer points out that grapes become "ripe" at different sugar levels, depending on the vintage and vineyard site. Shafer not only measures the grape sugar as harvest approaches, but also tastes the grapes. A winemaker instructing a grower only to pick at a certain sugar or acid level would be isolated from information that might make the difference between a merely good wine and a wine of excellence.

Some Oregon winemakers emphasize the delicate fruit flavors of the grape. Others prefer a style that emphasizes the transformation of these ethereal flavors and scents into more rounded, fuller flavors, with less fruit of the grape, but more complex character. Although such dichotomies are inevitably oversimplified, Shafer largely falls into the latter category.

The difference in style is evident in Shafer's Chardonnay. Shafer ferments the Chardonnay in oak barrels rather than stainless steel. He uses Montrachet yeast, a strain that has a reputation for extracting fuller flavors, but at the risk of an undesirable hydrogen sulfide byproduct. Guarding against hydrogen sulfide, Shafer applies no sulfur after July, and racks the wine (removes it from the remaining grape solids) immediately after fermentation is complete. Shafer's Chardonnays display the positive aspects of Montrachet yeast without its undesirable byproducts.

Instead of fermenting his Pinot Noir in the more convenient stainless steel tanks, Shafer, like many Oregon winemakers, ferments in bins four feet square and two feet deep. Lined with food grade plastic, the maraschino cherry brining bins are ideal fermentation containers. As Pinot Noir ferments, the skins and pulp rises to form a cap. In tanks, wine is pumped over the cap to resubmerge it. In the bins, the cap is punched down, squeezed, and macerated by the physical action, a process thought by some to be superior for extracting flavors from the grape. Shafer's Pinot Noir is then aged in Allier oak barrels.

In addition to Pinot Noir, Riesling, and Chardonnay, Shafer was among the first winegrowers to produce Sauvignon Blanc. According to viticultural texts, the grape ripens late, and thus would not be ideally suited to the Willamette Valley climate. In Shafer's experience, however, the grape ripens as early as Pinot Noir. In cool years, like other varieties, it suffers from lack of ripeness, but unlike some varieties, varietal flavors begin to show early. The grape, particularly at lower levels of ripeness, has a pronounced grassy-herbaceous character. Shafer produces Sauvignon Blanc only in small quantities—his specialty remains Pinot Noir and Chardonnay.

The Shafer winery.

SISKIYOU VINEYARDS

6220 Caves Highway
Cave Junction, Oregon 97523
(503) 592-3727

Wine Production
6,000 cases

Vineyards
12 acres

Year First Planted
1974

First Vintage
1981

Leading Wines
Cabernet Sauvignon, Semillon, Pinot Noir

Located in the Illinois Valley of southernmost Oregon, not far from the California border, Siskiyou Vineyards is in a climate quite different from northern Oregon's Willamette Valley, or even the Umpqua Valley near Roseburg in the southerly portion of the state. Chuck and Suzi David moved from southern California to the Illinois Valley in the early 70's, and established the area's first commercial vineyard and winery in the modern era. Widowed in 1983, Suzi David continues to run the vineyard and winery operations, assisted by Donna Devine, Siskiyou's winemaker.

The climate is quite warm compared to the other growing areas of western Oregon, although not quite as warm as the nearby Applegate Valley to the east, the site of southern Oregon's other major winery. At 1,800 feet above sea level, Siskiyou is higher than most other Oregon vineyards. Because summers are warm, and the soil, a Josephine loam, runs only three to five feet deep, holding little water, irrigation is a necessity. In the spring, cool air drains from the steep hillsides surrounding the vineyard, and spring frosts can be a problem. Siskiyou's overhead sprinkler systems not only provide irrigation for the vineyards during summer, but also protection against frosts in the spring.

A few old vines, remnants of the winegrowing era prior to Prohibition, still remain, but the Illinois Valley lay viticulturally stagnant until Charles Coury of the now defunct Charles Coury winery in the northern Willamette Valley came to Rogue Community College in 1972, and taught a course on enology and viticulture. As a result of the course, several area residents got cuttings from Coury and later planted vineyards. Most of the first plantings were modest, a few vines for a hobby, but the outcome was predictable and inevitable. The previous owner of David's property had attended the lectures and planted a few vines. After acquiring the property, David planted a vineyard large enough for a commerical winery.

Siskiyou's grapes come from several growing areas in southern Oregon, but eventually, as David's own vineyards and others in the valley mature, all Siskiyou's wines will be made from grapes grown in the Illinois Valley. Growing conditions vary considerably from vintage to vintage, but generally, grape ripening is about two weeks ahead of the Roseburg area, and Cabernet Sauvignon does especially well.

Situated on the highway to the famous Oregon Caves National Monument, the Siskiyou winery offers an attractive side stop for visitors. The new tasting room is finished in redwood, and features the work of local artists. In the spring, Siskiyou holds an art, music, and wine festival on the winery's two acre trout lake.

SOKOL BLOSSER WINERY

Sokol Blosser Lane
P.O. Box 199
Dundee, Oregon 97115
(503) 864-2282

Wine Production
21,000 cases

Vineyards
45 acres

Year First Planted
1971

First Vintage
1977

Leading Wines
Chardonnay, Pinot Noir, Riesling

In 1974, Bill and Susan Blosser sold the first grapes from their vineyard to neighboring wineries. By 1977, the Blossers' plans for a winery took shape. The Blossers formed a limited partnership consisting of Bill and Susan Blosser as general partners, and members of Susan Blosser's family as limited partners. The Blossers built a winery, hired a winemaker, and crushed their first vintage.

At a time in the Oregon wine industry when most wineries were very small, marginally financed operations, Sokol Blosser was different, one of the first to start with a modern, well-financed operation. Instead of a garage or expediently built shed to serve as a winery, the Blossers built their winery of prestressed concrete, set into a rocky knoll. For their winemaker, they hired Bob McRitchie, then chief chemist for Franciscan Vineyards.

Instead of a makeshift table to serve as a tasting room, the Blossers hired John Storrs, a noted architect, to design an attractive, modern winetasting and visitors building adjacent to the winery. Equipped with a kitchen, the building is available for dinners and receptions. One of Oregon's most popular wineries for touring, 25,000 visitors pass through the Sokol Blosser Winery each year.

Supplementing production from their own estate vineyard, 60 percent of Sokol Blosser's grapes are purchased from other growers. Most of Sokol Blosser's grapes come from the Willamette Valley in western Oregon. Sokol Blosser's largest supplier is Hyland Vineyards, a 65 acre vineyard about 15 miles southwest of the winery near the town of Bellevue.

Initially, a third of Sokol Blosser's grapes came from the Columbia Valley in Washington state, but now that Willamette Valley grape growers can satisfy their needs, Sokol Blosser buys few grapes from the Columbia Valley. Sauvignon Blanc is one of the grapes, a popular Sokol Blosser wine, and a variety that grows better in the Columbia Valley.

Most of the vast arid Columbia Valley is in Washington state, but a part of the valley dips into northern Oregon, east of the Cascade Mountains. Until recently, virtually no grapes were grown on the Oregon side of the border, but the land promises to be a major producer of wine grapes. When Washington winegrowers petitioned the Bureau of Alcohol Tobacco and Firearms (BATF) to formally recognize the Columbia Valley as an American viticultural area, Bill Blosser filed a supplemental petition to have the Oregon portion included.

The American taste in recent years has run toward white wines. In certain respects, this trend has aided wineries. Most white wines require less handling than red wines and can be released much sooner, tying up less capital and providing much needed cash flow to keep investors and bankers happy. Nearly 70 percent of Sokol Blosser's wines are white. Riesling is Sokol Blosser's largest selling wine.

Of the white wines, Chardonnay is Sokol Blosser's best. Popular taste runs toward lower acid wines. When such wines are consumed alone, they have a certain appeal, but when consumed with food, as most wine is meant to be, lower acid wines grow dull and cloying as the meal progresses, failing to cleanse and refresh the palate. Oregon wines are inherently higher in acid, but there is a tendency to release wines at lower acid levels to satisfy popular taste. Sokol Blosser's Chardonnay bucks this trend. Typically, the wine is tightly structured, and has sufficient acid to age well and marry well with food. Selected Chardonnays are released as reserve bottlings in some years.

Sokol Blosser is participating in several research projects. Four acres of Chardonnay are trellised by two different methods. Half the vines are trained on a single wire five feet high, the other half on a complex Geneva Double Curtain system. Balancing complexity, cost, maintenance, and support for the vine and grape crop is always a trade off. Sokol Blosser's experiment with two of the many trellising systems will help determine which systems are best for Oregon.

Sokol Blosser's vineyard is planted in a volcanic clay loam soil known as Jory. Distinctive in appearance, the red soil provides a colorful backdrop for the vineyard's lush green foliage. Some growers in the area say grapes from this soil produce more robust, fuller flavored wines than grapes from more delicate soils found elsewhere in the Willamette Valley. In spite of the temptation offered by their distinctive soil, the Blossers do not subscribe to this view, believing that soil character does not affect the taste of the wine.

Pinot Noir is widely regarded as Oregon's finest wine grape. Unlike many Oregon winemakers, McRitchie ferments his Pinot Noir in stainless steel tanks instead of the smaller, several hundred gallon, open top containers. This

The Sokol Blosser winery and tasting room.

method is one of the factors in the Sokol Blosser style. Some winemaking techniques that work well in the smaller open containers create different results when the wine is fermented in the tanks.

Since his first vintage, McRitchie has experimented with various Pinot Noir winemaking techniques, including leaving the stems with the grapes during fermentation, and letting the skins macerate with the fermented wine for a length of time before pressing. Neither technique worked well with the tank fermentation, and McRitchie gravitated to a style that emphasized more of the fruit character of the grape.

The 1983 harvest brought in perhaps Oregon's best ever Pinot Noir vintage. Such an intense and classic vintage usually calls for lengthy barrel aging to bring out the wine's best—or at least barrel aging no shorter than usual. In that year, McRitchie took a different approach than most Oregon winemakers, aging his Pinot Noir in barrels six months less than usual.

The effect was particularly notable in his 1983 Red Hills Pinot Noir, a wine with intense extract and at the same time a fresh fruity quality. Time in the cellar will show what this style of Pinot Noir will do with bottle age, but it has proved its merit in a noted New York wine tasting, comparing 1983 French Burgundies with 1983 Oregon Pinot Noirs. The top two scoring wines were both made by McRitchie.

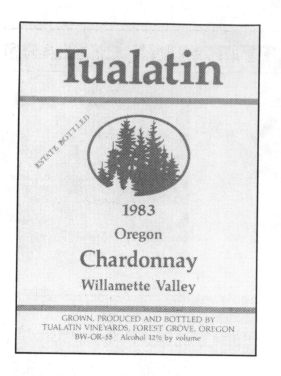

Tualatin

ESTATE BOTTLED

1983

Oregon

Chardonnay

Willamette Valley

GROWN, PRODUCED AND BOTTLED BY
TUALATIN VINEYARDS, FOREST GROVE, OREGON
BW-OR-55 Alcohol 12% by volume

TUALATIN VINEYARDS

*Route 1, Box 339
Forest Grove, Oregon 97116
(503) 357-5005*

Wine Production
20,000 cases

Vineyards
83 acres

Year First Planted
1973

First Vintage
1973

Leading Wines
Chardonnay, Riesling, Gewurztraminer

When wine is discussed, conversation often turns to the growing climate that produced the grapes, sometimes to the specialized climate of the vineyard itself. At the Tualatin vineyard, theoretical abstractions are grounded in a grassroots reality. The vineyard is one of the warmer growing sites in the area. Local residents remember a time when strawberry picking always began earliest at the Spangler farm. The children who worked for Spangler were often let out of school early to pick the already ripe berries. The

warmer Spangler farm climate is now the Tualatin vineyard. Now grapes instead of strawberries ripen earlier. In cooler, rainier years, Tualatin's warmer climate has a decided advantage.

In the early 1970's Bill Fuller and Bill Malkmus completed their search for a viticultural region suited to cooler climate, earlier maturing varieties of vinifera grapes, and founded Tualatin Vineyards. The two have different but complementary backgrounds. Malkmus is a graduate of Stanford University and Harvard Business School. Formerly an investment banker in San Francisco, Malkmus is in charge of business operations and marketing, working out of Tualatin's California office.

Fuller holds an M.S. in Enology from the University of California at Davis and has long been involved with the wine industry. From 1964 to 1973, he was chief chemist and wine production manager with California's Louis M. Martini winery. Fuller, in charge of winemaking and vineyard operations, lives on the Tualatin estate with his wife, Virginia.

From his nine years at Louis M. Martini, Fuller brings to Oregon much of the style and philosophy of a larger California winery. A centrifuge and other modern technology are regarded as basic to the winery operation. Instead of planting vineyards and waiting for them to bear fruit, Fuller broke an unwritten rule, and immediately

Bill Fuller.

began making wine from Washington grapes. The practice was subsequently adopted by most other northern Willamette Valley winemakers, though it is now fading as Oregon grape production is better able to meet the needs of Oregon winemakers.

From the beginning, Tualatin emphasized cooler climate, white wine grapes. Eighty percent of the vineyard is planted to white wine varieties. More acreage is planted to Riesling than any other grape. In view of the white wine boom, Tualatin's wine selection has played well to consumer tastes. Tualatin specializes in white wines in a Germanic style, low alcohol with some residual sweetness. Riesling is the principal wine in this style. Gewurztraminer, planted more heavily than at most Oregon vineyards, is another major variety for Tualatin made in the Germanic style. Fuller is also experimenting with vinifera crosses developed at the University of California at Davis, including Early Muscat, a grape that lives up to both parts of its name, ripening early with a pronounced muscat flavor, and Flora, a cross between Gewurztraminer and Semillon.

The Burgundian grape varieties, Chardonnay and Pinot Noir, are receiving increasing emphasis, and Tualatin's most recent vineyard expansion was devoted entirely to these two grapes. Tualatin's wines reflect the relative warmth of the growing climate. The Pinot Noir has a riper, fuller-bodied quality, sometimes showing better in moderately cooler vintages. Chardonnay is perhaps Tualatin's best wine, made in a rich, ripe, complex style. The Germanic-style wines, too, often have a riper character than their counterparts from other Willamette Valley vineyards.

TYEE WINE CELLARS

26335 Greenberry Road
Corvallis, Oregon 97333
(503) 753-8754

Wine Production
1,000 cases

Vineyards
6 acres

Year First Planted
1983

First Vintage
1985

Leading Wines
Chardonnay, Pinot Noir

A partnership of two couples, Dave and Margy Buchanan, and Barney Watson and Nola Mosier, Tyee Wine Cellars promises to become one of Oregon's more interesting new wineries. Barney Watson, one of the partners, is enologist at Oregon State University's Department of Food Science and Technology. Watson is a leading figure in Oregon wine research and development.

Oregon State University is bringing in and testing new clones and grape varieties from European research stations. Watson is charged with chemically analyzing the grapes and juice, making experimental batches of wine, and conducting sensory evaluations of the wines. As good as Oregon wine already is, the new clones and varieties promise even more.

Most of Oregon's grape varieties and clones were brought in from California, and are not necessarily the best selections for the Oregon climate. The Davis 108 clone of Chardonnay, for example, Oregon's most widely planted clone of the grape, ripens mid to late season with relatively high acidity—ideal for California, but not always the best for Oregon.

The new clones and grape varieties are virtually unavailable commercially, but they will eventually become a major focus for Tyee Wine Cellars. From the Espiguette research station in France, Tyee intends to plant the Espiguette 352 clone of Chardonnay, so far one of the most promising clones of the grape. The Espiguette clone will play a key role in Tyee's sparkling wine cuvees.

Tyee will also be planting Pinot Gris, and probably Ehrenfelser. Pinot Gris, a white wine relative of Pinot Noir, produces excellent, full-bodied, dry, white wine. Ehrenfelser is a cross of Riesling and Sylvaner from Germany's Geisenheim Institute. Ehrenfelser produces a Riesling-like wine with a more pronounced muscaty character. Tyee will be planting other new clones and varieties as well.

Tyee's vineyard and winery are located on the foothills of the Coast Range, on the Buchanans' 460 acre family farm. As a child, Dave Buchanan, the third Buchanan generation on the farm, milked cows in the barn that is now the Tyee winery. Future plans call for a fall harvest festival featuring wine and freshly harvested filberts from the Buchanan farm.

VALLEY VIEW VINEYARD

1000 Applegate Road
Jacksonville, Oregon 97530
(503) 899-8468

Wine Production
7,000 cases

Vineyards
26 acres

Year First Planted
1972

First Vintage
1976

Leading Wines
Cabernet Sauvignon, Merlot, Chardonnay

In 1972, the Wisnovsky family planted grapes in the Applegate Valley in southwest Oregon, marking the rediscovery of one of the Northwest's earliest viticultural regions. Western Oregon is known for its year-round temperate climate, richly foliaged landscapes, cloudy skies, and wet weather. Although this conception is substantially true for much of western Oregon, it does not apply to the Applegate Valley, a climatic region in the Jacksonville area of southwest Oregon.

Not far from the California border, the

Applegate Valley is considerably sunnier, warmer, and drier than anywhere else in western Oregon. Grasses, long needle pines, and the absence of ubiquitous foliage demonstrate that this is indeed a much different climate.

Valley View Vineyard is situated in the Applegate Valley at an elevation of 1,500 feet, an area known as Sunshine Village. The soil in the 26 acre vineyard varies, but is predominantly a Ruch sandy loam. Most of the vineyard needs no irrigation, but in the shallower portions the soil is only 18 inches deep, and, in most years, these shallower areas require irrigation. Bud break occurs in mid-April. The growing season is relatively short, and frost can be a problem in fall as well as spring.

Most areas in the Applegate Valley, including the Valley View vineyard site, are too warm for Gewurztraminer, Riesling, and Pinot Noir, so most of the grapes for these wines are purchased from vineyards in the cooler Illinois Valley to the west. In their own vineyards, Valley View is focusing on Cabernet Sauvignon, Chardonnay, and Merlot.

As in northern Oregon, Merlot does not set fruit well, and its yields are small and sporadic. At least one grower in the area, however, has had consistently good yields from the grape. Better clonal selection may be the key to more consis-tent crops. Merlot ripens well in southwest Oregon, but the grape is prone to lose acidity and gain sugar quickly as ripeness approaches. The grape requires careful attention by the grower to insure that the fruit is picked at optimum quality.

In this warmer growing area, the grapes are not as high in malic acid as those from northern Oregon, and malolactic fermentation, the conversion of malic acid to the less acidic lactic acid, is not as dramatic. Malolactic fermentation, however, does not merely lower the acidity of wine, it changes its character in a way that is beneficial for most dry red and many dry white wines.

All of Valley View's oak aged wines go through malolactic fermentation. Malolactic bacteria, once it is present in the barrels, multiplies and becomes active again as the barrels are filled with new wine. Valley View's malolactic fermentations recur of their own accord, and the wines do not require inoculation from commercial cultures.

Cabernet Sauvignon and Chardonnay show particular promise. Sauvignon Blanc has also been very good, but Valley View has so little, the wine is blended into their white table wine. More Sauvignon Blanc may be planted.

Valley View Vineyard also operates a tasting and sales room at 690 North 5th Street in Jacksonville.

The Valley View winery.

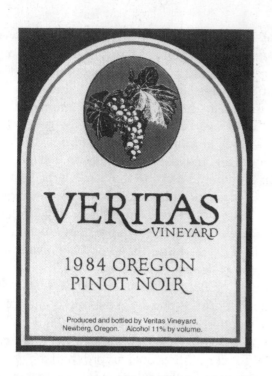

VERITAS
VINEYARD

1984 OREGON
PINOT NOIR

Produced and bottled by Veritas Vineyard,
Newberg, Oregon.   Alcohol 11% by volume.

VERITAS VINEYARD

31190 N.E. Veritas Lane
Newberg, Oregon 97132
(503) 538-1470

Wine Production
3,100 cases

Vineyards
20 acres

Year First Planted
1983

First Vintage
1983

Leading Wines
Pinot Noir, Chardonnay

Traveling Highway 99 West, from the Portland metropolitan area toward Oregon's famed coastal beaches, Veritas Vineyard is one of the first of many estate wineries along the northern Willamette Valley wine route. The Veritas tasting room is also a tasting and sales outlet for The Eyrie Vineyards and Adelsheim Vineyard, two wineries that have no regular public hours of their own.

Owned by John and Diane Howieson, a vineyard was planned as a retirement project for John Howieson, a physician at a Portland area medical school. Howieson wanted to plant near the Sokol Blosser winery, and have Sokol Blosser produce the wine for his winery label. In a major shift in plans, a 40 acre parcel and house closer toward Portland became available. Howieson bought the land, and planted his first vines in 1983. Sokol Blosser made the wines for Veritas's first vintage, but since 1984, Howieson has made all the wines at Veritas. Until the Veritas vineyard comes into full production, the majority of the grapes are purchased from nearby vineyards.

Pinot Noir and Chardonnay are Veritas's leading wines. Howieson ferments his Pinot Noir in 3,000 gallon stainless steel tanks instead of the more prevalent open-topped bins. As with most tank fermentations, the fermenting must is pumped over the floating cap of skins and pulp rather than punching the cap down into the must as is done with the open bins. Many favor punching down in the open bins for extracting more of the flavor nuances from the grapes. Howieson prefers a very warm 90 degree fermentation temperature for Pinot Noir to achieve the best color and flavor extraction.

With small open bins, a fermentation temperature this high is difficult to maintain for long, if it can be reached at all, but the larger fermenting mass in a tank achieves that temperature readily. Exceeding the 90 degree temperature risks volatile `acidity and stuck fermentations because of injury to the yeast cells, but the

John Howieson.

temperature of the fermenting must can be readily lowered with the heat exchanging jackets that surround the tank.

The Veritas estate vineyard follows the multiple curvatures of Rex Hill. Only a small portion of the vineyard is visible from the winery. The soil is a Laurelwood silt loam, a soil of volcanic and sedimentary origins, slightly richer and more water retentive than the purely volcanic Jory soils found in many other northern Willamette Valley vineyards. Planting the vines to run up and down the hillsides is easiest for cultivation, but topsoil runoff is a growing concern. Veritas is one of the newer vineyards with drainage terraces and vines planted to run across the slope. In the newest portion of the vineyard, the vine rows actually follow the contour lines of the hillside. Aesthetics as well as soil conservation benefit. The artistic curvatures of the vine rows, integrated with the natural flow of the land, echo the spirit and essence of the Oregon winegrowing experience.

WASSON BROTHERS WINERY

41901 Highway 26
Sandy, Oregon 97055
(503) 668-3124

Grape Wine Production
900 cases

Fruit And Berry Wine Production
1,200 cases

Vineyards
7 acres

Year First Planted
1978

First Vintage
1982

Leading Wines
Riesling, Gewurztraminer

A partnership of twin brothers, Jim and John Wasson, Wasson Brothers Winery grew out of the success of the brothers' homemade fruit and berry wines in judgings at the Oregon State Fair. The two planted a small vineyard in Clackamas County near Oregon City and opened a winery. Restrictive local regulations prevented the

Wassons from having an active tasting and sales room, so the two moved their winery to the town of Sandy. Almost immediately, a shopping center development forced yet another move to another location nearby.

Most Willamette Valley vineyards and wineries are in the western part of the valley. Wasson Brothers Winery and vineyard is one of the few east of the Willamette River in Clackamas County. Situated outside the mainstream of Willamette Valley wine country, Wasson's average winery visitor prefers the fruit and berry offerings to the grape wines. With an eye to their winemaking roots and their customers, more than half of the Wassons' wine production is fruit and berry wine.

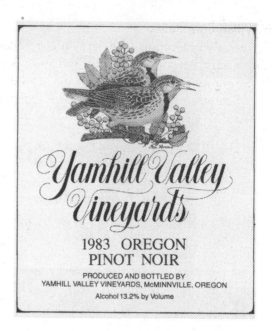

YAMHILL VALLEY VINEYARDS

16200 S.W. Oldsville Road
McMinnville, Oregon 97128
(503) 843-3100

Wine Production
7,500 cases

Vineyards
50 acres

Year First Planted
1982

First Vintage
1983

Leading Wines
Pinot Noir, Chardonnay, Riesling

In the fall of 1982, Denis Burger and his wife Elaine casually went looking at vineyard property. Within a week, they owned 34 acres of vineyard land. Joined by David and Terry Hinrichs, the partners now own 100 acres southwest of McMinnville, in the northern Willamette Valley. Nestled against the foothills of the Coast Range, the vineyard is sheltered from the onshore flow of Pacific marine air. Rain clouds tend to pass by on either side of the vineyard, and the site is slightly warmer and drier than many others in the northern Willamette Valley.

Unusual for Oregon, the vines are cordon pruned rather than cane pruned. Short spurs are left on permanent lateral arms (cordons), and the season's growth emerges from the buds on the short spurs. Oregon's cool, cloudy, early season climate can cause cropping problems with this method, but cordon pruning has advantages too, requiring less time to maintain each of the many thousands of vines, and allowing less experienced workers to do the pruning.

The young vines only began producing grapes in 1985. The first two vintages were made at other wineries from grapes purchased from other vineyards. Bob McRitchie at Sokol Blosser Winery helped make Yamhill Valley's 1983 Pinot Noir. An intense wine in an outstanding Pinot Noir vintage, the 1983 Pinot gained widespread recognition by placing first in a New York tasting of 1983 Burgundies and 1983 Oregon Pinot Noirs.

Like McRitchie, Denis Burger ferments his Pinot Noir in stainless steel tanks. Burger prefers a very warm, 90 degree fermentation temperature for his Pinot Noir to get the most body, and extract from the grape. Hot fermentation temperatures run the risk of spoilage problems, but Burger, a microbiologist, counters this concern by fermenting in the enclosed stainless steel tanks, a method he favors over the smaller, open topped containers that is the norm for most of Oregon's winemakers.

The winery, designed to accommodate a production of up to 10,000 cases, was designed by Burger's brother, Ed, a San Francisco architect. Bob Burger, another brother, designed the label and named the winery.

WASHINGTON

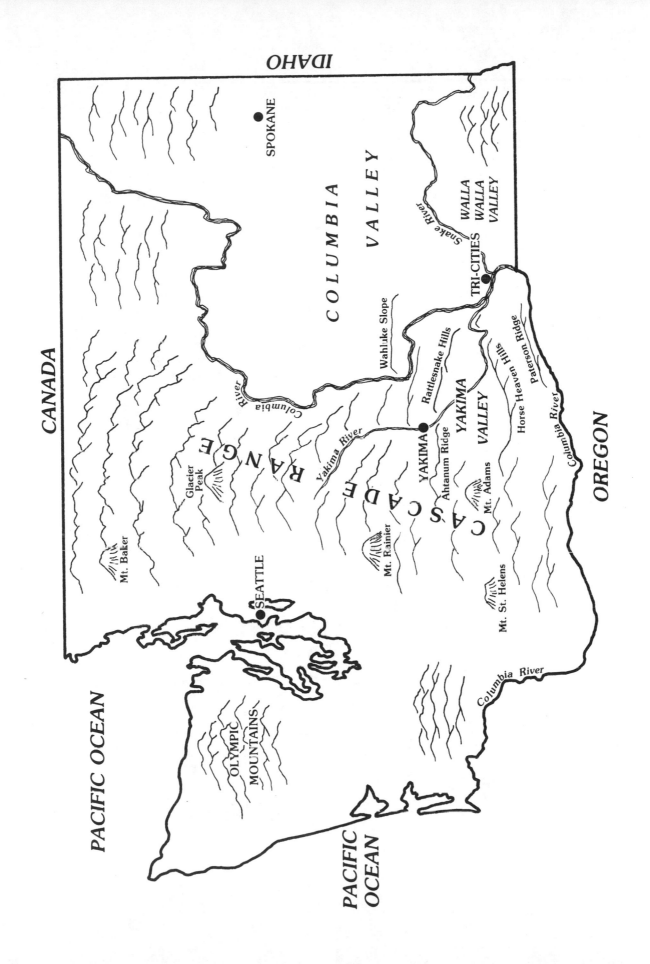

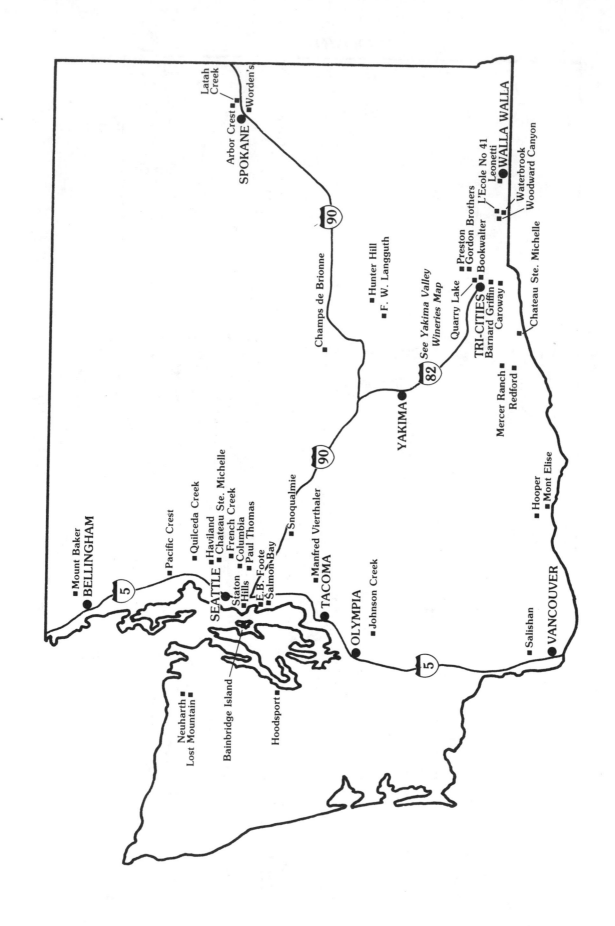

Latah Creek
Worden's
Arbor Crest
SPOKANE

WALLA WALLA
L'Ecole No 41
Leonetti
Waterbrook
Woodward Canyon

90

Preston
Gordon Brothers
Bookwalter
Chateau Ste. Michelle

Hunter Hill
F. W. Langguth

Champs de Brionne

Quarry Lake

See Yakima Valley
Wineries Map

82

TRI-CITIES
Barnard Griffin
Caroway

YAKIMA

Mercer Ranch
Redford

90

Quilceda Creek

Haviland
Chateau Ste. Michelle
French Creek
Columbia
Paul Thomas

Snoqualmie

Manfred Vierthaler

Pacific Crest

Mont Elise
Hooper

Mount Baker
BELLINGHAM

Seaton
Hills
E. B. Foote
SalmonBay

SEATTLE

TACOMA

OLYMPIA

Johnson Creek

5

VANCOUVER
Salishan

Neuharth
Lost Mountain

Bainbridge Island

Hoodsport

5

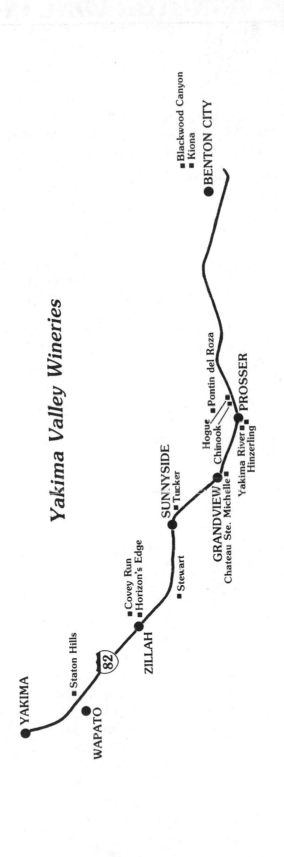

Yakima Valley Wineries

THE WASHINGTON WINE INDUSTRY

WINE GRAPE ACREAGE
11,000 acres
WINEGROWING REGIONS
Columbia Valley, Yakima Valley, Walla Walla Valley,
Columbia Gorge, Puget Sound, Southwest Washington
MAJOR GRAPE VARIETIES
Riesling, Chardonnary, Chenin Blanc, Cabernet Sauvignon,
Sauvignon Blanc, Semillon, Merlot, Gewurztraminer
LEADING WINES
Cabernet Sauvignon, Chardonnary, Semillon,
Sauvignon Blanc, Merlot, Lemberger, Riesling,
Chenin Blanc, Gewurztraminer

Washington produces more premium *Vitis vinifera* wine grapes than any state in America, except California. Wine grapes have been grown in Washington since the 1800s, but until the state's wine renaissance in the late 1960s, the Washington wine industry had little interest in premium wines or wine grapes. Washington had long been a large producer of grapes, but these were mostly *Vitis labrusca* varieties, principally Concord, used for grape juice products or for making indifferent, often fortified, wines.

Since the early 1800s, grapes have been planted at various locations both east and west of the Cascade Mountains. The first grapes were mostly non-vinifera varieties, often serving the multiple purposes of juice, jelly, table grapes, and sometimes wine. The early industry was primarily located in the wet, temperate, Puget Sound area of western Washington. As irrigation projects opened agricultural land in the Columbia Valley, east of the Cascades, grape growing shifted away from western Washington to the Columbia Valley, and the grape of choice shifted from Island Belle, a local variant of Campbell Early, to Concord.

Prior to Prohibition, Washington had an active grape growing industry, but no wine industry, as such. The Repeal of Prohibition and favorable state laws instantly created one. By 1937, 42 wineries were operating in the state. Wine quality, however, was poor. Most of the wines were made from Concord or other labrusca grape varieties. Protectionist state laws kept competition away. In the Yakima Valley, east of the Cascade Mountains, William B. Bridgman made a careful study of winegrowing climates, planted and purchased vinifera grapes, hired a German winemaker, and attempted to produce premium vinifera wines. Unfortunately, as wine authority Leon D. Adams reports, from personal experience, the wines were poorly made and were withdrawn from sale. Grape growers continued to cultivate a few vinifera grapes, only to have winemakers blend them with labrusca varieties. A viable premium wine industry was still decades away.

After the initial flurry of winegrowing activity following Repeal of Prohibition, the industry sank into a long decline. The number of wineries steadily decreased. The wines were still made mostly from labrusca grapes, with some occasional vinifera thrown into the blend for good measure. The rebirth of the Washington wine industry, based solely of premium *Vitis vinifera* grape varieties, did not come until the late 1960s. Catalysts for the Washington wine renaissance were an unlikely combination of a wine writer, some amateur winemakers, and the removal of protectionist state wine laws at the urging of wine retailers who were openly hostile to the state's wine industry and had little interest in premium wines from the state.

To abbreviate what is a rather elaborate story, a group of amateur winemakers began, in the late 1950s, purchasing vinifera grapes from Columbia Valley grape growers, rescuing them from fortified blends with *Vitis labrusca* grapes. In 1962, to insure a steady supply of grapes, the group purchased vineyard acreage and became a bonded winery, Associated Vintners. In 1966, Leon D. Adams, the noted authority on American wines, visited Associated Vintners. Impressed with some of their early efforts, Adams suggested that they become a commercial enterprise. In 1967,

Associated Vintners produced their first commercial vintage.

With the expected removal of protectionist wine laws, another winery, American Wine Growers, one of the state's largest, and the corporate predecessor of Chateau Ste. Michelle, was becoming interested in developing premium table wines. At the suggestion of Adams, Andre Tchelistcheff, the legendary California winemaker, visited the state, tasted the wines of the two wineries, and ultimately became consultant to American Wine Growers. In 1967, the same year that Associated Vintners "went public," American Wine Growers, under the label Ste. Michelle, produced their first commercial release of *Vitis vinifera* wine. Today, Chateau Ste. Michelle dominates the Northwest wine scene, producing more than 20 times as much wine as the Northwest's next largest winery. As a secondary effect of its marketing acumen and market presence throughout America, Chateau Ste. Michelle has opened new markets and stimulated consumer interest in other wines and wineries from America's Northwest.

Until recent years, the Washington wine industry was a paradox, having a relatively large number of grapes, but very few wineries, and at first, most of the state's winemaking was located in the urban areas west of the Cascades, far from the source of the grapes. By mid 70s, the industry began shifting toward a better balance. More wineries began opening to give the grapes a home. Estate wineries became more common. The Wallace family established Hinzerling Vineyards, a small vineyard and winery in Washington's Yakima Valley. Along the Columbia River Gorge, the Hendersons, with other partners, founded Bingen Wine Cellars (Mont Elise Vineyards). Near Pasco, on a much larger scale, the Prestons founded Preston Wine Cellars, still the Northwest's largest family-owned winery.

By the mid 80s, the Washington wine industry finally became truly diversified. Western Washington wines joined Columbia Valley wines on the merchant's wine shelves. The largest wineries grew still larger. Many small and medium size wineries began operation. Numerous vineyards and estate wineries stretched from one end of the Yakima Valley to the other. New and distinct growing regions entered the scene, and wineries were opening all across the state. Chateau Ste. Michelle expanded operations with a 26 million dollar winery and planted a single vineyard that stretched, literally, for miles, and the state's wine industry attracted its first foreign money with partial German financing of the F. W. Langguth Winery. For the first time since the years immediately following Repeal of Prohibition, the number of wineries exceeded 42, and this time around, the wine industry was based entirely on premium vinifera wine grapes—more than 10,000 acres of them.

The decades preceding the wine renaissance were not entirely wasted. Many of the first vinifera grapes were not good wine varieties or were poorly suited to the growing climate, but frosts and winter freezes offered winegrowers important lessons on cultivation practices, winegrowing sites, and the hardiness of various vinifera grape varieties.

In the late 1930s, Dr. Walter Clore, Washington State University horticulturist, among his other duties, began grape research at the Irrigated Agricultural Research and Extension Center at Prosser, in the Yakima Valley. In the coming decades, Clore helped refine grape growing practices, identified grape varieties best suited to the growing climates, and developed experimental vineyard test sites in selected growing areas. Nearly 50 years after he began his research, Clore, professor emeritus, working as a private consultant, submitted a petition to the BATF for the Columbia Valley viticultural area. On December 13, 1984, the BATF approved the petition, and the 18,000 square mile Columbia Valley viticultural area, the Northwest's largest, became a reality.

Riesling has been and still is the backbone of the Washington wine industry. Riesling is the most cold hardy of all the major vinifera varieties. Consumer demand for white wines, and for crisp, semi-sweet white wines in particular, makes Riesling readily marketable. No other American winegrowing region can so easily produce quality Riesling on such a scale, and the grape fits the perception that Riesling would be one of the best grapes for one of America's northernmost states. For all these reasons, Washington grape growers planted heavily to Riesling—probably too heavily.

Demand is shifting toward the traditionally dry white varieties such as Chardonnay and Sauvignon Blanc, and more recently, Semillon. Red wine grapes, principally Cabernet Sauvignon and Merlot, are increasingly in demand as consumers and winegrowers become more aware that Washington is not just a "Riesling" or "white wine" state. Arguably, Washington's best wines are the red Bordeaux varieties and dry whites, not Riesling. Although what "sells best" is not always what "is best," Washington already has an overbalance of Riesling, and a shift, already in progress, toward dry whites and reds is healthy for the industry, and a boon to the wine aficionado.

This shift, however, has neither been smooth nor predictable, nor has the overall size of recent grape harvests. A series of frosts and winter freezes have struck the industry in recent vintages. Riesling has come through in the best shape with closer to normal crop levels, but the dry white and red varieties are more tender, and in some cases, their harvests have been substantially reduced.

The Washington wine industry is in the midst of major growth and transition, and the frosts and freezes have come at a difficult time. On the one hand, vineyard expansion has been extraordinarily rapid, new vineyards are reaching maturity at about the same time, and grape production threatens to overwhelm the industry, producing far more grapes than can possibly be absorbed by existing wineries. At the same time, the curse and salvation of a series of unexpected frosts and freezes have reduced grape crops from prior harvests. Instead of overwhelming the industry with excess production, grapes have been in short supply, particularly the dry white and red varieties.

In anticipation of major growth, wineries expanded facilities, purchased new equipment, and prepared distribution and marketing programs for major thrusts into new national markets. Plans have been set aside, and equipment lays idle, awaiting a time that is still to come, but sometime

soon, Washington wine production will double, possibly quadruple. It is a tumultuous time for the Washington wine industry. If grape production, wine production, and marketing proceed without getting too far out of balance, Washington wines will achieve a major presence on the national wine scene.

Large-scale agricultural interests and family-owned farms and ranches are the economic backbone of the Columbia Valley. When it became clear that premium wine grapes were fast becoming an important crop, local farmers and ranchers were quick to respond. Unlike western Oregon, Washington has all the prerequisites for rapid and large-scale expansion. The 18,000 square mile Columbia Valley, the state's principal grape growing area, is not densely populated. Choice vineyard land competes less with residential sprawl. Land is relatively cheap, and vast acreage is available and suitable for grape growing. The major expansion of the 1980s is tiny compared to the state's capacity for expansion.

Washington state is divided into two distinct and radically different climates, the major grape growing climate east of the Cascade Mountain Range in the vast drainage basin of the Columbia River Valley, and the much cooler and wetter climate west of the Cascade Range. In the Northwest's three state grape growing region, the Columbia Valley's growing climate is the sunniest and warmest. Western Washington's is the coolest and rainiest.

Because of the climate and economics, very little acreage is devoted to wine grapes in western Washington. By contrast, Columbia Valley grapes and wines dominate not only Washington, but the entire Northwest wine industry. More than 99 percent of Washington wine is made from Columbia Valley grapes. More premium wine grapes are grown in the Columbia Valley than in all other grape growing areas of the Northwest combined, and the Columbia Valley is second in quantity only to California in the production of premium vinifera grape wines. Within its boundaries, the expansive Columbia Valley encompasses many grape growing regions, including the Yakima Valley and Walla Walla Valley.

COLUMBIA VALLEY

In December of 1984, the Bureau of Alcohol, Tobacco, and Firearms (BATF) formally recognized the Columbia Valley as an American viticultural area. One hundred and eighty-five miles wide and 200 miles long, the Columbia Valley covers approximately 23,000 square miles. Except for a portion of land between Banks Lake and the Snake River Valley which has a growing season too short for wine grapes, all of the Columbia Valley is included in the designated viticultural area. Encompassing 18,000 square miles, the Columbia Valley viticultural area is by far the Northwest's largest, covering a nearly a third the land mass of Washington.

The open, gently undulating terrain is bordered on the west by the foothills of the Cascade Mountain Range, on the north by the Okanogan Highlands that extend into Canada, on the east by the rolling hills of the Palouse, and on the south, in Oregon, by the Blue Mountains and their foothills, and the foothills of the Cascade Range. Most of the Columbia Valley's land and nearly all its grape growing is in Washington, but some of the land and grape growing activity extends into Oregon as well. Within its boundaries, the Columbia Valley includes two other viticultural areas, the Yakima Valley and Walla Walla Valley.

As a winegrowing climate, the Columbia Valley is unique. A short distance from the Pacific Ocean, the towering peaks of the Cascade Range thrust more than 12,000 feet above sea level. The Cascade Range runs north to south through Washington and Oregon, forming a continuous wall of mountains, blocking the flow of Pacific marine air, and creating a giant rain shadow extending across the Columbia Valley for hundreds of miles. The rain shadow renders the vast Columbia Valley a near desert. Much of the valley receives less than ten inches of rain a year. Ex-cept near rivers and streams, the land is natural-ly treeless. Grasses and sagebrush are the most common natural vegetation, but the famed Columbia River and its tributaries provide ample irrigation water, transforming the Columbia Valley into a rich agricultural region.

The growing season ranges from a low of 150 days, to a high of just over 200 days. Contrary to expectations for this northerly American winegrowing region, cool climate wine grapes are not the only suitable grape varieties. Measured in terms of heat summation units, the Columbia Valley encompasses the full range of the University of California's climatic regions, from the coolest Region I through the warmest Region V. All Columbia Valley vineyards, however, are on growing sites classified as Region I, II, or III, most in Regions I and II.

The U. C. Davis climate classification system is only a rough guide, and far from adequately captures the unique nature of the Columbia Valley's grape growing environments and their effect on the grapes and wine. The classification system, however, begins to illustrate how the Columbia Valley, often associated with Riesling, can consistently produce excellent wines from warmer climate varieties such as Cabernet Sauvignon and Semillon.

In many respects, the Columbia Valley growing climate is ideal. Under cloudless skies, warm sunny days are followed by cool clear nights. Because of the northerly latitude, day length is longer during the growing season. Rain during harvest is rare. Winter freezing presents the only major critical problem for grape growers, but better viticultural practices have greatly lessened the danger.

The growing season is relatively short and intense. At midsummer, during the height of the grape vine's vegetative period, the Columbia Valley averages two more hours sunlight than the Napa Valley. Temperatures remain in a range ideal for photosynthesis and vine growth, and grape sugars rise rapidly. As fall and the final grape ripening approaches, day length rapidly decreases and the intense heat of the summer gives way to rapidly moderating temperatures. Because the final ripening of the grapes does not take place under conditions of intense heat, the grape's volatile aromatics and flavoring components are preserved.

In the cloudless, near desert climate, nighttime temperatures are relatively cool, even in the middle of summer. Nighttime coolness becomes increasingly pronounced as fall approaches. Because acid reduction is mostly dependent on warm temperatures, but increases in grape sugar depend on both warm temperatures and sunlight, the combination of cool nights and warm sunny days produces grapes that retain adequate acidity even at relatively high sugar levels. The Columbia Valley can produce grapes with higher sugar levels usually associated with more southerly growing climates, but because of the Columbia Valley's unique climate, adequate acids, and complex fruit flavors and aromatics are preserved.

Every winegrowing region has characteristics that are both problems and opportunities for the winegrower. In Europe's premium winegrowing regions, winegrowers work with grapes that tend to be low in sugar and high in acid, Californians with grapes that tend to be high in sugar and low in acid. Columbia Valley winegrowers work with grapes that can be abundant in both sugar and acid. Although one of the Columbia Valley's assets, this is sometimes too much of a good thing. One of the challenges for the Washington wine industry has been to develop viticultural practices that insure the grapes will not be simultaneously overripe with too high an acid content, and to develop winemaking practices to handle grapes with these tendencies.

Frost and winter cold present the only serious problem for Columbia Valley winegrowers. Not totally an inland climate, some marine air still reaches the Columbia Valley to moderate temperature extremes. The Columbia River Gorge, cutting through the Cascade Range, provides a pathway for the marine air to reach the inland valleys. The marine influence is enough to allow the grape vines to survive the winter cold, but not enough to totally free the winegrower from the concerns of frosts and winter freezes.

The same Cascade Mountains that block the onshore flow of marine air and help create ideal grape growing conditions during the summer months, also block the moderating marine influences in winter. The rain shadow of summer becomes the snow shadow of winter, and the frequent lack of insulating snow cover leaves the vines more vulnerable to cold. Spring and fall frosts can also be a problem, damaging the newly budded vines, shortening the growing season, and preventing the vines from hardening their wood for the winter cold. In winter, cold

Frosts and freezes can hit hard in some vineyards. Here, the damaged cordons (lateral arms) have been cut away. The main trunk is left in hopes of recovery, but sucker growth is trained upward in case it must be used to replace the trunk. The root structure remains healthy.

110

temperatures can freeze the nascent buds, vine trunks, and even kill the vines at their roots.

Improved grape growing practices have greatly lessened the threat and severity of winter damage. Winegrowers can expect some vine damage or crop reduction several times a decade in most growing sites, but total vine kill is rare; and for most winegrowers following proper cultural practices, frosts or severe winters mean little more than a temporary reduction in the crop level. An unusual series of frosts and freezes in the mid '80s damaged vines and reduced the grape crop, but, at the same time, further proved that winegrowing in the Columbia Valley is viticulturally and economically viable. The continuing survival of vines from the last century, remnants of an earlier winegrowing era, offer the weight of history to the Columbia Valley winegrowing enterprise.

The Columbia Valley is the Northwest's most versatile winegrowing region. More varieties grow well in the Columbia Valley than in any other Northwest climate. With proper site selection, virtually all the major grape varieties will ripen, develop good varietal flavors, and maintain desired acid levels. And as a bonus, warm days of sunshine, nighttime cooling, and the control of moisture through irrigation provide an excellent climatic environment for sweet botrytised wines.

Vineyards can be pruned for modest yields for premium wines, yet because the climate allows high yields while maintaining good acid balance and varietal definition, the region lends itself well to the production of premium "jug" wines. The large blocks of land available for cultivation and the typically gentle slopes make mechanical harvesting easily feasible. Premium wines, however, gave birth to Washington's modern wine industry, and premium wines continue to be the industry's foundation as well as its glory.

Columbia Valley growing areas include the Yakima Valley; the Walla Walla Valley; Paterson Ridge, close to Paterson near the Columbia River and Oregon border; the Pasco Basin area, north of the city of Pasco, in the wide "U" of land formed by the confluence of the Columbia and Snake Rivers; and further north along the Columbia

Newly harvested grapes await the crusher.

River, Cold Creek Valley; and the Wahluke Slope.

In the last ten million years, the northward movement of coastal land masses folded and buckled the western portion of the Columbia Valley, creating a series of high ridges. Running east to west, the ridges act as barriers to the winter arctic air from the north, and many of their lower slopes offer ideal vineyard sites with extended south facing exposures and good air drainage. Examples of these ridges are the Saddle Mountains, Rattlesnake Hills, Ahtanum Ridge, and Frenchman Hills.

Some of the ridges already figure prominently in viticultural activity. Most Yakima Valley vineyards, for example, are situated on the lower slopes of the Rattlesnake Hills. The Wahluke Slope, near the town of Mattawa, on lower southern slope of the Saddle Mountains, has only recently seen viticultural development, but is already recognized as a major grape growing area. Other sites, such as the Royal Slope on the lower reaches of the Frenchman Hills, are promising, but have had little development.

The Columbia Valley viticultural area covers many thousands of square miles. Only a very small portion has been developed for grape growing. The climate is so unique and the region so diverse that the Columbia Valley's full potential as a winegrowing region is scarcely known, and may not really be understood for decades.

YAKIMA VALLEY

In May of 1983, the BATF formally recognized the Yakima Valley viticultural area, the first viticultural area in the Northwest. Wholly contained within the more encompassing Columbia Valley appellation, the Yakima Valley is the most intensely developed agricultural region in the Columbia Valley. Nearly 75 miles long and 22 miles wide at broadest point, the Yakima Valley encompasses slightly more than 1,000 square miles.

One of the Columbia River's major tributaries, the Yakima River emerges from the Northwest in the Cascade Mountains, meeting the Columbia River near the southern border of the state, just before the Columbia angles abruptly westward toward the Pacific Ocean. The Yakima Valley is the most geographically distinct of the Columbia Valley's major grape growing areas. The Yakima Valley is shaped not so much by the course of the river itself, but by ridges formed from basaltic uplifts in the terrain millions of years ago. Running in a generally east to west direction, the ridges define the shape of the valley.

Just south of the city of Yakima, the Ahtanum Ridge and Rattlesnake Hills define the Yakima Valley's northern boundary. The Toppenish Ridge and Horse Heaven Hills form the southern boundary, and the foothills of the Cascade Mountains form the western boundary. On the east, the southeastern extension of the Rattlesnake Hills, Red Mountain, and Badger Mountain separate the Yakima Valley viticultural area from the rest of the vast Columbia Valley. Most of the valley's vineyards are located on gently sloping sites on the eastern side of the Yakima River, on the lower slopes of the Rattlesnake Hills.

Much of the Columbia Valley is desolate, but the Yakima Valley is dotted with many small cities and towns. The terrain is dry and naturally treeless. Sagebrush and grasses cover the higher slopes of the golden brown hills, but since the early 1900s, irrigation canal systems have opened up much of the land for intense agricultural development. The irrigation systems turned the Yakima Valley into an agricultural center, home for a wide range of crops, including many tree fruits, vegetables, hops, mint—and grapes.

Native American grape varieties, mostly Concord, predominate, planted not for wine, but for grape juice. Approximately 20,000 acres of native American grapes are planted in the valley. The native American varieties have been widely planted since the early 1900s, but vinifera wine grapes did not become an important crop until the 1970s. One of the valley's many fruit crops, demand for native American grapes and grape juice is waning. Native American grape varieties still greatly outnumber wine grapes, but they play no role in the Yakima Valley wine industry.

In terms of the grape growing climate classification system developed at U. C. Davis, most of the Yakima Valley is classified as Region II. The growing season averages approximately 190 days. An outstanding wine producing region, the Yakima Valley is slightly cooler than most of the Columbia Valley's other major grape growing areas. Frost and winter cold damage can be problems, so careful selection of vineyard sites is key to wine quality and consistent crop yields.

Although the cooler climate or earlier ripening varieties such as Riesling and Gewurztraminer are especially well suited to many growing sites, the Yakima Valley has earned an excellent reputation for warmer climate varieties such as Cabernet Sauvignon. So far, most of Washington's best Cabernet Sauvignons have been made from Yakima Valley grapes.

WALLA WALLA VALLEY

In March of 1984, the BATF formally recognized the Walla Walla Valley viticultural area. Part of the more encompassing Columbia Valley appellation, the Walla Walla Valley, like the Columbia Valley, includes land in both Washington and Oregon. Also like the Columbia Valley, most of Walla Walla Valley winegrowing is centered on the Washington side of the border, in the southeast portion of the state. A dormant wine industry awaiting rebirth, some of Washington's first grapes for wine were grown in the Walla Walla Valley during the last century.

The Walla Walla Valley viticultural area is relatively small, encompassing approximately 280 square miles. Slightly moister and more temperate than most of the Columbia Valley, a variety of grasses share space with the Columbia Valley's ubiquitous Sagebrush. Several wineries are located in the Walla Walla Valley, but as yet few acres are planted to wine grapes. The Walla Walla Valley winegrowing climates are quite varied. So far, Cabernet Sauvignon has shown exceptional promise. Early indications suggest that the Walla Walla Valley will become an important source for quality wine grapes.

COLUMBIA GORGE

The confluence of the Columbia and Klickitat Rivers near the town of The Dalles marks the eastern boundary of the Columbia Valley. To the west, the Columbia River courses through the Columbia River Gorge, a geologically and climatically dramatic area. Here the Columbia River cuts through the otherwise unbreachable barrier of the Cascade Mountain Range. Along the narrow Gorge, the radically different climates of the hot, dry Columbia Valley and the moist temperate western marine climate converge and collide. Winds race incessantly through the Gorge, and major climatic differences occur within short distances.

Land suitable for vineyards is limited, but both the Washington and Oregon side of the border are home for wineries and vineyards. Grenache grows well in the warmest growing sites in the eastern part of the Gorge. Further west, a number of varieties, including Cabernet Sauvignon, Pinot Noir, Gewurztraminer, and Chardonnay grow successfully. Gewurztraminer from the Bingen and Hood River areas is particularly notable.

WESTERN WASHINGTON PUGET SOUND

In Washington, unlike Oregon, few wine grapes are grown in the western part of the state. Most of the wineries located in western Washington make wine from Columbia Valley grapes, not from western Washington grapes. The amount of wine made from western Washington grapes is insignificant compared with the volume of wine produced by all of Washington's wineries from Columbia Valley grapes.

Western Washington winegrowing is significant not because of its impact on the marketplace, but for the uniqueness of its wines. Western Washington has the coolest winegrowing climate in America. Most of the wine grapes grown in western Washington are vinifera—usually not the more familiar vinifera varieties such as Cabernet Sauvignon and Riesling, but less familiar varieties more suited to the long but very cool growing season—varieties such as Madeleine Angevine, or the somewhat more familiar Muller-Thurgau.

Oregon's major winegrowing region is situated in western Oregon between a coastal mountain range and the Cascade Range. The Coast Range partially interrupts the direct flow of marine air, rendering most of western Oregon warmer, sunnier, and drier than most of western Washington. In Washington, the Olympic Mountain Range and Canada's Vancouver Island help temper the onshore flow of air from the Pacific Ocean, but western Washington does not have

Oregon's continuous coastal barrier to the marine air. Consequently, most of western Washington is cooler, less sunny, and more moist than western Oregon.

In general, western Washington's warmest growing sites are located further away from the coast, on the slopes of Cascade foothills. The warmest sites, however, are also rainier and have shorter growing seasons. The best growing sites are situated where these conflicting tendencies are balanced, or in localized climates offering special advantage. Grapes are grown on selected sites all along western Washington from the Canadian to Oregon border. Vineyards are typically very small. The principal Puget Sound grape growing areas include the Nooksack, Puyallup, and Carbon River Valleys, and Bainbridge Island in Puget Sound.

SOUTHWEST WASHINGTON

The southwest corner of Washington is an exception to the general rule that western Washington is significantly cooler and moister than western Oregon. Here the land juts southward behind the northern reaches of Oregon's coastal mountains. The area, principally in Clark County, is very similar to Oregon's Willamette Valley climate. Grape varieties such as Pinot Noir and Chardonnay predominate, rather than the Puget Sound varieties such as Madeleine Angevine and Muller-Thurgau. For more information on southwest Washington's grape growing climate, refer to the Oregon sections in this book pertaining to the Willamette Valley.

WASHINGTON GRAPE VARIETIES

COLUMBIA VALLEY GRAPE VARIETIES

The Columbia Valley, including its secondary valleys, the Yakima Valley and Walla Walla Valley, produces more than 99 percent of the state's wine grapes. The small Columbia Gorge Region is included in this section of the book for convenience, although it is technically not part of the Columbia Valley.

All the grape varieties are *Vitis vinifera* (Riesling, Chardonnay, Cabernet Sauvignon, etc.). French-American hybrids drew slight interest in the earliest years of the industry because of their proven winter hardiness, but when vinifera varieties proved adequately winter hardy interest in the lower quality French-American wine grapes vanished. Only a few acres of these hybrids remain. None are released as varietal wines.

Three-quarters of the grape acreage is planted to white varietals. The quantitative predominance of white wine is even more pronounced, however, since the white varieties produce higher yields than the red varieties. More than four-fifths of Washington wine is white. Riesling is by far the most widely planted white variety, but its dominance is lessening with a shifting interest toward the traditionally dry white varietals such as Chardonnay, Sauvignon Blanc, and Semillon. Cabernet Sauvignon is the most widely planted red variety, followed closely by Merlot.

ALIGOTE, a high yielding, lesser quality white grape of Burgundy, produces a pleasant dinner wine, particularly if blended with another grape for additional character. Very little acreage is planted in Washington.

CABERNET SAUVIGNON, now an outstanding Washington varietal, has not been the easiest grape to tame, but Cabernet Sauvignon is arguably Washington's finest wine. This is not to say that Washington Cabernet Sauvignons are uniformly as good as the state's traditional white varietals. The quality of the Washington Cabernets is much more variable, yet the best are truly outstanding. To a greater degree than most other varieties, careful selection of growing sites, good vineyard practices, and winemaking skill and art are keys to excellence in Washington Cabernet Sauvignon.

Cabernet Sauvignon's potential was evident from the earliest years, but excellence was long in coming. The first wines did not go through malolactic fermentation, a virtual necessity for quality Washington Cabernet Sauvignon. The grape variety itself is prone to high pH, and lesser growing sites yield grapes that exceed desirable limits. Overfertilizing, overwatering, overcropping, and picking overly ripe are other detriments to quality Cabernet. Cabernet Sauvignon has such a distinctive varietal profile, that it is possible to produce a fairly flavorful wine from relatively poor quality grapes, but such wines are loosely structured and lack concentration and extract.

Washington Cabernets are typically deeply colored and flavored, full bodied, rough, tannic, and inaccessible when young, frequently requiring several years bottle aging to begin showing their best. Hard, relatively high in acid, and unyielding in their youth, the best Washington Cabernet Sauvignons are often misunderstood by winemaker and consumer alike. To make the wines drinkable sooner, winemakers have sometimes diluted the essential strengths of the wine to its inevitable detriment. The best Washington Cabernets, with good structure and ample acidity, benefit from long cellaring.

Cabernet Sauvignon is sensitive to winter cold damage, but the vine itself is vigorous and recovers readily. Fortunately, the same careful growing practices that protect the vine from winter also produce the best quality wine grapes.

The newly developing Walla Walla Valley shows excellent promise for the grape. Of the established growing areas, the Yakima Valley produces exceptionally good Cabernet Sauvignon. Yakima Cabernets often have a distinctive berrylike component. Very pronounced in the fruit of some vineyards, the berrylike element more typically shows itself as one of many nuances. Cabernets from the warmer eastern end of the valley tend to be fuller bodied and more textural. Further up the valley, toward the northwest, the Cabernets are less supple, but tightly knit with good concentration and extract. Individual growing sites throughout the valley, however, often contradict any general case statement.

CHARDONNAY, makes fine wine, though it has proven to be one of the more difficult white varietals for winegrowers. The grape is reasonably winter hardy and ripens without difficulty, but requires care in the vineyard to protect against mildew, and care in site selection and cropping to bring in grapes with sugars and acids in balance.

Washington Chardonnays are reliably very good, if sometimes slightly coarse. The best can be excellent. Unlike Oregon, few Washington winemakers put Chardonnay through malolactic fermentation, preferring more of the fruit of the grape rather than the alternate complexities offered by the secondary fermentation.

Most Washington Chardonnays are fermented in stainless steel tanks at moderately cool temperatures, and aged for relatively brief periods in oak. Perhaps as a result of the newness of many of the wineries, the oak barrels are new and impart distinctive oak character even though the aging period is brief. This fresh, unoxygenated style is highly successful, fits well with current consumer trends, and demonstrates inherent strengths of the region. At the same time, the enduring, and perhaps ultimately more interesting, complexities of traditional Burgundian styled Chardonnays are sacrificed.

A small but important counter trend toward a more Burgundian style is emerging. Both styles, and variations in between, have their place. For the moment, the fresher, fruity style predominates. If not always the easiest white wine to make, Chardonnay has proven to be among the more rewarding, and Chardonnay is also playing a role in Washington's increasing interest in sparkling wine production.

CHENIN BLANC produces high yields with good sugar and acid balance. Twelve tons an acre are not uncommon. In America, specifically, in California, Chenin Blanc is considered a lowly varietal with little character, a grape to provide the basis for cheap jug wines. Although the grape is not in the same league as Chardonnay, in its native France and in Washington, the wines are distinctive and worthy of interest.

Chenin Blanc was among Washington's earlier commercially produced varietals, but because of the grape's mediocre reputation, Chenin Blanc was largely ignored until the 1980s. Although some Washington winemakers are experimenting with Chenin Blanc in the French style, most is made in the manner of Washington Rieslings, slightly sweet, no wood, and fermented at cool temperatures in stainless steel to emphasize the fresh fruit of the grape.

For those who find the character of Riesling sometimes overly insistent and cloying, Chenin Blanc offers a different tasting, similarly styled wine. Although quite rare, botrytised Chenin Blanc shows yet another dimension of the grape. Chenin Blanc can be fairly cold hardy, but because the variety is typically cropped very high, and because of the vine's high vigor, Washington Chenin Blanc often suffers severely in a winter cold snap and in fall and spring frosts.

GEWURZTRAMINER was one of the state's early successes, helping to make a name for Washington white wine. This is not to say that all Washington Gewurztraminers are exceptional. The grape is fickle and must be picked at just the right ripeness. Picked too early, the spicy varietal character is lost. Picked too late, the wine is heavy, flat, dull, and bitter. The grape is naturally low in acid, and cooler growing sites are best. Slightly sweet Gewurztraminer is the most popular, but the successful dry Gewurztraminers, unaided by sugar to mask flaws in the wine, best demonstrate the region's capabilities. The wine is an ideal match for more aggressive food courses.

Gewurztraminer is one of the earlier ripening varieties and stands up well to the winter cold. Unlike other grape varieties grown in the state, a modified form of cane rather than cordon pruning is sometimes recommended. Although Washington produces fine Gewurztraminer, the distinctive character and intimidating name keeps the wine from being as universally appealing as many other varieties. The Yakima Valley and Columbia Gorge area have earned a reputation for producing Washington's best Gewurztraminers.

GRENACHE wines have characteristic flavors of black pepper and spice. The grape is made into soft red wines for easy quaffing, as well as flavorful roses. Grenache requires a hot growing climate and a long season. Planted only in small quantities, the vine's sensitivity to winter cold and subsequent erratic crops do not endear it to winegrowers. With the newest Grenache vineyards, special planting and cultivation measures will hopefully insure more regular and reliable harvests.

LEMBERGER, sometimes spelled Limberger, is a little known red wine grape grown in small quantities in several European countries. Best known as a wine from the Wurttemberg region of Germany, the grape came to Washington from Hungary via British Columbia in the late 1930s as part of Washington State University's research program.

Dr. Walter Clore, horticulturist emeritus from Washington State University, worked with the grape from the early years and has long been an ardent advocate. Winemakers, however, have been much less enthused, in part, because of the inherent marketing problems for an unknown variety with a name reminiscent of a foul smelling cheese.

Lemberger has been called Washington's Zinfandel, a characterization not too far from the truth. German Lemberger is generally undistinguished, but in Washington, Lemberger can be made into darkly colored, robust, flavorful wines.

Berrys and vanilla characterize its aroma and flavor. In Washington, Lemberger adapts to a wide range of styles from light and fruity to big and tannic.

Lemberger can be a prolific producer, but if the vines are overcropped and the growing season is not the best, the loss in quality is significant. Recent interest in the grape for generic blends as well as premium bottlings has created a demand that tempts overcropping. Most of the pruning wood goes to plant new vines. Lemberger has a naturally low pH and does well in most growing sites. Young Lemberger vines are particularly susceptible to winter cold, but once established, Lemberger is quite cold hardy. At present, Washington has very little acreage planted to the grape.

MERLOT, one of the Bordeaux grape varieties, when grown outside its homeland, is often either light and lacking in intensity or else "big," but low acid and one dimensional. The inherently higher acidity of Washington Merlot complements the grape. The best Washington Merlots are full-bodied but tightly structured wines of distinction. Merlot can easily become overripe, however, and must be carefully monitored as harvest approaches. Merlot produces slightly larger crops than Cabernet Sauvignon, ripens earlier, and is more cold hardy. It is often added to Cabernet wines for texture and suppleness. Washington Merlots are reliably good, and the best are excellent.

MORIO MUSCAT, also spelled Morio Muskat, a German cross of Sylvaner and Pinot Blanc developed by Peter Morio. The grape ripens early and produces high yields. The appealing wine has pronounced muscat flavor and aroma. Very little acreage is planted in Washington.

MUSCAT CANELLI, the principal muscat variety grown in Washington, is typically made in a fairly sweet style, balanced with adequate acidity. Although not extensively planted, the grape makes a flavorful dessert wine and rounds out the market line for many wineries.

PINOT NOIR, according to latitude and heat unit measurements, should have been a good grape for the Columbia Valley. Regrettably, the wines are seldom distinguished, and are usually no more successful than most California Pinot Noirs. Very little new acreage is being devoted to the grape. Although the track record has not been encouraging, it is premature to dismiss Columbia Valley Pinot Noir. Occasionally there have been significant successes, and new growing sites may yet produce high quality Pinot Noir. The Columbia Gorge area along the state's southern border is among the more promising sites. On a small scale, the grape is regularly successful in sparkling wine.

RIESLING, also known as White Riesling and Johannisberg Riesling, is the state's most widely planted variety. It is a winegrower's dream. Riesling, the most winter hardy of all the vinifera varieties, produces good yields, and grows successfully in a wide variety of growing sites, from the coolest areas in the Yakima Valley to the warm Wahluke Slope. Although Riesling is a late season grape, varietal character develops early in the ripening cycle, and good wine can be made even under adverse growing conditions.

Washington Rieslings are intensely fruity, and usually finished slightly sweet, with a counterpoint of crisp acidity. They are typically riper and fuller bodied than their German counterparts. Washington late harvest Rieslings, particularly those that acquire their higher sugars from additional ripening rather than botrytis, take on a muscat-like character. The organic compound linalool, the principal component associated with muscat, is present to a greater degree in riper Riesling grapes.

Riesling has also been been the basis for very fine ice, botrytised, and sparkling wines. Although the grape has become a bread-and-butter mainstay of the Washington wine industry, and perhaps no other growing region in America can so easily produce high quality Rieslings on such a large scale, the state's wine industry may have overcommitted itself to the grape.

While several other Washington varieties seem destined to compete with the best in the world, Washington Riesling does not achieve that elusive delicacy and finesse associated with the finest German Rieslings, nor, arguably, does Washington Riesling make a wine of equivalent breed in a different style. If not outstanding, Washington Rieslings are nevertheless routinely very good to excellent, and the grape is likely to continue playing a major role. The more recent shift in attention to other varieties only serves to bring about better balance in the wine industry.

SAUVIGNON BLANC, also known as Fume Blanc, is an increasingly popular grape. In Washington's cooler growing climate, the the character of the grape is sometimes even more pronounced than California's Sauvignon Blancs, yielding wines with a typically herbaceous, grassy, varietal character.

Nationally, the grape is gaining increasing favor, and Washington offers fine examples for those who enjoy the more varietally pronounced renditions of the grape. Many Washington winemakers are releasing Sauvignon Blanc with slight residual sugar for a more supple and rounder texture for this aggressively charactered varietal. This style, with a threshold level of sweetness, has proven popular with consumers and critics alike, but finds less favor with those more accustomed to the bone dry character of European wines. See Semillon.

SEMILLON, in America, more specifically, in California, is viewed as a lesser, secondary grape of white Bordeaux, as a grape of modest distinction that is not in the same league as Sauvignon Blanc. In Bordeaux, the view is quite the opposite. In recent years, there has been more emphasis on Sauvignon Blanc for fresher, earlier drinking wines, but for "serious" white Bordeaux, particularly those made by the best Chateau and intended for longer aging and development in the bottle, Semillon is the predominant grape.

The taste of Semillon and Sauvignon Blanc is quite similar, but Sauvignon Blanc has less finesse, and is more aggressively herbaceous. Because the warmer California growing climate burns away much of Semillon's varietal character,

the more pronounced and persistent flavors of Sauvignon Blanc have proven better suited to the California climate. In the Washington growing climate, Semillon shows intense varietal character.

If anything, Washington Semillon may be too varietally grassy for those accustomed to the wines of Bordeaux, but this is partly a function of Washington's prevalent winemaking style that emphasizes the crisp, varietal fruit of white wines, as well as a tendency by Washington wineries toward less wood and early release of the wines. In acreage, Sauvignon Blanc predominates over Semillon, but Semillon is gaining favor as it sheds its California reputation. One of Washington's earliest commercial wine grapes, Semillon is only recently gaining the acceptance and interest it deserves. Semillon is one of Washington's finest white varietals.

WESTERN WASHINGTON GRAPE VARIETIES

Very few acres of wine grapes are planted in western Washington. The economic impact of western Washington winegrowing on the Washington wine industry as a whole is nearly nil. Qualitatively, however, western Washington's very cool growing climate can produce interesting and worthwhile varieties not suited to the Columbia Valley.

A few hybrids and native American varieties, holdovers from an earlier era of winegrowing, are still made into wine, but cool climate vinifera varieties are the major focus, particularly the modern vinifera crosses from Germany, as well as older and unusual vinifera varieties from France. A few traditional varieties such as Gewurztraminer, Chardonnay, and Riesling, are grown with varying degrees of success. Experiments with specialized rootstocks may make a few of these varieties additionally viable.

A portion of southwest Washington dips south behind Oregon's coastal mountain range, and the climate is very similar to Oregon's northern Willamette Valley. For information on the characteristics of southwest Washington wines and grape growing, refer to the Oregon sections on the Willamette Valley climate and grape varieties. Except for Pinot Noir grown in southwest Washington, virtually all western Washington varieties are white. Numerous varieties, including some of the most promising, are grown in tiny experimental plots. The more widely planted, commercially available varieties are listed below.

MADELEINE ANGEVINE, also spelled Madeline Angevine, a French vinifera variety bred in the Loire Valley in the 1850s from two older vinifera varieties, Precoce de Malingre and Madeleine Royale, crops reliably, ripens well, and yields abundant fruit. The grape's pleasant fruitiness shows well in wines that are nearly dry, with slight residual sweetness. It is one of western Washington's principal varieties.

MADELEINE SYLVANER, an old French vinifera cross probably bred from Madeleine Royale and Sylvaner, has not established a clear role in Washington. The grape is less fruity than Madeleine Angevine and is often blended with other wines.

MULLER-THURGAU, a cross of Riesling and Sylvaner, was developed a century ago by Prof Dr. Hermann Muller-Thurgau. Today, it is the most widely cultivated variety in Germany.

Muller-Thurgau is a high yielding, low acid, early ripening variety, generally similar to Riesling, but without Riesling's varietal intensity and distinguished character.

The current mainstay of western Washington winegrowing, Muller-Thurgau produces wines similar to those of Germany. Muller-Thurgau is the grape of the ubiquitous Liebfraumilch, but when cropped more conservatively and grown in cool growing areas, the grape shows the ability to produce more distinguished wines.

OKANOGAN RIESLING, also spelled Okanagan Riesling, a traditional Canadian wine grape, is making its way south into western Washington. Of uncertain origin, Okanogan Riesling is now generally believed to be an interspecific hybrid and not a true vinifera. In Canada, the grape has a mixed reputation, and is generally falling out of favor. A number of clones exist, some tending to emphasize more or less of the non-vinifera characteristics, both in growing habit and in the taste of the wine.

Okanogan Riesling can have a coarse aggressiveness, and requires careful handling in the winemaking process. Given the right clone, growing climate, and winemaking methods, however, Okanogan Riesling can yield interesting, flavorful wines. The Washington efforts have done exceptionally well with the grape, demonstrating its potential and merit if handled properly.

WASHINGTON WINE NOTES

The wines from Washington's Columbia Valley, the state's major winegrowing region, are unique. The intensely sunny growing season, warm days, very cool nights, and rapidly moderating fall temperatures, produce grapes with crisp acidity, intense fruit flavors, and, potentially, high sugars. Most winegrowing regions either have a tendency to produce grapes with high sugars and low acids, as in many California winegrowing regions, or low sugars and high acids, as in many European winegrowing regions. Rarely does a region produce grapes that are frequently high in both acid and sugar, but Washington's Columbia Valley is such a region.

In the recent past, many grape varieties, particularly Riesling and Chenin Blanc, were harvested at moderately high sugars. The wines, as befitting the nature of the region, still had ample acidity, but they surrendered some of the fruity nuances for the riper flavors, and the wines were moderately high in alcohol for the type, or fairly sweet.

Today, the prevalent white wine style showcases the unique character of Columbia Valley wines. Increasingly, winegrowers are harvesting many white varieties, particularly Riesling and Chenin Blanc, at lower sugar levels, releasing the wines at a moderate 10 or 11 percent alcohol, with crisp acidity balanced by some residual sweetness. Typically, the white wines are fermented in stainless steel at cool temperatures, further emphasizing crisp acidities and the intense, fresh fruitiness of the grape. Chenin Blanc, made in this style, is especially notable. Washington Chenin Blancs have a character and interest that betrays the grape's lowly American reputation.

The traditionally dry white varieties, such as Chardonnay, Sauvignon Blanc, and Semillon, are often treated similarly to emphasize the fruity character of the grape. Some of the "dry" wines are are not totally "dry." Sauvignon Blanc and Semillon are the most frequent recipients of this treatment, using slight residual sweetness as a counterpoint to the crisp acidity and grassy-herbaceous character.

The fresh fruitiness of the traditionally dry varietals is accomplished through one or more of a variety of winemaking techniques, including stainless steel fermentations at cool temperatures, avoidance of malolactic fermentation, only brief aging in new oak barrels, removal of grape solids before or immediately after fermentation, avoidance of oxygenation (keeping the wine in a "reduced" state), and immediate and frequent racking of the wine away from the lees.

These methods are part of "modern winemaking technique" and are by no means unique to Washington, but the crisp acidities and intensely fruity character of Washington grapes makes the effect of these methods all the more apparent.

Made in this fresh, intensely fruity style, the dry white wines clearly articulate the Columbia Valley's winegrowing climate. Yet, for those accustomed to the classic European renditions of these varieties, the fresh, fruity style can sometimes seem coarse and simplistic, not wearing well through the course of a meal.

The fresh, fruity style remains a valid (and tasty) expression of the region, but winemakers are increasingly employing some of the more traditional methods, and bringing welcome diversity to the Washington wine scene. A few of the methods that give up some of the fresh, fruity flavors in favor of alternate complexities include, fermenting the wine in small oak barrels, fermenting the wine without first clarifying the juice, warmer fermentation temperatures, a secondary malolactic fermentation, longer aging in older oak barrels, and more extended contact with the lees.

A winemaker can choose one or several of these methods to make wines with enduring, complex flavors that still express the intense varietal character of the region's wines. As the number of Washington wineries increases, wineries are seeking a stylistic signature to distinguish themselves from the rest of the crowd. The growing diversity of wine styles is all to the good, satisfying all tastes and moods.

Riesling has been and will continue to be the backbone of the Washington wine industry. The grape resists winter damage, the wines are popular with consumers, and no other American winegrowing region so easily produces Rieslings of such high quality. Yet, except for the occasional, exotic ice wines and highly botrytised renditions of the grape, the glory of the Washington wine region does not lie with Riesling. Washington produces Rieslings to a routine high standard, but the wines are seldom truly outstanding or exciting.

More and more clearly, Cabernet Sauvignon is emerging as Washington's stellar grape variety. Cabernet showed promise and sporadic excellence from the earliest years, but not until the vintages of the early 1980s did the wine begin to achieve consistent excellence by a range of winemakers. So far, the best Cabernets have come from the small to medium size wineries.

Wines made from overcropped Cabernet grapes lack extract, varietal intensity, and the proper structure for aging, but because Cabernet vines are particularly sensitive to winter cold, and overcropping greatly increases the chances of winter damage, growers have an additional motivation to limit their crop.

The best Washington Cabernet Sauvignons have immense fruit extract. They are deeply colored, with a good acid armature to carry them through long cellaring. Although Washington Cabernet Sauvignons have their own set of flavors, and are often slightly riper and higher in alcohol than the wines of Bordeaux, the structure of Washington Cabernets is not unlike the old style Bordeauxs in many respects, and they often require similarly lengthy cellaring.

Some winemakers pick the grapes very ripe to make high alcohol, low acid, full-bodied wines, sometimes with lots of tannin to give an added impression of "bigness." This style of wine is sometimes popular with consumers, and often does well in wine judgings, but it does not show the region at its best. Despite their "bigness," such wines do not develop well with age. A solid acid, low pH structure with fruit intensity and extract are the keys to quality Cabernet with long aging potential. These Cabernets are the current and future glory of the Washington wine industry.

The character of Cabernet Sauvignon wines is closely tied to the vineyard and growing site, and many of the state's best Cabernet winemakers have actively searched for the choice sites and entered into extended contracts with the growers. For us fortunate consumers, more and more Washington winemakers are producing outstanding Cabernets.

Washington Chardonnays are becoming increasingly refined as winemakers gain experience with the grape. Chardonnay is an inherently textural wine without a highly defined varietal profile. It tends to lend itself less well to the fresh fruity style of winemaking than does Sauvignon Blanc, for example. Washington Chardonnays made in a more traditional Burgundian fashion show the grape at its best. Washington Chardonnays made in this style demonstrate the region's potential, and easily hold their own in any company.

Many American winegrowing regions produce fine Chardonnay, but Washington lays special claim to Semillon. A white wine companion to the red Bordeaux variety, Cabernet Sauvignon, Semillon has found a special home in Washington's Columbia Valley.

In California, Semillon is largely shunned in favor of Sauvignon Blanc, but in Bordeaux, Semillon is considered the superior grape. In the best white Bordeauxs, intended for long aging, Semillon frequently predominates. Most American Semillons lack distinction, but Washington Semillon is distinctively varietal, yet more refined and less herbaceous than Sauvignon Blanc. Semillon is emerging as one of Washington's finest white wines.

Washington has long been considered a white wine, and especially, a Riesling wine producing state. Washington's most important qualitative impact, however, lies not with Riesling, but with the dry white varietals, principally Chardonnay and Semillon. And arguably, Washington's best wine is not even white, but red—Cabernet Sauvignon.

WASHINGTON WINERIES

ARBOR CREST

East 4506 Buckeye
Spokane, Washington 99207
(509) 927-9463

Wine Production
25,000 cases

Vineyards
88 acres

Year First Planted
1982

First Vintage
1982

Leading Wines
Sauvignon Blanc, Merlot, Chardonnay, Cabernet Sauvignon

For three generations, the Mielke family has grown and processed fruit near the city of Spokane. David Mielke continued operating the family business, while brother Harry Mielke pursued a medical career, becoming director of the Institute of Cancer Research at San Francisco's Pacific Medical Center.

In the late 1970s, the brothers started a joint project centered around Harry's interest in wine and the family's association with fruit growing. The Mielkes planted forty different kinds of vinifera, native American, and French-American hybrid grapes in a small six acre experimental vineyard on the family farm.

Interest in grape growing stimulated interest in a winery, and in 1982, the Mielkes hired Scott Harris, a U. C. Davis graduate in enology, and then assistant winemaker at California's Davis Bynum winery. The Mielkes moved their cherry processing operations to other buildings on the farm, and moved in the winemaking equipment.

The experimental vineyard showed them that the Spokane area was not suitable for premium vinifera wine grapes, the kind of grapes they wanted for Arbor Crest's wines. Arbor Crest buys grapes from several growers throughout the Columbia Valley. The Mielkes also joined a grape growing partnership and planted a vineyard on the Wahluke Slope, one of Washington's most promising new grape growing areas.

What does Scott Harris, a U. C. Davis graduate and California winemaker for five years, think of Washington grapes and Washington wine? "What amazes me so much," says Harris, "is that the grapes are damn near perfect. The acids and sugars need little or no correction."

In California, the grapes are usually very warm when they come into the winery, and the winery, unless cooled, is warm as well. "I was unprepared for my first crush at Arbor Crest," says Harris. "The grapes were cool, and we had a cellar temperature of 48 degrees. In California, for the white wines, we always had to chill the must before we could ferment. Here, we just start making the wine."

For most medium-size, and larger, Washington wineries, Riesling is the predominant wine, and Riesling is the first wine shipped to out-of-state markets. At Arbor Crest, the approach is different. White wines comprise 80 percent of Arbor Crest's production, but Chardonnay and Sauvignon Blanc, not Riesling, account for nearly half the winery's production. "Instead of Riesling," says Harris, "we use Chardonnay to put us into new markets."

Only French oak is used for barrel aging. In typical Washington style, the white wines emphasize crisp acidity and the fruit of the grape. But within this style, Arbor Crest's whites have a fuller, more textural quality. Arbor Crest's Sauvignon

Blanc is finished with a slight amount of residual sugar, contributing more of a full-bodied, textural impression, and toning down the grape's naturally aggressive character. A leader in this style, the wine has been exceptionally popular regionally and nationally.

The Cabernet is made in a style meant for long aging. Fermentation temperatures are allowed to reach 90 degrees, and, beginning with the 1983 vintage, the cap of skins and pulp are punched down into the fermenting must instead of resubmerging the cap by pumping the must over it. The skins and pulp are not removed until the wine has finished fermentation. The Cabernet is then aged for two years in French oak, mostly Never, and another year in the bottle before release.

The winery is very well equipped, but the corrugated steel, one-time cherry processing building is not the last word in esthetics, and new space will soon be needed to accommodate Arbor Crest's growth. For the winery's future home, the Mielkes purchased Spokane's historic Riblet mansion and estate. The mansion, renamed Arbor Crest Cliff House, is located on a basalt outcropping below Mount Spokane and overlooks the Spokane River, the surrounding countryside, and northern Idaho in the distance.

For years, Seattle area wineries in the more cosmopolitan western part of the state have dominated the Washington wine industry.

Arbor Crest is among the new wave of Spokane area wineries adding balance and diversity to the states burgeoning wine industry.

Scott Harris.

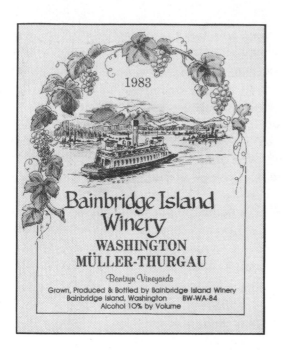

1983

Bainbridge Island Winery

WASHINGTON
MÜLLER-THURGAU

Bentryn Vineyards

Grown, Produced & Bottled by Bainbridge Island Winery
Bainbridge Island, Washington   BW-WA-84
Alcohol 10% by Volume

BAINBRIDGE ISLAND WINERY

682 State Highway 305 N.E.
Bainbridge Island, Washington 98110
(206) 842-WINE or 842-6711

Wine Production
2,000 cases

Vineyards
1 ½ acres

Year First Planted
1978

First Vintage
1981

Leading Wines
Muller-Thurgau, Siegerrebe

Bainbridge Island Winery, the only island winery in the northwest, is a 30 minute ferry boat ride from Seattle's picturesque waterfront. Located a quarter mile from the Bainbridge Island ferry terminal, Jo Ann and Gerard Bentryns' Bainbridge Island Winery is dedicated to the production of premium vinifera wines from western Washington grapes.

The first vines were planted in 1978. Because the Bentryns' own vineyard is very small,

1 ½ acres, additional grapes are purchased from other western Washington growers, and growers from the Columbia Valley east of the Cascade Mountain Range. Approximately half of the winery's production comes from Columbia Valley grapes, but the wine styles of western Washington grapes set the pace for the winery. Committed to the cool climate grape varieties suited to the Puget Sound area of western Washington, the Bentryns have spurred others on Bainbridge Island to grow grapes for their winery.

Western Washington, particularly the Puget Sound area, is a very cool, moist, growing climate, and the grape varieties and wine styles are quite different from those grown east of the Cascade Mountains in Washington's Columbia Valley. Most of the Bentryns' grapes are of German origin, and the wines are Germanic in style, low alcohol, crisp, off-dry to slightly sweet white wines, emphasizing delicate fruit flavors and fragrances. Muller-Thurgau is the principal variety, but Bentryn is also working with other cool climate vinifera varieties such as Siegerrebe, and relatively unknown varieties of French origin such as Madeleine Sylvaner and Madeleine Angevine, both now popularly grown in England as wine grapes. Siegerrebe itself is a cross of Madeleine Angevine and Gewurztraminer.

The Puget Sound growing climate has simi-

Gerard Bentryn.

larities to both Germany and England, but is not quite the same as either, being cooler and less sunny than Germany, but warmer and drier than England. The Bentryns believe that the cool Puget Sound growing area is ideal for preserving floral intensity and the delicate fruit esters of grapes carefully chosen for the climate.

In the Bentryns' view, Muller-Thurgau does not have the reputation it deserves because it is usually grossly overcropped and grown where it is too warm and the varietal character is burned out of the grape. The Bentryns crop their vines to a moderate 4½ tons an acre, thinning the clusters down to two per shoot in most years. Grown in this way, the Bentryns describe Muller-Thurgau as having pronounced varietal character with a distinct musky flavor.

Bentryn has picked Muller-Thurgau from as low as 15 Brix up to 22 degrees Brix, and Madeleine Angevine as high as 25 degrees Brix. According to Bentryn, the grapes taste better at higher sugars, but the best wines are made from grapes picked at about 17 degrees Brix to preserve the complex and delicate fragrances. Even in the warmest years, Bentryn picks the grapes at about 17 degrees Brix and chaptalizes the wine to the desired sugar level.

Ferryboat White, a varying blend of Columbia Valley and western Washington grapes, Bainbridge Island Winery's least expensive wine, often displays more interest than the ubiquitous and sometimes overly insistent Columbia Valley Rieslings.

Ardent supporters of the vertically integrated, small, family winery, an ideal exemplified by the many small German winegrowers, the Bentryns quit their other jobs to operate all aspects of the winery, from grape growing to winemaking to marketing. As in the European model, nearly all the wine is sold directly from the winery. An attractive winery, tasting room, and small wine museum adjoin the vineyard.

BARNARD-GRIFFIN WINERY

P.O. Box 6273
Kennewick, Washington 99336
(509) 586-6987

Wine Production
1,000 cases

Vineyards
none

First Vintage
1983

Leading Wines
Chardonnay, Fume Blanc

Rob Griffin is winemaker and general manager for for The Hogue Cellars, one of the Yakima Valley's leading wineries. In partnership with his wife, Deborah Barnard, Griffin also makes wine for their own, small Barnard-Griffin Winery.

Larger wineries, and even wineries of moderate size, need to make wines that appeal to a broad range of consumers, and they need to sell the wines at relatively inexpensive, competitive prices. The Barnard-Griffin wines are made in a distinctive style for a narrower range of consumers. Broad appeal is not a critical factor, nor is competitive price an overriding concern. The Barnard-Griffin wines require more hand labor, and they are priced accordingly.

Griffin makes three wines, Chardonnay, Sauvignon Blanc, and Riesling. Of the three, the Chardonnay and Sauvignon Blanc receive most of the special treatment.

The Chardonnay and Sauvignon Blanc are fermented in small French oak barrels. The fermentation temperatures start at about 50 degrees, and peak at about 68 degrees. Most Washington Sauvignon Blancs and Chardonnays are fermented at cooler temperatures.

Griffin does need to control the temperature so that it does not reach any higher than about 68 degrees, however. "I couldn't have fermented the wines this way in California without refrigeration," says Griffin, formerly a California winemaker. "In Washington, when I want to cool down the fermentation temperature in the barrels, I just open the winery doors to the cold October night."

The Chardonnay and Sauvignon Blanc are given extended lees contact. The wine is left in the barrel on the lees (the sediment of dead yeast cells and grape solids) and stirred once a month. The Chardonnay is left on the lees for nearly a year, and goes through a malolactic fermentation.

Typical Washington winemaking methods would have the wines fermented at cooler temperatures in stainless steel tanks, and would have the wine immediately racked off the lees. In stainless steel tanks, the wine is in a reduced state ("starved" for oxygen). In a reduced state, if the wine were left on the lees, hydrogen sulfide and other undesirable nastiness would be the likely result. With barrel fermentation, and careful technique, the wines have just enough oxygen (but not so much they get oxidized) to prevent off flavors from forming while allowing the beneficial flavors of the lees contact to develop.

The Barnard-Griffin style emphasizes winemaking technique rather than simply the fruit of the grape. The technique requires both technical skill and the artistic hand of the winemaker. Griffin is among a small, but increasing number of Washington winemakers looking toward this winemaking approach.

But what are the benefits? Why make wines in this riskier, less efficient way? These methods are associated with the more traditional European, particularly Burgundian, winemaking methods. Made in this way, the wines trade some of the simplistic fruitiness of the grape for more interesting and enduring flavors and scents. The wines are more rounded, fuller, textural, and complex.

BLACKWOOD CANYON VINTNERS

Route 2, Box 2169H
Kiona, Washington 99320
(509) 588-6249

Wine Production
15,000 cases

Vineyards
51 acres

Year First Planted
1984

First Vintage
1982

Leading Wines
Chardonnay, Cabernet Sauvignon, Semillon

At the far eastern end of the Yakima Valley, the the Yakima River runs into Red Mountain, taking an abrupt turn northward before turning back south to join the Columbia. Situated on the grass and sagebrush covered slopes of Red Mountain, the Blackwood Canyon winery and vineyards overlook the Yakima River, and the long view westward up the valley.

At a time when many Washington wines, particularly the whites, have evolved into a stylistic formula, the wines of M. Taylor Moore, Blackwood Canyon's iconoclastic winemaker and vineyard manager, are distinctly different. The predominant Washington dry white wine style emphasizes the crisp fresh fruit flavors of the grape, employing such methods as fermentation in temperature controlled stainless steel tanks, "clean," cool fermentations, the absence of a

secondary malolactic fermentation, perhaps brief aging in new oak, and occasionally, bottling "dry" wines with slight residual sugar.

While few Washington wineries match this formula exactly, these are the elements of an overriding theme. The style is valid and successful, yet to some, this style sacrifices too much of the enduring complexities and nuances for overly insistent, simple, fresh fruit flavors.

Moore's wines make no such sacrifice. His winemaking methods employ many of the techniques of traditional European winemaking practices. Moore's white wines are fermented in small oak barrels. The wine is not racked off the lees (grape solids and sediment) for up to nine months, and undergoes a gradual malolactic fermentation in the barrel. Different barrels are fermented with as many as four different yeast strains for added complexity before being blended together for bottling.

Moore likes to ferment his Chardonnay with about ten to fifteen percent solids in the must. To achieve this, he sometimes scrapes out the grape remnants in the crushing tank to add to the barrels. Moore believes that the fear of off flavors from lengthy contact with the lees evolves out of poor vineyard practices and problems arising out of the reductive (starved for oxygen) effects of keeping wines in stainless steel tanks. All Moore's white wines are barrel fermented.

Moore's red wines are also made in a unique style. Moore leaves the wine on the skins for two weeks after the fermentation has completed. Alcohol and water extract different flavors from the grape, and Moore likes the character obtained from the alcohol extractions that predominate after the fermentation has finished. Ironically, the wine is not more tannic for its additional time on the skins. The tannins polymerize and fall out as sediment, reducing the overall tannin to moderate levels. The fermentation temperature is a warm 85 to 90 degrees. To avoid excessive oak flavors, the Cabernet is aged in older oak barrels.

Moore's methods do not fit the Washington norm, but the quality and complex flavors of his wines articulately validate his approach. A graduate in enology from Davis with additional

M. Taylor Moore.

Tragically, an October 1985 fire burned Moore's home and winery to the ground. Most of his Cabernet was destroyed just as it was about to be released for sale. Moore rebuilt the winery and is continuing operations. His vinous statements to the wine world are only delayed.

training in viticulture, Moore worked with several California wineries before coming to the northwest in search of a cooler growing climate to start his own winery. After a lengthy search, Moore settled on the Red Mountain area at far eastern end of the Yakima Valley and formed Blackwood Canyon Vintners, a family partnership.

Only a part of his 180 acre site is in vine, planted one third each to Cabernet Sauvignon, Chardonnay, and Chenin Blanc. The undulating land is comprised of several vineyard areas. The Chardonnay is planted on a slight north slope, Cabernet Sauvignon on a warmer, south facing slope. Similar in certain respects to some of Europe's premium vineyard soils, Blackwood Canyon's soil contains high amounts of calcium carbonate, and is a high 8.2 pH.

While Moore's own vineyards mature, he is buying grapes from other Washington growers, including some from other vineyards in the Red Mountain area. Other winemakers embrace a few of the same winemaking methods, but for now, Moore stands nearly alone in the totality of his approach. The net result of Moore's winemaking methods are complexly flavored, well-balanced wines with characteristics that echo their traditionally styled European counterparts. Blackwood Canyon is specializing in Chardonnay, Cabernet Sauvignon, Semillon, and sweet late harvest desert wines from several grape varieties.

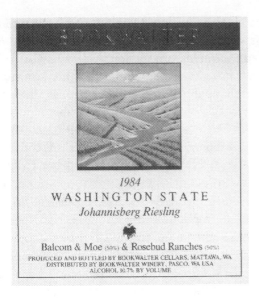

1984
WASHINGTON STATE
Johannisberg Riesling

Balcom & Moe (50%) & Rosebud Ranches (50%)
PRODUCED AND BOTTLED BY BOOKWALTER CELLARS, MATTAWA, WA
DISTRIBUTED BY BOOKWALTER WINERY, PASCO, WA USA
ALCOHOL 10.7% BY VOLUME

BOOKWALTER WINERY

2505 Commercial Avenue
Pasco, Washington 99301
(509) 547-8571

Wine Production
3,000 cases

Vineyards
none

First Vintage
1983

Leading Wines
Chardonnay, Riesling, Chenin Blanc

From 1976 to 1983, Jerry Bookwalter managed Sagemoor Farms, the Northwest's largest, independent, wine grape, vineyard operation. In 1983, Bookwalter left Sagemoor to start his own grape and wine marketing services—and to start his own winery.

Bookwalter has no vineyards of his own, and prefers it that way. In Bookwalter's view, buying grapes on the open market allows for much greater flexibility. Knowing grape growing areas, vineyards, and grapes is an intrinsic part of Bookwalter's consulting and brokerage services — an advantage when it comes to choosing and buying grapes for his own winery.

Bookwalter has bought grapes from many parts of Washington's vast Columbia Valley, in-cluding the Royal Slope, one of the state's newer and more northerly growing areas, located on the lower slopes of the Frenchman Hills, east of the community of Vantage. Most of Bookwalter's grapes, however, come from vineyards within a 15 mile radius of his winery.

"I think that great wine is made in the vineyard," says Bookwalter. "There is high art to winemaking, but a winemaker can't create quality that isn't in the grapes. The best he can do is capture 100 percent of what the grapes offer. We try to locate pockets of greatness in the vineyards, and turn them into the best wines possible."

Unlike many Washington winemakers, Bookwalter puts his Chardonnay through a malolactic fermentation, in the Burgundian tradition. Bookwalter likes malolactic fermentation for the softer, more rounded character it gives to the wine.

Bookwalter makes some of the wine himself at his own winery. The rest is made to his specifications at the Langguth winery near Mattawa and at the Coventry Vale custom crushing facility at Grandview. Bookwalter could easily produce a wide range of wines, but he chooses to focus on only three, Chardonnay, Riesling, and Chenin Blanc. Bookwalter also makes small amounts of Cabernet Sauvignon, and an occasional specialty wine, such as Grenache Nouveau.

Bookwalter sees his winery as very consumer oriented. He wants to make high quality, popularly styled wines, rather than esoteric wines that appeal only to wine aficionados with esoteric tastes.

CAROWAY VINEYARDS

P.O. Box 6273
Kennewick, Washington 99336

Wine Production
1,000 cases

Vineyards
40 acres

Year First Planted
1980

First Vintage
1983

Leading Wines
Chardonnay, Riesling

The Caroway winery was born as a result of the tumultuous growth of Washington's wine-growing industry. Washington's industry is expanding so rapidly that grape supply, winery crushing capacity, and market demand are rarely in balance. In 1983, Washington produced more grapes than wineries could handle. In that year, vineyard owners Carol and Wayne Miller opened a winery to insure all their grapes would have a home.

The upcoming vintages promised even more difficulty for growers trying to find a home for their grapes, but a series of unexpected winter freezes and spring and fall frosts greatly reduced the grape harvests. Grapes, particularly some varieties, quickly became scarce. Supply and demand may again rapidly shift balance, but for now, most grape varieties are in demand.

The Caroway vineyards and winery are located near the town of Finley, in the broad horseshoe formed by the Columbia River, as it bends back westward toward the Pacific Ocean. The vineyard is in the foothills of the Horse Heaven hills, within five miles of the Columbia River. In recent vintages, many vineyards have been hard hit by frosts and winter freezing, but Caroway has been less affected than most.

In some years, Caroway does not make any wines of its own. Grape commitments to other wineries are met first. Caroway takes the remaining grapes for its own wines. If Caroway continues to operate as a winery, the Millers plan to expand its production capacity.

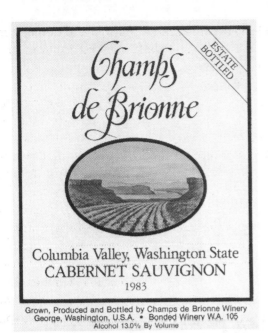

Columbia Valley, Washington State
CABERNET SAUVIGNON
1983

Grown, Produced and Bottled by Champs de Brionne Winery
George, Washington, U.S.A. • Bonded Winery W.A. 105
Alcohol 13.0% By Volume

CHAMPS DE BRIONNE

98 Road West N.W.
Quincy, WA 98848
(509) 785-6685

Wine Production
6,000 cases

Vineyards
130 acres

Year First Planted
1980

First Vintage
1983

Leading Wines
Semillon, Riesling, Cabernet Sauvignon

On a high bank, overlooking the Columbia River and the massive basalt cliffs cut by its course, the Champs de Brionne estate embraces one of the most scenic views in Washington's wine country—but the site was not chosen merely for the view. Several trips to Europe and a conviction in the excellence of Washington winegrowing climates prompted Vince and Carol Bryan to travel Washington seeking a site for their vineyards.

From their studies, the Bryans made a list of eleven key characteristics for their vineyard site.

Their European travels lead them to give more than usual emphasis on soil type. Working with soil test reports prepared by the Army Corps of Engineers for the Grand Coulee Dam project, their quest led them outside the already established growing areas to the center of the state, and a vineyard site near Quincy Washington. Champs de Brionne's soil is high in calcium carbonate with an ideally high pH of 7.8.

Situated on Evergreen Ridge, 900 feet above the Columbia River, the vineyard's soils are not the only factor that makes the site special for growing grapes. Tempered by the nearby Columbia, Champs de Brionne has a 195 day growing season.

Comparing the growing climate with the Yakima Valley, for example, a more established growing region, bud break (the seasons new growth) is two weeks later, and spring frosts are not a threat as they are in the Yakima Valley. At 2,800 heat units, the growing climate has a greater heat accumulation than many Yakima growing sites, but the greater accumulations occur in the summer, during the grapevine's vegetative period. In the fall, during the final ripening of the grapes, when overly warm temperatures can burn out delicate flavors, the temperatures are actually cooler than many sites in the Yakima Valley. Chilling late fall temperatures come abruptly, however, making fall frosts and the vine's final energy gathering period before winter all the more critical.

Vince Bryan—in the background, the basalt cliffs of the Columbia River.

Prompted by similarities in soil, and climate, particularly during the ripening period, with France's Burgundy district, the Bryan's are enthusiastic about the prospects of Pinot Noir and Chardonnay. Calcium Carbonate is the principal limestone type found in Burgundy (particularly in the Cote d'Or). Calcium Carbonate also predominates at Champs de Brionne.

Champs de Brionne is virtually the only winery in the Columbia Valley focusing on Pinot Noir. The winery's main Pinot Noir vineyard is planted on a slightly north facing slope overlooking the Columbia River. The vines are closely planted at a distance of four feet between each vine. When in full production, the Pinot Noir will be cropped at a modest two to three tons an acre to preserve varietal intensity.

Semillon is another variety that is emerging as a winery specialty. In California, Sauvignon Blanc predominates, a more herbaceous variety capable of standing up to the heat. In Europe, Sauvignon Blanc is not as highly regarded, and Semillon has a much more important role. Semillon is proving very successful in Washington's Columbia Valley. Champ de Brionne's style of Semillon has a restrained, grassy, varietal character touched with French oak. In cooler years, the wine emphasizes the crisp fruitiness of the grape balanced with a touch of residual sugar.

Champs de Brionne is a partnership comprised of 35 limited partners with Vince and Carol Bryan as the general partners and principal owners. A neurosurgeon by profession, Vince Bryan's enthusiasm and commitment to the winery is genuine and profound, extending from the technical aspects of grape growing to the esthetic experience of the natural setting.

"Do you like the smell of sage?" asks Bryan picking a sprig from a nearby bush. "I love the smell. When we first came here and walked the fields, I slept with my shoes by my pillow." Just past the Pinot Noir vineyard, a natural amphitheater is set into a bluff overlooking the Columbia and its basalt cliffs, cut by the river into the ancient volcanic basalt. The acoustics and view are unsurpassed. The first concert in this relatively remote area drew 1,800 visitors.

CHATEAU STE. MICHELLE

14111 N.E. 145th
P.O. Box 1976
Woodinville, Washington 98072
(206) 488-1133

P.O. Box 231
Paterson, Washington 99345
(509) 875-2061

West 5th and Avenue B
P.O. Box 580
Grandview, Washington 98930
(509) 882-3928

Wine Production
750,000 cases

Liqueur Production
12,000 cases

Vineyards
2,930 acres

Year First Planted
1942

First Vintage
1967

Leading Wines
Fume Blanc, Riesling, Chardonnay, Muscat Canelli, Semillon

By far the Northwest's largest winery, the roots of Chateau Ste. Michelle reach back to the era immediately following Prohibition, when two companies, Nawico and Pommerelle, began producing wines from hybrids and native American grape varieties such as Concord.

Chateau Ste. Michelle's Woodinville winery.

In 1954, the companies merged to form American Wine Growers. In 1967, American Wine Growers made Semillon, Cabernet Sauvignon, Pinot Noir, and Grenache Rose, the winery's first systematic pursuit of premium vinifera grape wines, and the first wines to bear the Ste. Michelle name. In 1973, a group of local investors headed by Wallace Opdycke purchased American Wine Growers. The following year, Ste. Michelle became a wholly owned subsidiary of the United States Tobacco Company.

Within a decade, the massive infusion of capital by the winery's parent company transformed Chateau Ste. Michelle into one of America's major premium wineries. From a production of 15,000 gallons in 1967, Chateau Ste. Michelle has grown to a production of well more than a million gallons a year. By the end of the decade, the Ste. Michelle organization expects production to exceed two million gallons a year.

In 1976, Chateau Ste. Michelle built a modern showcase winery near the community of Woodinville, not far from the city of Seattle. Situated on a 87 acre estate once owned by Seattle lumberman Fred Stimson, the attractive chateau-style building houses corporate offices and visitor facilities. Scarcely visible from the winery grounds, the 140,000 square foot produc-

tion facility is set on a lower plane, maintaining the estate's pastoral ambience.

The grounds have been carefully preserved, designed in the early 1900s by the Olmstead brothers of Boston, designers of New York's Central Park and Seattle's Arboretum. The Stimson home, a National Historical Monument, is available to groups for wine tastings. Approximately 150,000 people visit Chateau Ste. Michelle's Woodinville winery every year.

As large as the Woodinville winery must have seemed when it was first built, Chateau Ste. Michelle rapidly outgrew it. In 1983, Chateau Ste. Michelle completed construction of River Ridge, a modern, 26 million dollar winery overlooking the Columbia River near Paterson.

River Ridge is perhaps Chateau Ste. Michelle's boldest move to date. Nearly three times the size of the Woodinville winery, River Ridge symbolizes Chateau Ste. Michelle's commitment to Washington wine, the economic confidence of the winery's parent company in the success of the enterprise, and more broadly, an affirmation of the importance of Washington wine on the future of the American wine scene.

For River Ridge, Chateau Ste. Michelle planted a new 1,780 acre vineyard adjacent to the winery. Some of the vineyard is irrigated by conventional drip irrigation systems, but part of the vineyard's system is unique, patterned after

The red wines age in oak barrels stacked in long racks.

135

The River Ridge winery in Paterson.

Chateau Ste. Michelle's red wines are fermented at a third winery, the small, original Nawico facility at Grandview, in the Yakima Valley. Refinished and refurbished, the Grandview winery's open top tanks proved ideal for fermenting red wines.

From a winemaking standpoint, Chateau Ste. Michelle does not view itself as a monolithic entity, but as an aggregate of several specialized wineries and winemakers. Peter Bachman, formerly of Monterey Vineyard in California, is winemaker at Paterson and director of winemaking operations. Cheryl Barber is winemaker at Woodinville, Doug Gore at Grandview.

The River Ridge winery produces Chateau Ste. Michelle's blended wines for the Farron Ridge label, and specializes in Riesling, Chenin Blanc, sparkling wines, and other white varietals not

traditional agricultural practices of the area. The vines, planted in circular vineyards of roughly 100 acres each, are watered by center-pivot irrigation systems. Irrigation pipe is suspended above the vines on mobile towers on wheels, and, like the hand of a clock, the irrigation pipe and its sprinkler heads sweeps across the circular vineyard, irrigating the vines as it passes.

Chateau Ste. Michelle is moving toward increased direct control of its grape supply, and the River Ridge vineyard is a major step in this direction. Chateau Ste. Michelle owns a fourth of the state's vineyards. Looking ahead, Chateau Ste. Michelle purchased 17,000 acres of land for future expansion.

Much of the winemaking area at River Ridge is on a lower level, partially underground. Only a small part of the winery is now in use, underscoring the magnitude of growth Chateau Ste. Michelle will experience in the next few years. As large as it is, the winery in no way resembles a tank farm at an oil refinery in the fashion of some of California's largest "premium" wineries.

River Ridge's fermentation tanks are no bigger than 12,000 gallons, and some are only a quarter that size. For such a large winery, the relatively small tanks offer the opportunity to treat separate lots of grapes differently, make different blends from the separate lots, or simply to sell a distinctive batch of wine as a special bottling. The finely furnished visitor's building is designed in the manner of a rustic country estate.

The frosty tanks tell that the wine inside is being cold stabilized.

The historic Grandview winery.

requiring oak aging. River Ridge also produces Columbia Crest, a proprietary label and blend of Riesling, Gewurztraminer, and Muscat Canelli, and crushes Chateau Ste. Michelle's Chardonnay and Sauvignon Blanc grapes, clarifies the juice, and sends it to Woodinville for fermentation and wood aging. After fermentation, Grandview sends its red wines to River Ridge to age in oak.

Until the late 1970s, all Chateau Ste. Michelle's Cabernet Sauvignon and Merlot were aged in American oak. In 1978, Chateau Ste. Michelle released its second reserve bottling of Cabernet Sauvignon, their first red wine aged entirely in French oak. The French oak favorably enhanced the character of the wine, and in 1981, Ste. Michelle began putting some of its "regular" Cabernet and Merlot in French oak. With each successive year, French oak comprises an increasing percentage of the cooperage.

For Washington, and for Chateau Ste. Michelle, consistent success with red wine was long in coming, but by the late 70s, much had been learned about growing the grapes and making the wine. Selecting the right growing site is particularly critical for Cabernet Sauvignon. The site needs to be warm, yet the grapes must maintain good acidity and low pH. Chateau Ste. Michelle's best Cabernet grapes routinely come from their Cold Creek Vineyard in the Rattlesnake Hills. The vineyard has a very slight 5 degree southerly slope and receives an average 3,300 heat units during its 210 day growing season.

Development of the red wines dates back to Ste Michelle's inception. In 1967, Andre Tchelistcheff, the legendary California winemaker, visited American Wine Growers, the corporate predecessor to Chateau Ste. Michelle, to discuss Washington's future in the premium wine industry. Tchelistcheff agreed to act as special consultant, and to this day continues in that role, visiting Chateau Ste. Michelle four times a year.

From the beginning, Tchelistcheff advocated a "secondary," malolactic fermentation for Ste. Michelle's red wines. This secondary bacterial fermentation converts malic acid to less acidic lactic acid, softening and rounding the wine, and contributing to its complexity. In 1974, Chateau Ste. Michelle achieved their first complete malolactic fermentation, marking an important turning point in the quality of their red wines.

Merlot, another Bordeaux grape variety, had been planted in 1972 to soften the Cabernet's higher acidity and harshness, but by the time the Merlot was ready for its first harvest in 1976, it was no longer needed for the Cabernet. Washington Merlot has proven to be a very good wine on its own, and Ste. Michelle sells its Merlot as a 100 percent varietal bottling.

The white wines have been Chateau Ste. Michelle's most successful. Riesling, finished with some residual sweetness, is by far Chateau Ste. Michelle's most popular wine. While other grape varieties took some learning and development, Chateau Ste. Michelle's Rieslings were very good from the start, and immediately appealing to a broad spectrum of consumers. Riesling continues to play a dominant role at Chateau Ste. Michelle.

For the wine aficionado, Chateau Ste. Michelle's dry white wines are becoming increasingly noteworthy. Both the Chardonnay and Fume Blanc are partially fermented in French oak tanks or barrels, then aged briefly in oak prior to bottling. The 1978 vintage of Chardonnay was put through a malolactic fermentation, but since then, Chateau Ste. Michelle has emphasized the fruit of the grape in all its dry white wines, and the Chardonnay is prevented from going through a malolactic fermentation.

The Ste. Michelle name was born more than a decade and a half ago with the release of a Semillon-Blanc. The Semillon grape has not garnered much attention in America, but Washington Semillon has proven exceptionally distinctive, perhaps the best Semillon grown anywhere. At Chateau Ste. Michelle, Semillon-Blanc is becoming an increasingly important variety. In years when a particularly good lot of Semillon is made, the wine is set aside for wood aging and the "Reserve" designation. A genetic relative of Sauvignon Blanc (also called Fume Blanc), Semillon displays similar crisp, grassy flavors, but with less herbaceous insistence.

Washington is quite capable of producing wines in the fat, unctuous, overripe style that became popular in the 1970s, but Chateau Ste. Michelle is aiming toward a more restrained style for its wines, wines made in an unoxygenated style with crisp acid structure to marry well with food. In particular, the Chardonnay and Sauvignon Blanc benefit from additional bottle aging to open up their restrained character and develop complexity and texture.

Chateau Ste. Michelle views itself as a premier American winery, a leader and innovator in grape growing and winemaking at the frontier of a new and important wine region, as a winery not constrained by its large size, but all the more capable because of its resources. Special wine releases have included botrytised Chenin Blanc, Riesling Ice Wine, a loganberry liqueur made from the winery's loganberry farm on Whidbey Island in Puget Sound, port made from Cabernet Sauvignon grapes, and a continuing series of reserve wines and bottle fermented sparkling wine.

Chateau Ste. Michelle is a dynamic enterprise, constantly changing itself to meet its own changing needs. In 1983, Chateau Ste. Michelle president Wallace Opdycke, one of the early organizers of the enterprise, resigned his post to pursue other business interests. A specialist in finance, Opdycke played the principal role in acquiring a faltering winery in Seattle's industrial

district, and within a decade, transforming the winery into the dominant showcase for Northwest wine.

Allen Shoup is Chateau Ste. Michelle's current president. The winery's tremendous expansion, coming at a time when the American wine market is experiencing a flat growth period, requires consumate marketing acumen. Shoup's credentials are impressive. After receiving a bachelor's degree in marketing and a master's degree in psychology, Shoup became marketing manager for the Ernest and Julio Gallo winery, then a director of marketing for Max Factor in the highly competitive cosmetics industry. Chateau Ste. Michelle has overcome much in its brief existence. A skillfully run company, failure is not an issue, only the magnitude of success.

For much of the wine drinking world, Chateau Ste. Michelle is synonymous with Washington wine. Far larger than any other Northwest winery, and distributed in every major metropolitan market in America, Chateau Ste. Michelle has become the de facto representative for the wines of Washington. Chateau Ste. Michelle's size and marketing clout insures recognition not only for itself, but for the entire Washington wine industry. By the 1990s, Washington will be firmly established in the American wine scene, and Chateau Ste. Michelle will have done much to pave the way.

CHINOOK WINES

P.O. Box 387
Prosser, Washington 99350
(509) 786-2725

Wine Production
2,000 cases

Vineyards
none

First Vintage
1983

Leading Wines
Sauvignon Blanc, Sparkling Riesling

The joint effort of Kay Simon and Clay Mackey, Chinook Wines came into being when the two left their positions with Chateau Ste. Michelle, began independent wine consulting businesses, got married, and opened their own winery. Simon was formerly winemaker at Chateau Ste. Michelle's 26 million dollar River Ridge winery at Paterson. Mackey was formerly vineyard operations manager at Paterson, then manager of all vineyard operations for Chateau Ste. Michelle.

Once responsible for a major share of the wines and vineyards in Washington state, the shift in scale and perspective from one of America's larger premium wineries to a small boutique winery was dramatic. Simon and Mackey now operate a winery that will grow no larger than

6,000 cases a year. "We wanted," says Mackey, "to do something that was entirely our own. At Chinook, we do everything from renovating the winery building to winemaking and marketing."

Although Mackey worked most of his career in vineyard operations, he was trained in enology at U.C. Davis. Both Mackey and Simon continue their consulting and lab work for other northwest wineries.

Situated near a freeway exit, the winery still manages to convey a rustic atmosphere, looking out across the width of the Yakima Valley toward the Rattlesnake Hills to the north. A converted private residence, the pathway from the house to the garage is covered by an arbor of old, thick-trunked Concord and Black Monukka vines. The backyard is now a picnic area for visitors.

Until their own winery was bonded, the first wines, from the 1983 and 1984 vintages, were made by the two at other Yakima Valley wineries. Chinook wines are made in a dry, crisp, fruity style with minimal oak. The ubiquitous semi-sweet Riesling is missing from the Chinook line of wines, as is Chenin Blanc. Unlike most Washington wineries, Chinook produces no semi-sweet wine to broaden its marketing base.

The term "food wine," heavily overworked and claimed by all, is quite apt for Chinook's wines. The absence of residual sweetness and the crisp acidity match the wines well with food. Sauvignon Blanc, Chardonnay, and Topaz, a proprietary blend of Semillon and Sauvignon Blanc, are fermented in stainless steel (except for occasional experimental lots) and aged only briefly in French oak barrels or tanks. Little oak is apparent in the wines. The Sauvignon Blanc is blended with about 25 percent Semillon to tone down the Sauvignon herbaceousness and contribute fruitiness and the typical Semillon fresh cut grass character.

None of the white wines are put through a malolactic fermentation. Merlot, Chinook's only red wine, is put through malolactic fermentation and aged in French oak. The Merlot carries through Chinook's stylistic theme, emphasizing the fruit of the grape with sufficient acidity to age and marry well with food.

Produced in very limited quantities, Chinook is advancing a new wine style with a bottle fermented sparkling Riesling. Left on the yeast only briefly, approximately six months, the fruit is emphasized rather than the yeast. The strong varietal Riesling character is muted, however, and the wine is nicely balanced with no single flavor predominating.

COLUMBIA WINERY

1445 120th Avenue N.E.
Bellevue, Washington 98005
(206) 453-1977

Wine Production
45,000 cases

Vineyards
none

First Commercially Released Vintage
1967

Leading Wines
Cabernet Sauvignon, Merlot, Semillon,
Gewurztraminer, Riesling

In 1984, Washington's oldest, continuously operating, premium, grape winery changed its name from Associated Vintners to Columbia Winery. In its more than two decades of existence, the winery has gone through many changes. Its beginnings are now legendary.

In the early 1950s, Lloyd Woodburne, then a professor of psychology at the University of Washington, began making homemade wine. Interest spread among Woodburne's colleagues, and before long, a number of the University's faculty were buying grapes and making wine. The group purchased a grape crusher that Woodburne kept in his garage. To comply with legal restrictions, the winemakers formed a corporation and bonded a winery. In 1962, the association of vintners became Associated Vintners.

David Lake.

In 1966, the noted wine authority, Leon Adams, tasted one of Woodburne's Grenache roses, found it excellent, and suggested that Associated Vintners should become a commercial winery. In 1967, the most famous and respected of all American winemakers, Andre Tchelistcheff, tasted a Gewurztraminer made by Phil Church, another home winemaker in the group, describing it as the best Gewurztraminer made in the United States.

Spurred by this enthusiastic response, the group moved the crusher from Woodburne's garage to a small facility in Kirkland, Washington, a suburb of Seattle. In 1967, Associated Vintners produced their first commercial vintage.

Phil Church, a meteorologist, and one of the original ten shareholders, made early studies of Washington's climates, showing, among other things, that parts of Washington east of the Cascades have virtually the same heat units as parts of France's Burgundy region. Although it is now recognized that heat unit measurements are only a partial indication of viticultural comparability, Church's early studies provided much of the impetus for vinifera grape growing in Washington. Woodburne credits Church, now deceased, for pioneering work that helped launch Washington's rapidly growing wine industry.

In 1976, the winery moved from its small building in Kirkland to a much larger, more modern facility in nearby Redmond. By 1980,

production had increased to more than 10,000 cases a year, and it was becoming increasingly apparent that Associated Vintners was outgrowing itself.

The time had come for a transformation to preserve and enhance the vitality of the original enterprise without compromising its fundamental and sustaining spirit. The winery generated new capital by selling its vineyards and increasing the number of shareholders to 30. Included in the new group were key members with business and marketing expertise.

In 1981, Associated Vintners moved to the adjacent community of Bellevue, to a building three times the size of the Redmond facility. The winery purchased much needed new equipment. The old, horizontal, fermenting tanks for white wines were replaced by modern, temperature controlled vertical tanks. After the changes, the wines were fresher, retained more of their fruit, and were less prone to oxidation.

In 1984, Associated Vintners changed its operating name to Columbia Winery, reflecting the winery's transformation, and echoing its ties with the Columbia Valley, Washington's most important winegrowing region.

When a winery sells its vineyards, takes on new investors, greatly increases production, emphasizes business and marketing concerns, and changes its identity, decline in quality and commitment to excellence is a certainty—almost a certainty. For Columbia Winery, the effect was quite the opposite.

David Lake, Columbia's winemaker and vice-president, played a key role in the winery's transformation. Lake holds what is undoubtedly the wine world's most distinguished title—Master of Wine from Britain's Institute of Masters of Wine. Although the institute has been in existence for some 30 years, only about 100 persons have been certified as Masters of Wine.

Lake came to the United States after ten years in the British wine trade. He studied for a year at the University of California at Davis, and worked for a time with David Lett at Eyrie Vineyards in Oregon, who subsequently recommended him to Woodburne.

Whether consumer or member of the wine trade, we become most familiar with a particular wine style, judging all other wines against that frame of reference. Lake brings a unique perspective to the Washington wine scene. By definition, as a Master of Wine, Lake has developed a highly eclectic palate, a comprehensive familiarity with the diverse wines and wine styles of the world.

In Lake's view, there has been too much of a tendency to down play some of the distinctive characteristics of Washington wines, attempts to mold Washington wine into more familiar styles, to the inevitable detriment of the wine and the winegrowing region. There is a growing trend, he notes, for Washington winemakers to allow the wines be themselves, a trend that has done much to further the quality of Washington wines and advance the region's state of the art.

Lake does not attempt to level out the differences from vintage to vintage to create a uniform "house style" by bolstering lighter vintages, or, figuratively speaking, watering down classic wines from outstanding vintages that happen to be hard and inaccessible in their youth. Strengths are not minimized for the sake of uniformity, and excellence is not sacrificed at the altar of cash flow and immediate consumer appeal.

Columbia does not always release wines sequentially, but in accordance with the vintage and character of the wine. Wines from lighter, fruity vintages may be released earlier than wines with a deeper structure that need and benefit from lengthier aging.

Matching current market interests and perceptions is the safest business path. Leading the market and shaping it through a commitment to the best is much riskier. Columbia Winery is not blind to current market trends, but neither is it a blind follower of those trends.

"The conventional wisdom," says Lake, "is that this is a white wine region. We obviously have potential for very good white wines, but red, I think, will be even more exceptional. My own feeling is that in ten years time, or twenty years time at least, we are going to see that this is even a more outstanding region for red wine."

Lake's red wines offer convincing evidence for his view. In 1979, his first vintage as winemaker, Lake produced a Cabernet Sauvignon that remains a benchmark. Of the wine, the great American winemaker Andre Tchelistcheff said, "This is one of the best Cabernets I have ever tasted. It is a wonderful wine, deep, with a velvety texture, enormously complex, very much in the style of a classic Medoc—a lovely wine, perfect in every way; not one single flaw that I could find; artistically complete, balanced and perfect."

The 1979 vintage was exceptional, and Columbia had decided to release the Cabernet with a special designation, "Millennium," a wine to be laid down until its twenty-first birthday, in the year 2000. Lake asked Tchelistcheff if he thought Columbia was justified in its claim that the wine would continue to develop in the bottle until the arrival of the new century. Tchelistcheff's reply was succinct, "Of course, without any doubt."

Columbia Winery produces a higher proportion of red wine than any other Washington winery of its size, and Lake hopes to increase the proportion even further. Systematically, Lake searches out and enters into extended contracts with some of Washington's best Cabernet vineyards.

Two of the vineyards are routinely released as separate bottlings. From fan trained vines, nearly three decades old, Otis Vineyards grapes produce a fine, but often atypical Cabernet, sometimes displaying a distinctive weedy, black cherry flavor and aroma. Cabernet grapes from Red Willow Vineyards yield a complex, textural wine with flavors more closely resembling the wines of Bordeaux. Columbia winery releases as many as four different Cabernets each vintage.

Washington Cabernets are inherently rough and tannic in their youth, but Lake does not purposely soften them for early drinkability. "Softened" Cabernets inevitably sacrifice quality. On the other hand, Lake does not produce immensely tannic, high alcohol, low acid, overripe beasts. Such wines promise a long life, but their lack of acidity and balance prevents them from developing well with age.

Lake's Cabernets are tightly structured wines

with concentrated flavors, low pH, and good acidity—a structure not unlike traditionally made Bordeaux, though sometimes with a slightly riper quality befitting Washington's growing climate. The wines are reasonably accessible in their youth, but benefit greatly from bottle age.

Columbia produces other red wines besides Cabernet Sauvignon. Merlot plays a role in blends with the Cabernet, and is released as a single varietal bottling as well. From the Columbia Gorge and from southwest Washington, Columbia produces Grenache and Pinot Noir. Lake has made experimental batches of Petite Sirah and other red varieties.

Lake was admittedly uncomfortable with the sale of the winery's vineyards, and the loss of immediate and direct control over the grapes. In retrospect, the decision was a good one. Columbia is not locked into a single growing area for all their wines. Different grape varieties are purchased from the vineyards that grow them best.

Lake insists on pH readings as well as sugar and acid figures when buying grapes. Lake works closely with Columbia's grape growers throughout the season. As harvest approaches, Lake visits the vineyards at least once a week, looking at the condition of the vines, and tasting the grapes. Sugar, acid, and pH readings do not tell the whole story, and tasting the grapes, particularly Gewurztraminer, Riesling, and Semillon, gives important indications of ripeness, quality, and character.

The taste of Gewurztraminer is not for everyone, and it is not an easy wine to make well, but Columbia has justly earned a reputation for this variety, made in a dry Alsatian style. Lake likens the arid growing environment of Washington's Columbia Valley to France's Alsace region, noting that the drier areas of Alsace produce the best Gewurztraminer.

Many American growing regions, including some in the Northwest, produce Gewurztraminer with a floral, perfumy, and sometimes bubble gum-like flavor. Lake particularly likes Washington's Yakima Valley for Gewurztraminer, feeling that the wines are better structured and spicy, along classic Alsatian lines.

Although Gewurztraminer is a Columbia Winery specialty, its production is limited. Chardonnay, Semillon, and a sweet Riesling called Cellarmaster's Reserve are Columbia's major white wines.

Columbia's focus on Semillon as a major variety is especially noteworthy. Largely ignored in America in favor of Sauvignon Blanc, Semillon holds a superior position in Bordeaux, where it is regarded as having a more refined character and the ability to age and develop much better than Sauvignon Blanc. In the best white Bordeaux destined for a long life, Semillon typically predominates. Sauvignon Blanc may be the best variety for California's warmer growing climate, but in Washington, Semillon demonstrates its superiority.

Increasingly popular as a Washington varietal, Columbia was the one of the first wineries to recognize its potential and produce it as a major wine, and not just as something to round out a line of wines. Lake's Semillon is made in an intensely varietal rendition of the grape, with a pronounced, crisp, grassy aroma and taste, but without the aggressive herbaceous edge of a Sauvignon Blanc. In Lake's opinion, nowhere else in the world does Semillon produce such a distinctive and flavorful wine of such high quality.

For a winegrowing region most commonly known for its ubiquitous Rieslings, Columbia's focus and success with three Bordeaux varieties, Cabernet Sauvignon, Merlot, and Semillon, defines an important direction for premium Washington wine.

More than two decades ago, a loose association of amateur vintners banded together, formed a winery, and became instrumental in the birth of Washington's premium wine industry. Much has changed, but the transformed Columbia Winery successfully preserves the pioneering, innovative, and independent spirit of the original founders. Just as more than two decades ago, Columbia Winery remains a leader in Washington's premium wine industry.

COVEY RUN VINTNERS

Route 2, Box 2287
Zillah, Washington 98953
(509) 829-6235

Wine Production
40,000 cases

Vineyards
180 acres

Year First Planted
1980

First Vintage
1982

Leading Wines
Chardonnay, La Caille de Fume,
Lemberger, Merlot, Riesling

One of the Yakima Valley's leading wineries, Quail Run Vintners changed its name to Covey Run Vintners in 1986. Litigation by a California winery of a similar name had threatened to embroil Quail Run in further legal proceedings. The name change relieves the Yakima Valley winery from further legal action, and allows it to continue with more substantive interests—like growing, making, and selling good wine.

Stan Clarke heads the partnership of twenty owners. Clarke graduated from U.C. Davis with a degree in viticulture, and worked for several California vineyards and Washington's Chateau Ste. Michelle before coming to Covey Run. Clarke is Covey Run's marketing director and viticulturist. Covey Run's two vineyards are owned separately by two of the winery's partners, who then sell the grapes to the winery.

Located just below the Roza Irrigation Canal, along the farthest reaches of Yakima Valley's agricultural land, Covey Run was the first well-financed, showcase, estate winery in the Yakima Valley. Situated on a hillside in the Whiskey Canyon area northeast of the community of Zillah, the modern Covey Run winery and visitor facility overlooks the valley and estate vineyard below. Pheasants and coveys of quail run amongst the vines.

Covey Run buys grapes from other Yakima Valley growers to supplement production from its own vineyards. Washington's larger wineries have traditionally developed their vineyards outside the Yakima Valley. Covey Run was the first winery of its size to produce wines solely from Yakima Valley grapes. One of Washington's most important grape growing regions, the Yakima Valley is generally cooler than the other major growing areas in Washington's vast Columbia Valley.

Covey Run's winemaker, Wayne Marcil, a graduate in enology from U. C. Davis, was winemaker for California's Monterey Peninsula Winery before coming to the Northwest. Marcil likes the intense fruitiness and crisp acidity of Yakima Valley grapes. He makes his wines to emphasize these characteristics.

Riesling and Gewurztraminer are almost always fermented at cool temperatures, but, in what is becoming a Washington style, Marcil ferments his other wines at relatively cool temperatures as well. His Chardonnay, as an example, is fermented at 55 degrees. Other winemaking styles call for Chardonnay fermentation temperatures as high as the eighties. Cool fermentation temperatures emphasize the fruity qualities of a wine.

Clarke's training and work as a viticulturist spurred his interest in less common grape varie-

The Covey Run winery.

ties, especially those that might do especially well in Washington's growing climate. Covey Run adds variety to the Washington wine scene by producing small quantities of wine from several of these lesser known grapes, Aligote, Morio Muskat, and Lemberger.

Aligote is a high yielding, white, Burgundian grape, somewhat similar to the more refined and aristocratic Chardonnay variety. Covey Run blends Chardonnay with their Aligote, then ages the wine briefly in French oak. Covey Run's Aligote is a less expensive alternative to Chardonnay.

Morio Muskat was developed in Germany from a cross of Sylvaner and Pinot Blanc. The linalool component of the Sylvaner is greatly emphasized in the crossing, yielding an appealing wine with a pronounced muscat character.

Lemberger is the most important of the three lesser known grape varieties. A German red wine grape, Lemberger holds excellent promise for Washington state. The variety yields relatively high quantities of darkly colored, low pH, intensely fruity wine. Dr. Walter Clore, a Washington State University horticulturist, advocated Lemberger even before Washington's premium wine industry was born. Covey Run was among the first few Washington wineries to produce the wine commercially.

Lemberger lends itself to a wide variety of styles. After trying several styles, Marcil settled on a less conventional approach for a red wine. To emphasize the variety's fresh, berrylike flavors,

Marcil ferments the Lemberger in stainless steel, then bottles the wine without wood aging, and without a malolactic fermentation. The wine is intensely colored, intensely fruity, and berrylike. Crisp, relatively high acidity contributes to the wine's fresh fruity character.

When the grapes are available, Covey Run makes La Caille de Fume, a proprietary blend of Semillon and Sauvignon Blanc. Washington produces excellent Semillon grapes. In the tradition of white Bordeaux, Covey Run blends Semillon with Sauvignon Blanc. The La Caille de Fume blend combines the refined grassy-citrusy character of Semillon with the more herbaceous intensity of Sauvignon Blanc. The two grapes complement each other well.

Most of Covey Run's wines are made from traditional grape varieties such as Chardonnay, Riesling, Chenin Blanc, and Cabernet Sauvignon. The less common grape varieties like Morio Muskat, Lemberger, and Aligote, and special blended wines such as the La Caille de Fume, offer additional interest for the wine consumer, while exploring some of the dimensions and directions of the Washington winegrowing industry. Covey Run has earned a well-deserved reputation for both its traditional and less common wine varieties.

Stan Clarke.

145

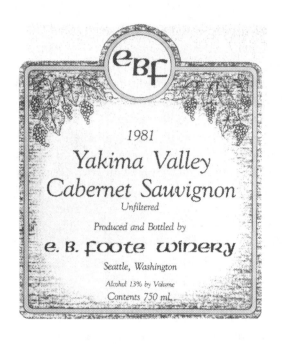

1981
Yakima Valley
Cabernet Sauvignon
Unfiltered

Produced and Bottled by

e. B. foote winery

Seattle, Washington

Alcohol 13% by Volume

Contents 750 mL

E. B. FOOTE WINERY

9354 4th Avenue South
Seattle, Washington 98126
(206) 763-9928

Wine Production
2,000 cases

Vineyards
none

First Vintage
1978

Leading Wines
Chardonnay, Gewurztraminer

A small family operation, the E. B. Foote winery is headed by Gene Foote, a senior engineer at Boeing. The winery is a natural outgrowth of Foote's interest in wines and winemaking, a pursuit that started innocently enough with a batch of blackberry wine. Foote quickly became interested in making fine wines from premium grapes. A small commercial winery followed some 10 years later.

As Foote says in retrospect, "I got started in commercial winemaking without appreciating what I was getting into. I underestimated the paperwork, financial backing, and time that was involved." The first year's production was only 1,300 gallons, but the commitment in time and energy were substantial for a person employed full-time in another occupation.

Foote's first winery facility was located in an industrial park in south Seattle. In 1983, Foote moved to a new location. Only eight blocks away from the old winery, the setting is greatly different. Foote's new winery is on part of the Joe Desimone farm, an island of agriculture in the industrial milieu.

The Southpark area once supplied fresh produce to nearby Seattle. The Desimone farm still does. Foote's winery is surrounded by fields of lettuce, basil, and pansies. Joe Desimone Sr. came to the area in 1916, and became one of the founders and directors of Seattle's famous Pike Place Market. Desimone's son still farms part of the original property.

All of Foote's grapes come from Washington's Yakima Valley. Foote prefers them. In his view, Yakima Valley grapes generally have more

Gene Foote.

146

varietal character and better balance than grapes from some of the warmer growing areas in the state. Foote emphasizes the importance of quality fruit. Poor wine, states the maxim, can be made from outstanding grapes, but outstanding wine can never be made from poor grapes.

Chardonnay is Foote's leading wine. The wine is fermented in stainless steel tanks at a temperature of 55 to 60 degrees, then aged in Limousin oak barrels. Foote dislikes the soft unctuous renditions of Chardonnay, preferring a wine with substantial body and a sturdy acid backbone to match. The fairly high acid level balances the wine and makes it a good accompaniment for food.

Foote makes all his wines to go with food. With rare exception, all of Foote's wines are made in a completely dry style, and all have enough acidity to refresh the palate throughout a meal. In 1985, Foote made his first sweet wine, a Riesling, from intensely sweet botrytised grapes. In this instance, the grapes dictated the wine style.

To insure that none of the flavoring components are stripped away, Foote's wines are only rarely fined, and none are filtered. Without fining and filtration, the wines must be carefully racked (the wine drawn off the sediment) numerous times.

In Foote's view, a winemaker must, above all, assign a stylistic signature to his wines. If a winemaker makes wines that, though good, taste like everyone else's, then he is really not exercising his art. Foote's wines bear his signature.

FRENCH CREEK CELLARS

15372 N.E. 96th Place
Redmond, Washington 98052
(206) 883-0757

Wine Production
5,000 cases

Vineyards
none

First Vintage
1983

Leading Wines
Cabernet Sauvignon, Merlot, Lemberger

For years, an informal group of home winemakers got together to buy grapes and exchange ideas about making wine. After a decade, a few in the group decided to start a commercial winery — French Creek Cellars. French Creek is run by a partnership of Hans and Trudi Doerr, and Bill and Fred Mundy.

French Creek was founded with a focus on dry wines that compliment food. In their first vintage, all the wines, including the Riesling, were fermented dry. Most consumers like and expect Riesling with some residual sweetness, so French Creek changed its style for the second vintage, only to find that the dry Riesling had created a dedicated following. Beginning with the 1985 vintage, two thirds of the Riesling is made with some residual sweetness, a third is fermented dry.

White wines are most in demand by consumers, and white wine grapes are more readily available, so a large percentage of French Creek's wine is white. But red wines are at the heart of the winery's purpose. Cabernet Sauvignon and Merlot are French Creek's leading wines.

French Creek also makes Pinot Noir, sometimes from Oregon grapes, and a small amount of Lemberger, a promising Washington red grape variety that may play a role similar to Zinfandel's role in California. Cellarmaster Richard Winter first made Lemberger in 1976, from a few experimental vines at Sagemoor Farms in the Columbia Valley. Some Washington Lemberger is made in a light, fruity style. French Creek's is not. "We don't make roses at French Creek," says Winter. French Creek's Lemberger is a substantive red wine, aged in French oak.

All of French Creek's red wines are made in a substantive style—red wines for red wine drinkers. French Creek's first Cabernet release epitomizes the style. An uncompromising wine, the 1983 reserve Cabernet Sauvignon is darkly colored and rich in extract from the grape. Although it has lots of tannin and 14.2 percent alcohol, it is not one of those simplistic, "big," overripe, loosely structured Cabernets with a thick tannic mask. Its high acidity, tight structure, and intense fruit extract balances perfectly with the alcohol and tannin. The wine demands lengthy cellaring, and promises corresponding rewards.

The 1983 reserve Cabernet Sauvignon was made from exceptional grapes from an excellent vintage. All French Creek's red wines are not as uncompromising, but they follow the same stylistic lead—traditionally styled wines made to age.

GORDON BROTHERS CELLARS

531 Levey Road
Pasco, Washington 99301
(509) 547-6224

Wine Production
2,000 cases

Vineyards
80 acres

Year First Planted
1981

First Vintage
1983

Leading Wines
Riesling, Sauvignon Blanc

Located a dozen miles northeast of Pasco, potato farmers Jeff and Bill Gordon decided to expand their agricultural interests into other crops. Part of their land is rocky and sloping, not the best for growing potatoes, but good for tree fruits, and especially good for wine grapes.

The Gordons' vineyard is situated on southerly slopes, on the bluffs overlooking the

Snake River. The river moderates the climate, and the sloping terrain keeps the air from pooling. The vineyard is more temperate than many other grape growing sites in the Columbia Valley. The vineyard is cooler in summer, frosts less in spring and fall, and freezes less in winter.

With their first crop, the Gordons experienced some of the trials of the Washington winegrowing industry—rapid, tumultuous growth, with supply and demand for wine grapes fluctuating widely and seldom in balance. Following their first harvest, a year when the supply of grapes exceeded demand for them, a series of unexpected frosts and freezes reduced Washington's grape crop. The balance suddenly shifted, and demand again exceeded supply— temporarily.

A grape grower, a director of the Washington Wine Grape Growers Association, and now a winery owner, Jeff Gordon advocates cooperation rather than divisive confrontation between grape growers and wineries. Ultimately, in his view, grape growers and wineries are dependent on the well-being of each other.

Except for Riesling, all Gordon Brothers' wines are made from grapes grapes grown in their own vineyards. The Gordons made a fortunate decision not to plant Riesling. Washington now has an overbalance of the variety. At the same time, varieties that the Gordons did plant, Sauvignon Blanc, Chardonnay, Cabernet Sauvignon, and Merlot, are in much more demand.

The Gordons continue to sell most of their grapes to other wineries, reserving part of the harvest for their own winery. A native of the area, winemaker Steve Phillips produces an unusual Sauvignon Blanc with three percent residual sugar, a low 10.5 percent alcohol, and crisp acidity to balance the sweetness. A popular winery specialty, Phillips plans to make the wine every year.

HAVILAND VINTNERS

19029 36th West
Lynnwood, Washington 98036
(206) 771-6933

Wine Production
20,000 cases

Vineyards
75 acres

Year First Planted
1961

First Vintage
1981

Leading Wines
Cabernet Sauvignon, Merlot, Chevrier

After battling Chateau Ste. Michelle over what Ste. Michelle considered traffic safety concerns, Haviland Vintners was finally issued building permits for a showcase winery across the road from Chateau Ste. Michelle's Woodinville winery. The area is zoned for industrial use, but Haviland is joining Chateau Ste. Michelle in preserving the pastoral setting with an elegant winery and grounds.

Haviland had planned to have the new winery built in time for the 1986 crush, but delays in getting approval for construction forced Haviland to continue operations in suburban Lynnwood's Colony Park Complex. Haviland's new winery is designed as a six million dollar, 10,000 square foot, victorian manor house with offices and visitor facilities, attached to a 30,000 square foot wine production facility—all surrounded by expansive grounds to preserve the pastoral atmosphere.

The manor house completes the vision of Haviland's founder, George DeJarnatt. Prior to the approval for construction of the Woodinville winery, the manor house existed only as a drawing on Haviland's label. Unlike some of the larger western Washington wineries, Haviland is a fully operational winery, crushing all its grapes on site.

Haviland came into being after the purchase of one of Washington's oldest producing Cabernet Sauvignon vineyards. Located near Benton City

George DeJarnatt.

in the Yakima Valley, half of the 11 acre vineyard was planted in 1961, the other half in 1965. The vineyard was the source of Chateau Ste. Michelle's first Cabernet Sauvignons. Haviland subsequently acquired land contiguous with the Cabernet vineyard. The new acreage, part of the former Corral Creek Ranch, is devoted principally to Merlot and Chardonnay.

While attending college, DeJarnatt managed a retail wine store. As part of his goal to have a winery of his own, DeJarnatt wrote his graduate thesis on the economics of winery operations. After several years as an accountant, DeJarnatt left his practice to operate Haviland Vintners.

While many new Washington wineries produce almost entirely white wines, primarily semi-sweet Rieslings, Haviland emphasizes red wines and dry or nearly dry white wines for the table. Haviland makes several semi-sweet Rieslings, but the emphasis is elsewhere. DeJarnatt is working toward a target of 30 to 40 percent of production in red wines.

Haviland's regular Chardonnay bottling is fermented in stainless steel. The reserve bottling is fermented in French oak barrels. Fermenting in oak sacrifices some of the fruit of the grape, but DeJarnatt prefers this slight sacrifice for the richer, fuller quality that barrel fermentation contributes. DeJarnatt does not put his Chardonnays through malolactic fermentation, however, believing that this process, while important for red wines, takes away too much of the Chardonnay fruit.

Haviland's Semillon is called Chevrier, another French name for the grape. The Chevrier is finished at about .5 percent residual sugar, approximately the threshold for perceptual sweetness for most people. The slight residual sugar does not make the wine taste particularly sweet, but it conveys a sense of roundness, smoothness, and texture, and a bit of sweet/sour piquancy.

Haviland's Woodinville winery is designed as a showcase visitor facility, encouraging guests with wine events, group functions, tasting and retail sales rooms, and picnicking on the six acres of grounds.

Hinzerling

1981
Yakima Valley
Cabernet Sauvignon
Estate Bottled

Produced & Bottled by Hinzerling Vineyards, Inc., Prosser, WA
Alcohol 12.5% by Volume

HINZERLING VINEYARDS

1520 Sheridan Avenue
Prosser, Washington 99350
(509) 786-2163

Wine Production
2,500 cases

Vineyards
30 acres

Year First Planted
1972

First Vintage
1976

Leading Wines
Cabernet Sauvignon, Late Harvest Gewurztraminer
and Riesling

One of the true pioneers of the Washington wine renaissance, Mike Wallace and his family left the metropolitan lifestyle of Seattle to establish a vineyard and winery in Washington's Yakima Valley. The first winter, a severe freeze killed many of the tender young vines. Others that planted grapes that year did not replant. The Wallaces replanted and persevered.

Now, with more than 10,000 acres of wine grapes and a thriving wine industry, it is hard to imagine that scarcely more than a decade ago the viability of Washington winegrowing was very much in question. Without the commitment of Wallace and the other pioneers, the Washington wine industry might not exist.

Hinzerling was one of the first premium Washington wineries located not in the Seattle metropolitan area, but east of the Cascade Mountains near the source of its grapes. Having a winery near the vineyards is not simply a matter of convenience. For Wallace, grape growing and winemaking are ineluctably intertwined.

Winegrowing, in its full sense, is a responsive relationship, quite different from the perspective of a winemaker awaiting delivery of a truckload of grapes purchased from a far away vineyard, knowing the sugar, acid, and pH of the grapes, but little else. For Wallace, this was not enough.

The Yakima Valley has suffered an unusual series of frosts and freezes. Hinzerling's vineyard has been affected less than most, partly because of excellent site selection, and partly because of careful protective measures. Irrigation is ceased in August to harden off the vines. Then at the end of the season, the vines are irrigated to drench the soil and roots, protecting them from drying. Wallace limits the crop yields, understressing the vines and allowing them to build a carbohydrate reserve that will later act as protective antifreeze.

Modest yields also preserve the intensity of the grapes, so that flavors are not lost in overcropping the vines. Sometimes, however, there can be too much of a good thing. Sacrificing yield and profit margin for quality, Wallace first cropped his Chardonnay vines to a very modest two to three tons an acre. The grapes ripened well and had good acidity—in fact, too much so. By the time the acidity dropped to acceptable levels, the grapes were overripe, and the wines were high in acid, or alcohol, or both. Wallace now crops the Chardonnay at 4½ to 5½ tons an acre. This moves maturity back about ten days, forcing the sugar levels to rise more slowly while the acids drop to the desired levels.

Hinzerling was among the first Washington winegrowers to work with botrytised wines. *Botrytis cinerea* is a fungus that, under the right conditions, concentrates the juice of the grapes by reducing their water content, and at the same time, contributing glycerol and flavors of its own to yield an intense, richly sweet wine.

Hinzerling's botrytised wines are made from Riesling and Gewurztraminer. According to Wallace, Gewurztraminer is more resistant to Botrytis than Riesling, but just enough so that it is more easily manageable.

Hinzerling's most heavily botrytised Gewurztraminer is called Die Sonne, a wine made by picking selected bunches of botrytised grapes and laying them in trays behind the winery. Bees and nighttime condensation help spread the botrytis, further desiccating the grapes and concentrating their essences. The grapes are not crushed until the sugars rise to nearly 40 degrees Brix. Hinzerling's most heavily botrytised Riesling is made from individual, hand-selected, botrytised berries. The botrytised wines are not made every year, but only when conditions are favorable.

Cabernet Sauvignon has not been the easiest grape for Washington to tame. In the early years,

with the exception of some sporadic successes, talk of the potential for excellence was more prevalent than the actuality. Wallace helped point the direction for Washington Cabernets, and was among the first to succeed with the grape. Hinzerling's Cabernets are typically "big" wines, very rough and tannic in their youth, requiring several years of bottle aging to smooth their edges and begin showing their best.

More recently, Wallace has been releasing a second Cabernet for earlier consumption. Usually a blend of Cabernet Sauvignon, Merlot, and Malbec, the wine is more immediately supple and elegant than the regular release. Unlike many wines intended for earlier consumption, it is far from insipid.

In France, Cabernet Sauvignon, Bordeaux's premier grape, is almost always blended with other related varieties. Merlot is the best known of these, but there are others. Wallace is experimenting with Cabernet Franc as well as Malbec.

Cabernet Franc, Wallace reports, is quite similar to Cabernet Sauvignon, though not as intense and flavorful. Malbec, on the other hand, is distinctive, combining pleasant herbaceous flavors with scents of violets and lavender. Malbec berries are large, and the clusters are straggly, a result of the variety's typically uneven berry set. Malbec is naturally high in malic acid. Wallace's experimental blends with Malbec have been very successful, but few grapes are yet available to provide more than a tiny percentage of the blend for a commercial release.

In the decade and a half since Wallace came to the Yakima Valley, Washington's winegrowing industry has become firmly established, but for the pioneering spirit, the winegrowing frontier is still close at hand.

Mike Wallace.

THE HOGUE CELLARS

Route 2, Box 2898
Prosser, Washington 99350
(509) 786-4557

Wine Production
45,000 cases

Vineyards
200 acres

Year First Planted
1975

First Vintage
1982

Leading Wines
Riesling, Chenin Blanc, Fume Blanc

In 1949, the Hogue family planted 40 acres of hops in Washington's Yakima Valley. The Hogues still harvest hops from the towering hop trellises, and process them at their own hop plant, complete with a traditional hop kiln to dry the moist, sticky, fragrant, hop buds, and pack them into bales.

Hops are still an important crop, satisfying the needs of the brewing industry, but Hogue Ranches also raises cattle, and grows a variety of crops, including spearmint, asparagus, potatoes —and grapes. For decades, the Hogues grew Concord grapes for the valley's grape juice processing plants. In the 1970s, the Hogues planted their first premium, vinifera, wine grapes.

Mike Hogue heads the ranch and winery operations. "We've always had a lot of pride in what we produce, but its identity always got lost as soon as we brought in the crop and sold it. Some of the gum you chew has our Scotch spearmint in it, but its not all our mint, and the gum says Wrigley's, not Hogue. Wine is different. Its our wine. Our pride is in it, and our label is on it."

The wine experience inspired exploration of some of Hogue's other agricultural products. In 1984, Hogue produced a limited amount of pickled asparagus and sold it at the winery with the familiar Hogue label and logo. The asparagus proved so popular, the Hogue's bought the cannery and expanded production.

Hogue's vineyard manager is Andy Markin. An agricultural economist, and graduate of Cornell, Markin wrote his Masters thesis on grape growing. Markin keeps his hands in the soil as well as in the books. The Hogue operation successfully blends business acumen with the traditional perspectives of a family close to the land. All agricultural crops, particularly hops and grapes, experience wide swings in market demand and price. The Hogues have earned a reputation for making the most of the changes.

Hogue was a leader in what is now the predominant Washington style for Chenin Blanc and Riesling. The two grapes, both delicate, floral/fruity varieties, respond well to the Yakima Valley climate. Hogue emphasizes the delicate, fruity quality of the grapes by keeping the alcohol content to a low 10 to 11 percent, fermenting at cool temperatures, and releasing the wines with crisp acidity to balance their residual sweetness. Chenin Blanc and Riesling comprise the majority of Hogue's production.

Rob Griffin is Hogue's winemaker. After receiving his degree in enology and viticulture from U. C. Davis, Griffin became a chemist for California's Buena Vista winery, then came to Washington as winemaker for Preston Wine Cellars, before joining Hogue in 1984.

Chenin Blanc and Riesling led the way into the marketplace for Hogue, but as Hogue's vineyards mature, other varieties are playing an increasing role. The Chardonnay and Semillon

Rob Griffin, winemaker, and David Forsythe, assistant winemaker.

are aged in French oak. For Sauvignon Blanc, Griffin likes a combination of French and American oak. The more aggressive American oak flavors act as an effective foil for the aggressive herbaceous character of the Sauvignon Blanc grape.

Similarly, Cabernet Sauvignon, an aggressively flavored red wine variety, is aged in air dried, fire bent, American oak barrels. Hogue's first Cabernet Sauvignon release, the 1983 Reserve, created a sensation at the Atlanta International Wine Festival. An intense wine with pronounced American oak character, Hogue's Cabernet was awarded "Best of Show" out of 1,667 entries. For a region best known for its Rieslings, Hogue's Cabernet Sauvignon was a revelation.

After Griffin made a successful test batch of bottle fermented sparkling Riesling, Hogue decided to produce the wine on a commercial scale. Griffin's sparkling Riesling is left only a short time on the yeast, emphasizing the fruit of the grape rather than the yeasty character.

Griffin, The Hogue Cellars' general manager as well as its winemaker, also makes wine for his own small winery. Drawing on the methods he explored at his own winery, Griffin decided to make a barrel fermented Semillon Reserve at Hogue. After the barrel fermentation is complete, Griffin leaves the Hogue Semillon Reserve in contact with the lees (the sediment of yeast cells and pulp). This method makes a less fruity wine, but one with more rounded, more complex flavors.

In California, most Semillon is relatively dull and undistinguished. Sauvignon Blanc is considered easily superior. Washington produces excellent, distinctive Semillons, wines that live up to the grape's European reputation. Some argue that Washington Semillon is superior to Sauvignon Blanc. Griffin makes wine from both grapes, and likes them both.

"They are really complementary grapes," says Griffin. "I don't think one should be ranked above the other. Fermented cool, Semillon is not too different from a Chenin Blanc. At higher temperatures, Semillon shows a fuller character. Some Semillon, depending on where and how the grapes are grown and how the wine is made, can be even more herbaceous than Sauvignon Blanc. From a winemaking standpoint, Washington Semillon is a versatile grape."

"The harvest" has many meanings at Hogue, from spring asparagus, to mint and hops. Wine expands the meaning of "the harvest" and makes the term more special. When the grape harvest goes out the door to market, the Hogue product and and pride are in it—and the Hogue label and logo are on it.

154

A Natural Wine
Red Wine

HOODSPORT
1984
WINERY

Island Belle Wine

Alcohol Content
12% By Volume

Bottled by Hoodsport Winery Inc., Hoodsport, Washington
BW-WA-76

HOODSPORT WINERY

N. 23501 Highway 101
Hoodsport, Washington 98548
(206) 877-9894

Grape Wine Production
2,500 cases

Fruit And Berry Wine Production
3,500 cases

Vineyards
3 acres

Year First Planted
1872 (historic vineyard)

First Vintage
1980

Leading Wines
Raspberry, Island Belle

On western Washington's Olympic Peninsula, along the Hood Canal, Edwin and Peggy Patterson operate a fruit, berry, and grape winery. Some of the grape wines are made from grapes grown in Washington's Columbia Valley, east of the Cascade Mountain Range, but Hoodsport's most interesting wine, from an historical standpoint, is Island Belle, a light red wine made from a non-vinifera, native American variety.

In the late 1800s, Adam Eckert came to Puget Sound's Stretch Island from New York and established a fruit and grape nursery. Eckert developed a grape he called Island Belle, a local variant of the grape Campbell Early (or perhaps, simply Campbell Early itself, with a different name). Very little Campbell Early is planted in America, but it is one of Japan's major grape varieties.

Island Belle enjoyed early commercial success as a table, jelly, and wine grape, before Concord from Washington's Columbia Valley gained popularity and took its place. With lack of interest and support, Island Belle, and Eckert's vineyard, fell to neglect. In 1975, Harry and Mary Branch and Bonnie Hanson purchased Eckert's Stretch Island vineyard. The new owners resuscitated the old vines and began selling the grapes on a "U-pick" basis to visitors and local residents.

In 1981, the Pattersons' discovered the grapes, and Hoodsport made their first Island Belle wine. The vineyard owners have since become shareholders in the Hoodsport winery, and Island Belle, one of Washington's oldest grape varieties from one of Washington's oldest vineyards, is a Hoodsport specialty.

CHARLES HOOPER FAMILY WINERY

Box 215, Spring Creek Road
Husum, Washington 98623
(509) 493-2324

Wine Production
800 cases

Vineyards
17 acres

Year First Planted
1979

First Vintage
1984

Leading Wines
Riesling

For more than twenty years, Charles and Beverlee Hooper lived overseas in England, France, and Germany, working for the Department of Defense foreign school system. During their last assignment, the Hoopers found time to work in the Mosel vineyards near Trier, Germany.

Returning to the states after their children were grown, the Hoopers settled in the Columbia Gorge, near the small community of Husum, and planted wine grapes. Situated on a very steep south facing slope, the Hooper vineyard looks out across the Columbia River to Oregon's Mount Hood, one of the Cascade Mountains' towering, snow covered, volcanic cones.

In the extremely steep vineyards of the Mosel, conventional wire trellising is impossible, and the vines are trained on individual stakes. Following the German practice, the Hoopers train their vines on stakes, a highly unusual practice in America. Hooper usually leaves two canes on each vine, arcing them downward, and tying them to the stake.

Also in the German tradition, all Hooper's wines are white, and the focus is on Riesling. The Hoopers purchase a few grapes, but all come from Columbia Gorge vineyards. While his own vines matured, Hooper learned winemaking by working at the nearby Mont Elise Vineyards.

The winery name, Charles Hooper Family Winery, accurately describes the operation. Very much a family enterprise, Hooper's wife, and Hooper's son and his wife are all part of the business, working in marketing, and the winery and vineyard.

CHARDONNAY
Columbia Valley
1985
ALCOHOL CONTENT 12.75% BY VOLUME

HORIZON'S EDGE WINERY

Route 2, Box 2396
Zillah, Washington 98944
(509) 829-6401

Wine Production
2,500 cases

Vineyards
18 acres

Year First Planted
1985

First Vintage
1984

Leading Wines
Chardonnay, Riesling

In the mid '70s, Tom Campbell graduated from the University of Montana with a degree in Zoology. At the time, career opportunities in his field were limited. Interested in agribusiness, Campbell went to U. C. Davis for more training. The subjects in the department of enology and viticulture sounded appealing. A year later, Campbell left, having completed the course work in enology.

In 1979, while working for a California winery, Campbell returned briefly to his native Montana and planted an experimental vineyard near Flathead Lake, in the western part of the state (see the entry for Mission Mountain Winery in Montana.) In the early 1980s, Campbell left California for Washington, working as consultant and winemaker for several Yakima Valley wineries. Four of Campbell's classmates from Davis came to Washington, Stan Clarke and Wayne Marcil of Covey Run, Brian Carter of Paul Thomas Wines, and M. Taylor Moore of Blackwood Canyon.

In 1985, Campbell and his wife, Hema Shah, bonded their own winery. After coming to Washington from England, Hema worked as a pharmacist for the Yakima Valley Farm Workers Clinic. The Campbells' vineyard is planted to 10 acres of Chardonnay, 5 acres Muscat Canelli, and 3 acres Pinot Noir. Muscat Canelli is easily damaged by winter cold, but with the control afforded by his own vineyard, Campbell hopes to achieve better winter hardiness by stressing the vines, reducing irrigation so that the vines will build their nutrient reserves and go dormant earlier in the fall.

Usually too warm for Pinot Noir, the Horizon's Edge vineyard is in a cooler section of the Yakima Valley, and the vines are planted on a slightly north slope. On hot days, Campbell cools the Pinot Noir with an overhead sprinkler system. The overhead sprinkler system is also used for irrigation, but it is then left on for longer periods

Tom Campbell displays a cluster of botrytised Riesling grapes.

so the water can soak into the soil.

Chardonnay is Horizon's Edge's flagship wine. Ninety percent of the winery's production will be white wine, and eighty percent of the white wine will be Chardonnay. Prior to bonding his own winery. Campbell made his first wines with M. Taylor Moore at Moore's Blackwood Canyon winery. Both share a similar perspective on Chardonnay, one that differs markedly from the general Washington trend.

Most Washington Chardonnays are fermented at cool temperatures in stainless steel tanks, removed immediately from the lees (sediment following fermentation), aged briefly in (usually) new oak barrels, then bottled for release. Malolactic fermentation is avoided. The emphasis is on freshness and fruitiness at the expense of texture and complexity.

Campbell takes a radical view in the opposite direction, fermenting Chardonnay in oak barrels at warmer temperatures using a combination of yeasts, putting the wine through malolactic fermentation, and aging in small oak barrels with the lees. Malolactic fermentation was not a part of Campbell's original technique, but more experience with the wines led him toward this method as well.

With malolactic fermentation, much of the wine's fruitiness is transformed into alternate complexities and flavors. In the view of its detractors, malolactic fermentation is criticized for a "canned corn" character that it sometimes imparts to the wine. Campbell now believes this is only a factor if the grapes are below par, flat tasting, high in pH, or shy on fruit character. Campbell's success with Chardonnay is a strong argument for his position. In the better vintages, Campbell's Chardonnays show fine texture and length with a complexity of flavors absent from the fruitier renditions of the grape.

HUNTER HILL VINEYARDS

Royal Star Route
Othello, Washington 99344
(509) 346-2607

Business Address:
4250 133RD S.E.
Bellevue, Washington 98006
(206) 746-1120

Wine Production
2,500 cases

Vineyards
28 acres

Year First Planted
1981

First Vintage
1984

Leading Wines
Riesling

Within the last 10 million years, the northward movement of the Northwest's coastal land mass buckled the Columbia Valley's basalt lava flows and formed folded high ridges. The ridges run in a generally east to west direction, offering shelter from the cold of the north—and sunny south facing slopes for grape growing.

Hunter Hill Vineyards is the first winery on one of the Columbia Valley's more northerly folded ridges, the Royal Slope, a grape growing area just north of the more familiar Wahluke Slope. In 1977, Airline pilot, Art Byron, bought a 233 acre farm at the far eastern end of the Royal Slope and turned part of it into a vineyard and winery. The vineyard spans the Adams and Grant county line. The winery itself is just off Highway 12 in Adams county, the county's first winery.

A Washington State University research farm is within a mile of the vineyard, but little is known about Royal Slope grape growing. So far, Byron reports that the grapes ripen about eight to ten days later than the Yakima Valley. The heat during the summer months is more intense than other parts of the Columbia Valley, but the growing season is slightly shorter and more compressed.

Byron consulted with noted Washington horticulturist, Walter Clore, before planting his vineyard to Riesling, Merlot, and Gewurztraminer. Byron plans to expand his vineyard with Chardonnay and more Merlot. The Riesling is made in a Germanic style with a low 10% alcohol. Byron also buys other varieties from other Columbia Valley growers to supplement production from his own vineyard.

European winegrowing has evolved over the course of some 2,000 years, but only within the last two decades have winegrowers begun systematically exploring Washington's highly unique winegrowing climates. The Royal Slope is one of the Columbia Valley's newest grape growing regions. Byron is one of the state's new pioneers.

JOHNSON CREEK WINERY

19248 Johnson Creek Road S.E.
Tenino, Washington 98589
(206) 264-2100

Wine Production
1,500 cases

Vineyards
3 acres

Year First Planted
1985

First Vintage
1984

Leading Wines
Riesling, Merlot

In the Skoocumchuck Valley, twenty-six miles southeast of the state capitol of Olympia, Vince and Ann deBellis own and operate Alice's Restaurant. Converted from a rural farm house, Alice's Restaurant features a six course, two hour dinner, Wednesday through Sunday. Fresh rainbow trout and fresh bread are served with every meal.

An outgrowth of the restaurant, the deBellis's planted a small vineyard and a started their own winery, Johnson Creek. The family owns 33 acres of land on Johnson Creek, but only three acres on the valley floor are suitable for vineyards.

Western Washington is a very cool grape growing climate. DeBellis planted his vineyard at a very dense spacing of five feet between each row and four feet between each vine within the rows. The dense spacing is typical of cool climate winegrowing, reducing the load on each vine for a better quality crop. His vine trellises are seven feet tall to catch the sunshine, a precious commodity in western Washington.

DeBellis is one of the few winegrowers working with grapes grown west of the Cascade Mountains. He has planted some experimental vines, but most of the vineyard is planted to Muller-Thurgau, a Riesling-like grape suitable to very cool climates like western Washington. DeBellis buys more grapes from other western Washington grape growers, but two-thirds of his grapes come from the Columbia Valley, east of the Cascade Mountains. DeBellis stems and crushes the grapes in the vineyard, bringing only the juice back to the winery to ferment.

Riesling is Johnson Creek's major wine, but the Chardonnay is of special interest. Made in a Germanic style, similar to Johnson Creek's Riesling, the Chardonnay grapes are picked for crisp acidity, finished with about two percent residual sugar as a counterpoint to the acidity, and bottled without oak aging.

DeBellis prefers Muller-Thurgau to the other typical western Washington grape varieties such as Madeleine Angevine and Madeleine Sylvaner, and he is focusing on this variety for his western Washington wines. Most of Johnson Creek's wines are sold directly from the winery. They are also available to accompany Alice's Restaurant's hearty dinners.

KIONA VINEYARDS

Route 2, Box 2169E
Benton City, Washington 99320
(509) 588-6716

Wine Production
7,000 cases

Vineyards
30 acres

Year First Planted
1975

First Vintage
1980

Leading Wines
Lemberger, Cabernet Sauvignon, Chardonnay

Just before merging with the Columbia, the Yakima River runs up against a short but determinant block of hills, and takes a brief, radical turn northward. One of the warmest and driest parts of the Yakima Valley, this area, on the northward turn of the river, at the far eastern end of the Yakima Valley, was nearly left to sagebrush when the Kennewick Irrigation District abandoned plans for an irrigation canal.

In 1974, however, the partnership that would later become Kiona Vineyards drilled a well 550 feet deep to a major aquifer, the first deep water well in the area. The following year, the

Kiona partners planted their vineyard on the lower slopes of Red Mountain, near the town of Kiona. Their pioneering success brought other grape growers and wineries to the area, and Red Mountain has emerged as an important sub-region of the Yakima Valley.

Kiona Vineyards is the partnership of two families, Jim and Pat Holmes, and John and Ann Williams. Since 1961, Holmes and Williams have worked together as engineers. Holmes, a native of San Francisco and long time home winemaker, describes the Kiona winery as a hobby that got out of hand. Kiona sold its first grapes to other wineries, but in 1979, the partners bonded the Kiona winery, and in 1980, Holmes crushed Kiona's first commercial vintage in the crowded confines of his garage. Since then, the winery has moved to a newly constructed facility on the vineyard site.

The soil is a Hezel silt loam, running 25 feet down to a 60 to 80 foot layer of sand and gravel. Clumps of calcium carbonate dot the soil. At 8.4, the soil's pH is one of the highest in the northwest, a desired characteristic for growing grapes. Unlike some vineyard sites in the Columbia Valley, the Kiona vineyard does not have a calcerous layer of hardpan near the soil's surface. Vineyard sites having this hardpan must be ripped and worked so that vine roots can penetrate far enough into the soil to be protected from winter cold.

Some of Washington's early vinifera grape plantings were fan trained. On a fan trained vine, several trunks emerge from the vine's base and spread upward forming a tall fan. In eastern European countries, soil is ploughed over the base of the fan trained trunks to protect the vine from winter cold. In the early years of Washington winegrowing, fan training was a recommended method of winter protection.

The training method has since been abandoned as unnecessary for winter protection, but at Kiona, the vines, including the newest plantings, are still fan trained, not for winter protection, but because Holmes and Williams see other advantages. In their view, the vines have fewer mildew problems, sunlight more evenly strikes the leaves near the grape clusters, and the grapes ripen earlier. For the winery visitor, the fan trained vines are a pleasing esthetic difference.

Chenin Blanc and Riesling are the winery's staples, both made in dry and slightly sweet renditions. Kiona's Chardonnay, fermented in French oak, is their premier white wine. Kiona makes Cabernet Sauvignon, aged in American oak, and also sells Cabernet grapes to other select wineries. Kiona is emerging as one of Washington's premier Cabernet Sauvignon vineyards. The Kiona grapes yield Cabernets with concentrated varietal fruit and a fine textural richness.

Kiona's unique specialty is Lemberger, a little known red wine grape with not much to recommend it in winegrowing traditions. Its most well-known viticultural roots are in Wurttemberg, Germany, a region not exactly known for exceptional red wines. From a commercial standpoint, Lemberger has no established market as does Riesling or Cabernet Sauvignon. Worse yet, the name is identified with a nasty smelling cheese. There is, it seems, little reason to bother with the grape—except that Washington State University

Jim Holmes displays Kiona's classic fan trained vines.

professor emeritus Dr. Walter Clore was more interested in performance on merit than in tradition or marketing.

Dr. Clore has long recommended the grape for Washington's wine industry, and his recommendations have long been resisted for understandable, though regrettable, reasons. Now comfortably established, Washington's wine industry can afford to explore new possibilities for its unique growing climate.

Planted in 1976, Kiona has the oldest commercial acreage of the grape in the state, and Kiona was the first winery to release Lemberger as a varietal wine. The grape can successfully be cropped higher than most red varieties. At Kiona, the vines are pruned for a yield of six tons an acre. Cropped much higher, however, the grapes lose fruit intensity.

Because Lemberger is unique, well suited to the growing climate, and highly versatile, it has been called Washington's Zinfandel. The grape lends itself well to wine styles ranging from fruity, Beaujolais-like wines to deeply colored, tannic, robust wines requiring lengthier aging. The flavors are typically berries and vanilla with a Merlot-like softness. Kiona's Lemberger is aged in American oak and made in a full-bodied, tannic style, calling for cellar aging. Now much in demand by other vineyards and wineries, all of Kiona's Lemberger pruning wood is saved for planting.

F.W. LANGGUTH WINERY

2340 Winery Road
Mattawa, Washington 99344
(509) 932-4943

Wine Production
60,000 cases

Vineyards
265 acres

Year First Planted
1981

First Vintage
1982

Leading Wines
Select and Late Harvest Rieslings

F. W. Langguth, a 5 million dollar winery in Washington's Columbia Valley, is the first winery in the Northwest substantially financed by a foreign wine company. Langguth's parent corporation is its namesake, F. W. Langguth Erben, GMBH, a huge winemaking operation headquartered at Traben-Trarbach in Germany's Mosel region. J. Wolfgang Langguth is the current head of the huge family-owned corporation that traces its corporate and winemaking roots back to 1789.

In the late 1970s, Langguth began looking around the world for a wine producing region to expand its operation. Such diverse areas as Brazil, North Africa, Australia, and California were considered, but on the advice of Dr. Helmut Becker, director of the famous German viticultural school at Geisenheim, Langguth chose Washington. Washington offered a climate suitable for growing Riesling and other German grape varieties, as well as local investment partners interested in the venture.

The cooperative investment arrangement is complex, but essentially the German firm has majority interest in a Washington corporation which, in turn, is general partner in Washington's F.W. Langguth Winery. Langguth does not own any Washington vineyards per se, but has contracted long-term arrangements with a partnership called Weinbau, formed for the purpose of planting new vineyards in Washington's Columbia Valley, on the Wahluke Slope near Mattawa. Seattle attorney, Alec Bayless, and retired folding-door manufacturer, Winslow Wright, two of the twelve principal partners in Sagemoor Farms, Washington's largest independent grape grower, are also general partners in Weinbau. The Langguths own one-third of the limited partnership interests in Weinbau.

The Weinbau vineyards are planted entirely to white wine grape varieties, primarily Riesling. The small amounts of Langguth red wines are made from grapes purchased from other growers. In Germany, although Riesling is by far the superior grape, growing conditions are marginal, and much acreage is planted to lesser Riesling-like grapes, primarily Muller-Thurgau. In the Columbia Valley, however, Riesling is the state's most reliable grape variety, consistently producing relatively large yields of good fruit. Because of Riesling's reliable success, Muller-Thurgau has little role to play, and Langguth is working with Muller-Thurgau only on an experimental basis.

Langguth's winemaker, Max Zellweger, received his training at the College of Technology, Viticulture, and Horticulture in Wadenswil, Switzerland. Before coming to Langguth, Zellweger was winemaker at Oregon's Chateau Benoit Winery. Zellweger's winemaking style emphasizes freshness, no oak, and the fruit of the grape.

White wines are fermented in a temperature range of 45 to 55 degrees. Immediately after

Irrigation pipe on the Wahluke Slope.

fermentation, the wines are centrifuged to remove all yeast cells. Prior to fermentation, the grape juice may also be centrifuged to remove unwanted grape solids, a practice that contributes to a lighter, more delicate character. Langguth purchased state-of-the-art winemaking equipment for its new Washington winery, including an enclosed membrane press that allows juice yields of 165 to 170 gallons per ton without heavy pressing pressure, giving Langguth some of the best of both worlds, high yields and good quality juice. In keeping with the marketing approach of the parent company, most of Langguth's wines are moderately priced at a fair value to the consumer.

Not unexpectedly for a winery with German parentage, Riesling is Langguth's leading wine. In keeping with the Germanic (and Swiss) perspective, Zellweger prefers to pick his grapes at lower sugar levels than many Washington winemakers. Earlier picking translates into wines with lower alcohol, a more delicate fruitiness, and less ponderous ripe flavors—desirable characteristics in Riesling wines. The trend toward earlier picking of Riesling grapes is increasing among Washington winemakers.

Centrifuging the grape must and minimizing phenolics and other elements contributing to bitterness or unclean flavors can also have negative effects, stripping away some of the wine's character so that it tastes flat, simple, or hollow. In Langguth's reserve and special release Rieslings, however, Zellweger achieves a fine balance of technique. The best of the special release wines are fresh and unencumbered by bitter or over-ripe elements, and at the same time, show intense fruit flavors and complexity, setting them apart from the average Washington Riesling. Although more expensive than the rest of the Langguth line, they represent a good value for wines of their quality.

Wines released under the Langguth label emulate the German style in grape variety and taste. Under the Saddle Mountain label, Langguth releases a line of moderately priced, less typically Germanic wines, including Gewurztraminer, Cabernet Sauvignon, and Chardonnay. Here still, the wines are in accord with the winery perspective. The Chardonnay and Cabernet are made in a fruity style for early drinking. None of Langguth's wines sees oak.

LATAH CREEK WINERY

13030 East Indiana Avenue
Spokane, Washington 99216
(509) 926-0164

Wine Production
15,000 cases

Vineyards
none

First Vintage
1982

Leading Wines
Chenin Blanc, Maywine, Semillon, Riesling

Spokane's first winemaker in the modern era, Mike Conway, an experienced California winemaker, came to the city in 1980 to make wine for Worden's Washington Winery. After two years at Worden's, Conway left to become wine-maker for Hogue Cellars in the Yakima Valley, commuting from Spokane by private aircraft. That same year, with financing from Hogue, Conway opened his own winery in Spokane, Latah Creek Wine Cellars. After an agreed transitional period, Conway left his winemaking role at Hogue to concentrate his efforts full-time at Latah Creek. The Hogue Ranches remain a major supplier of Latah Creek's grapes.

Unlike many new winemakers coming to Washington, Conway is a microbiologist, and not

Mike Conway.

a winemaking graduate of U. C. Davis. While attending school, Conway worked nights as a lab technician for California's Gallo Winery. After graduating, he went to work for Franzia, and soon became directly interested in winemaking. In 1977, Conway applied for an assistant winemaking position at Parcucci, not really expecting that they would hire someone without formal training in enology. At the time, however, Parducci was undergoing a massive expansion and needed someone who could insure the biological stability of their wines. Conway was hired, and became directly involved in the winemaking process.

One of Latah Creek's specialties is a direct result of Conway's association with Parducci. Joe Monostori, Parducci's cellarmaster, learned winemaking in Hungary from his grandfather. In the spring, to celebrate the planting of new crops, the local Hungarian winemakers made May Wine, a light, sweet, fragrant wine flavored with woodruff and strawberries. At Parducci, Monostori made small quantities for sale only at the winery. Conway learned the recipe from Monostori, and May Wine is now a Latah Creek speciality, released each spring to coincide with Spokane's Lilac Festival. The wine is intensely flavored and semi-sweet, with crisp balancing acidity.

Crisp acidity and fresh fruitiness are the mark of Washington's predominant white wine style.

The very nature of the winegrowing region lends itself to this wine style, and no one exemplifies and demonstrates it more than Conway. Conway's wines are very fruity, fresh and clean, and apparently low in phenols. The wines, especially Chenin Blanc and Riesling, are low in alcohol with residual sweetness balanced by fairly high acidity.

Conway's Chenin Blanc is especially notable. Normally a wine of modest interest, Chenin Blanc suffered greatly with its reputation as an indifferent jug wine grape in California's warm growing regions. Although Washington had produced good Chenin Blanc for more than a decade, Conway's dedication to the grape carried the wine an additional qualitative step further. Different than the Chenin Blanc of France's Loire district, Conway's Chenin Blanc is in a fruitier style, similar in profile, if not in taste, to a Washington Riesling.

Riesling and Chenin Blanc are Latah Creek's major wines. Both are fermented slowly at cool temperatures to preserve their fresh fruity qualities. Different yeast strains behave in different ways. Some yeast strains "stick" at low temperatures and cannot be readily restarted, causing many problems for the winemaker. Conway, especially for his delicate white varietals, prefers the Steinberg strain. Steinberg ferments slowly and reliably at low temperatures, yet can be easily stopped when the desired sweetness is reached. Most comes from California as a liquid culture, but Conway's is a German dry culture he obtains from Canada via the barter system, trading some of his grape juice for the yeast.

Sometimes chemical preservatives called sorbates are added to semi-sweet wines to insure their stability and prevent refermentation in the bottle and other such maladies. Sorbates, however, if used to any great degree, adversely affect the flavor of the wine. Because of Conway's training in microbiology, Parducci, for the first time, was able to completely eliminate sorbates in most of their wines. At Latah Creek, Conway is again employing his skills in microbiology to avoid chemical preservatives.

Conway likes to keep his delicate white wines cool from the onset of fermentation through the bottling process. Keeping the wine continuously cool traps carbon dioxide and makes the wine slightly 'spritzy" when the bottle is opened and the wine is served. The slight effervescence from the release of the trapped gas contributes to the wine's fresh taste.

Chardonnay, Muscat Canelli, Sauvignon Blanc, Semillon, and Merlot round out Latah Creek's line of wines. All carry through the Latah Creek style. Even the Merlot, bottled with only a brief time in wood, emphasizes the fresh fruit character of the grape. Conway is one of an increasing number of Washington winemakers enthused about Semillon. In Washington, Semillon is perhaps superior to Sauvignon Blanc, similar and intensely varietal, yet without the intrusive herbaceousness that is often present with Sauvignon Blanc. Conway's Semillon is released with moderately high acid and slight residual sugar. The wine tastes almost, but not quite, dry.

Conway has definite ideas about the kind of wine he wants to make. Taking a cue from Parducci, a winery that has long had a reputation for good wine at a reasonable price, Conway is not emphasizing expensive specialty wines, but good wines at modest prices.

L'ECOLE NO 41

41 Lowden School Road
P.O. Box 111
Lowden, Washington 99360
(509) 525-0940

Wine Production
3,000 cases

Vineyards
none

First Vintage
1983

Leading Wines
Merlot, Semillon

A vibrant, silver-haired couple with a wry wit and self-effacing humor, Baker and Jean Ferguson are cut from a different mold. A retired bank president, Baker Ferguson introduces his wife as L'Ecole's winemaker and CEO—chief executive officer, himself as president and CTO—chief talking officer. L'Ecole 41 specializes in two Bordeaux grape varieties, Merlot and Semillon.

For their retirement home—and winery, the Fergusons bought a large frame building that once housed classrooms and offices for School District 41—thus the winery name. For their label design, the Fergusons held a contest among all their nieces, nephews, and cousins under the sixth grade. The winning design effectively captures the winery's theme.

The Fergusons make their home on the building's third floor, the second floor houses the tasting room and public area, and the bottom floor, the winery. A restaurant, Barbara's 41, is also located in the winery. Barbara Mastin was formerly owner and chef of a highly acclaimed restaurant in California's wine country. Barbara's 41 is open for groups by prior arrangement, (509) 529-1159.

A rich-voiced, articulate, folksy orator, Baker Ferguson has a deep sense of history, and a sense of his roots in the Walla Walla Valley. His great-grandfather, a Washington pioneer, founded the oldest bank in Washington. In the modern era, winegrowing in the Walla Walla Valley is only just beginning, but Ferguson's research shows that the Walla Walla Valley was among the earliest wine-growing areas in the Northwest.

According to Ferguson, winegrowing in the Walla Walla Valley may have predated wine-growing in California's Napa Valley. Ferguson has identified three earlier periods of Walla Walla Valley winegrowing. Like other early winegrow-ing efforts in the Northwest, grape cultural prac-tices, winemaking, and timing did little to insure the continuance of the industry.

Ferguson hopes the time is now right. The Fergusons and the rest of the new wave of upstart Walla Walla winemakers are at the beginning of a winegrowing renaissance. The Walla Walla vine has lengthy roots and a promising future.

LEONETTI CELLAR

1321 School Avenue
Walla Walla, Washington 99362
(509) 525-1428

Wine Production
1,000 cases

Vineyards
1 acre

Year First Planted
1978

First Vintage
1978

Leading Wines
Cabernet Sauvignon, Merlot

Leonetti Cellar is one of Washington's easternmost winegrowing estates. Owned and operated by Gary and Nancy Figgins, Leonetti Cellar has a lengthy heritage. Figgins' grandfather, an Italian immigrant, settled in the Walla Walla Valley, growing grapes and making wines for family use. In the modern winegrowing era, Fig-gins opened the first winery in the Walla Walla Valley.

For a time, Figgins made wine from grapes grown on the original vineyard site, supplemented by grapes grown elsewhere in the Columbia Valley. The historic family vineyard is no longer a source of grapes, but Figgins tends a tiny one acre Merlot vineyard adjacent to his winery, rely-ing still on select growers in the Columbia Valley for most of his grape supply.

Figgins once made a Riesling, since discontinued, in favor of his fundamental mission—red wine. Figgins released Leonetti's first Cabernet from the 1978 vintage, and immediately gained recognition in major regional and national wine judgings. Leonetti's other red grape, Merlot, has had similar success. The wines are made in a ripe, moderate acid, fairly high alcohol style, with lengthy vatting to extract the most from the grape, and lengthy barrel aging to pick up additional tannins and complexity.

Except for the yearly September release of new wines, Leonetti is not open to the public, and the wines are available only locally, and in limited markets.

LOST MOUNTAIN WINERY

730 Lost Mountain Road
Sequim, Washington 98382
(206)683-5229

Wine Production
425 cases

Vineyards
none

First Vintage
1981

Leading Wines
Merlot, Cabernet Sauvignon

A research chemist, Romeo Conca revived his Italian family tradition and began making homemade wine, a practice learned as a child from his father. Upon retirement, Conca started his own tiny commercial winery near the town of Sequim, on Washington's Olympic Peninsula.

Conca makes only red wines. The Cabernet Sauvignon and Merlot are made from Washington grapes. Conca brings in Zinfandel and Petite Syrah grapes from California for his blended wines as well as his single varietal bottlings. An unusual Lost Mountain Red wine is made from a blend of Zinfandel, Petite Syrah, and Muscat. All Lost Mountain's wines are make in a robust, high alcohol, full-bodied style.

Lost Mountain also releases wines in a special Poetry Series. Each is a blended red wine featuring a poem by a local poet. The wines have a dominant grape, like Pinot Noir or Petite Syrah, complimented by the addition of other grapes for interest and complexity.

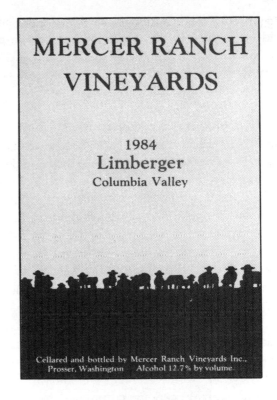

MERCER RANCH VINEYARDS

H.C. 74, Box 401
Prosser, Washington 99350
(509) 894-4741

Wine Production
1,000 cases

Vineyards
132 acres

Year First Planted
1972

First Vintage
1984

Leading Wines
Limberger, Cabernet Sauvignon

One of Washington's earliest commercial wine grape growers in the modern era, Don and Linda Mercer opened their own winery after more than a decade of grape growing. The Mercers still sell most of their grapes to other wineries, reserving enough of the harvest for their own small winery.

Although the winery has a Prosser mailing address, Mercer Ranch is actually located outside the Yakima Valley, on the other side of the Horse Heaven Hills. The winery and vineyards are five miles north of the Columbia River, 18 miles west of the town of Paterson.

The Mercer family has deep roots in the region. Until 1952, the Mercers were sheep ranchers. The original ranch, started in the late 1800s by Don Mercer's grandfather, is located just east of the present site. For decades, the family moved the sheep by rail to their summer range in Montana, then back again in the fall to the winter range along the Columbia River. For the long trip, the Mercers herded the sheep to the town of Whitcomb, on the Columbia River, loaded the sheep in stock cars, the wagons and trucks on flatcars, and the sheepherders and range hands in an old coach car. The Mercer's sheep ranching heritage is depicted on the Mercer Ranch label.

Steve Redford is Mercer's winemaker. Both Redford and Mercer are committed to Washington red wine—and Mercer Ranch makes only red wine, focusing on two varieties, Cabernet Sauvignon and Limberger. Mercer's Cabernet comes from four vineyards located within a half mile of each other. Each vineyard, according to Mercer, produces distinctly different wines. Mercer blends some of the Cabernets from the different vineyards, and releases some as individual vineyard bottlings.

Mercer Ranch currently has the largest Limberger vineyard in North America—12 acres. An uncommon grape variety, Limberger is becoming very popular in Washington. Acreage throughout the state promises to increase dramatically as planting wood becomes more readily available. Washington State University researchers Dr. Walter Clore and George Carter were early advocates of the grape. In the late 1960s, Mercer tasted some of their experimental wines and became an advocate as well.

Mercer's Limberger is fermented with about 20 percent whole grape clusters, emphasizing the variety's inherent fruity character. The wine is left on the skins for a week after it has fermented dry, then aged in a combination of French oak and neutral American oak barrels. About three percent Cabernet Sauvignon is blended into the Limberger. According to Mercer, three percent Cabernet added to the wine's complexity, but a test blend of five percent only detracted from the Limberger character instead of adding the desired complexity. "We were surprised," says Mercer, "that such small amounts made those differences in the wine." Mercer's Limberger is a darkly colored wine with good fruit extract—a wine made to age and develop in the bottle.

Mercer Ranch's focus on red wines is timely. The winedrinking world is finally acknowledging Washington as a premium red wine region. Washington's best wines may well be red. Mercer and Redford are anxious to furnish more of the proof.

Don Mercer.

1984 WASHINGTON
GAMAY BEAUJOLAIS
MONT ELISE VINEYARDS

PRODUCED AND BOTTLED BY MONT ELISE VINEYARDS, BINGEN, WA ALC. 11.5 % BY VOL.

MONT ELISE VINEYARDS

315 West Steuben
P.O. Box 28
Bingen, Washington 98605
(509) 493-3001

Wine Production
7,000 cases

Vineyards
55 acres

Year First Planted
1972
(test plot planted in 1964)

First Vintage
1975

Leading Wines
Gewurztraminer, Riesling, Sparkling Pinot Noir Brut

Charles Henderson has been involved with agronomy all his life, and for the past 20 years, has grown grapes in the Columbia River Gorge near the town of Bingen. In the early years of grape growing, Henderson worked closely with Dr. Clore and others from the Irrigated Agricultural Research and Extension Center at Prosser, Washington to evaluate the grape varieties best suited to the Bingen area.

From about 20 experimentally planted grape varieties, Pinot Noir and Gewurztraminer were selected as the best, and in 1972, Henderson planted his vineyard to them. A total of 200 acres of Henderson's property are suitable for wine grapes. Henderson's first wines were marketed under the name Bingen Wine Cellars, but in late 1978, the Hendersons bought out the other winery partners and became sole owners, changing the winery's name to Mont Elise Vineyards.

The Cascade Mountains and the Columbia River Gorge are remarkable geologic phenomena, and their climatic influence is no less profound. The Mont Elise vineyards are just east of where the Columbia River Gorge cuts through the line of the Cascade Range. The Cascades block the easterly flow of marine air, making much of eastern Washington a desert while leaving western Washington moist, temperate, and lushly vegetated. The Columbia River Gorge is a passageway along which the two dramatically different climates converge and collide. Understandably, radical climatic changes occur within relatively few miles. Parts of the gorge are characterized by this tempestuous mixing of climates.

In terms of the commonly used heat summation method of climate measurement, heat units at the Mont Elise vineyards range from 2,000 to 2,100 a year. A short distance west, and heat units measure 1,800 or less; a short distance east, and heat units measure 2,900 or higher. Thus, the Mont Elise growing climate is very tightly defined, one of the most highly localized grape growing climates in the Northwest. Climates, however, are much more complex than the measure of relative heat units. Henderson points out that Bingen receives slightly fewer heat units than growing areas in Oregon's Willamette Valley, yet Bingen grapes generally harvest one to two Brix higher in any given year.

Bingen is not troubled by frosts, but winters can be very cold. Henderson protects his vines by promoting deep root growth. The clay soil in Henderson's vineyard runs eight to twenty-five feet deep. The vines are not irrigated, and even new vines receive only one pail of water at planting. Although the young vines do not produce fruit as rapidly as they would with irrigation, their winter hardiness is increased. For reasons of grape quality as well as vine strength, the vines are limited to an average yield of 3½ tons an acre.

During the infamous severe winter following the 1978 harvest, the vines suffered little. Except for Gewurztraminer which is cane pruned, the vines are cordon pruned as is the practice in the Columbia Valley.

In 1985, Henderson's son, Charles Jr., completed his studies in enology at U. C. Davis and returned to Mont Elise to assume the winemaking duties, allowing Charles Sr. to devote more attention to the expanded vineyard operations. Mont Elise has been shifting focus in recent years, and that process is accelerating with the return of Charles Jr.

In accordance with market interest, Mont Elise is shifting emphasis more to white wines. Fully 90 percent of Mont Elise's production is now white. The principal red wine, Gamay Beaujolais, is made in a light, fruity style with slight residual sweetness. Largely replacing red Pinot Noir, a bottle fermented Brut-style sparkling Pinot Noir is Mont Elise's new flagship wine. The sparkling wine will play an increasingly important role at Mont Elise, eventually comprising a substantial portion of the winery's production. The Hendersons' expansion plans call for a 25,000 case winery by the end of the decade.

MOUNT BAKER VINEYARDS

4298 Mount Baker Highway
P. O. Box 626
Deming, Washington 98244
(206) 592-2300

Grape Wine Production
12,000 cases

Fruit And Berry Wine Production
500 cases

Vineyards
25 acres

Year First Planted
1977

First Vintage
1982

Leading Wines
Madeleine Angevine, Gewurztraminer,
Chardonnay, Okanogan Riesling,

Washington has two distinct climates. West of the Cascade Mountain Range, the marine climate is characterized by temperate summers, moderate winters, and frequent clouds and rain. East of the Cascades, the climate is cooler in the winter and much warmer in the summer. The skies are frequently cloudless, and there is little rain.

Al Stratton and Jim Hildt, tying dormant canes after pruning.

Although the first premium grape wineries in the modern era were located in metropolitan areas west of the Cascade Mountains, virtually all the grapes were grown east of the Cascades in Washington's vast Columbia Valley. The Columbia Valley will always remain the state's biggest winegrowing region, but western Washington's cool, temperate, winegrowing climate insures a niche for a unique range of wines.

Al Stratton, founder of Mount Baker Vineyards, and Jim Hildt, horticulturist and partner in the winery, are major proponents of western Washington winegrowing. A retired military physician, Stratton became involved with research projects at Washington State University's Research and Extension Unit at Mount Vernon, Washington. When the time came to make wine from the experimentally grown grapes, the research center's horticulturist, Bob Norton, turned to Stratton. The Mount Vernon area, averaging about 1,300 heat units during the growing season, is far from the best grape growing climate in western Washington, but Stratton was impressed that good quality wine could be made even in this very cool area.

Many areas west of the Cascades are far better suited to growing grapes. The site of Stratton's own vineyards is in one such area. The vineyard is located 11½ miles east of Bellingham, Washington, in a localized climate a quarter mile wide

and two miles long. Even though the vineyards are on the valley floor, nighttime thermal air currents keep the vines frost free during the growing season, a season that lasts from 210 to 240 days, longer than the growing season in most Columbia Valley vineyards.

Stratton's site averages approximately 2,200 heat units during the growing season. Heat units are by no means the only factor in choosing a grape growing area, but they are an important indicator. Stratton's site is quite warm for western Washington. The heat units are almost as high as some of the Columbia Valley's cooler growing sites, though Straton's site has more frequent cloud cover, warmer nights, and less intensely hot days.

Many of the grape varieties that grow best and produce the best wine in western Washington are not the same as Washington's Columbia Valley grape varieties. Mount Baker works with western Washington Gewurztraminer and Chardonnay, but Madeleine Angevine, Okanogan Riesling, and Muller-Thurgau, are the major varieties.

Madeleine Angevine is a French vinifera variety bred in the Loire Valley in the 1850s. It is a cross of two older vinifera varieties, Precoce de Malingre and Madeleine Royale.

A traditional Canadian wine grape, Okanogan Riesling was brought to the New World by Hungarian immigrants, and named after a Canadian Valley. A grape of mysterious origin, Okanogan Riesling is believed by many to be an interspecific hybrid and not a true vinifera variety. Because Okanogan Riesling's grape solids can contribute off flavors to the wine, Straton centrifuges the juice before fermentation, ferments the wine in four to five days at about 68 degrees, then centrifuges the wine again. With careful and correct winemaking technique, Okanogan Riesling makes a good wine, and Straton has been very successful in bringing out the best of the grape.

Muller-Thurgau is one of the most widely planted varieties in Germany. Straton makes the Muller-Thurgau in a Riesling-like style with some residual sweetness. Except for Riesling, Gewurztraminer, and Chardonnay, which have sometimes been made totally or partially from Columbia Valley grapes, all Mount Baker wines are made from grapes grown in western Washington. The most recent releases of Gewurztraminer and Chardonnay have been made entirely from western Washington grapes.

Like Oregon, and unlike most of California and Washington's Columbia Valley, Mount Baker's vines are cane pruned rather than cordon pruned, a more involved pruning method common in much of Europe, and more suitable to cooler climates. Soil is important. Most of Stratton's vineyard is a sandy alluvial soil, but a very small section is heavier and more clay-like. The vines planted in this section are more prone to excess vegetative growth, and the grapes ripen five to seven days later.

Of the more familiar grape varieties, Stratton believes that Pinot Noir will make a flavorful rose in cool years, and a Burgundian-style red wine in warmer years. Stratton is particularly enthused about the prospects of Chardonnay. In the western United States, except for pest resistance, there is little interest in specialized rootstocks, but growers in Europe's cooler climates work extensively with different rootstocks in conjunction with various grape varieties to bring out the best in the vine according to soil type and climatic conditions. Stratton is experimenting with different rootstocks for his Chardonnay, a variety he feels will benefit considerably from rootstock selection.

Cool fermentation temperatures and crisp, fruity, white wines are the rule for Washington winemaking. Mount Baker bucks this rule. Stratton believes that long, cool, fermentation temperatures leave an undesirable yeastiness in the wine. Stratton ferments all his white wines at about 68 degrees, cool enough, in his view, to preserve the fruit of the grape without a simplistic character and yeasty taste. As a result, Mount Baker's white wines are less immediately fruity, but more rounded and fuller than the Washington norm.

Stratton's experimentation extends beyond winegrowing. Some wineries flavor wines with oak chips as an expedient, either because the experimental wood they wish to test has not cured long enough to cooper into barrels, or is not physically suitable to cooper into barrels, or, more often, simply to avoid the expense of oak barrels.

Stratton's perspective is different. In his opinion, red wines may benefit from the controlled oxidation that takes place in wood barrels, but white wines suffer from such treatment. Stratton prefers to keep white wines in stainless steel, adding oak chips or oak extract to the tank if oak character is desired. He goes further in his assessment of oaks, suggesting that the denser harder heartwood is preferable for red wine while the softer sapwood is milder, marrying best with white wine.

More than two decades ago, Stratton planted several European oak species on his property. The trees have matured enough to thin, and now provide an abundant source of oak chips for his extracts. According to Stratton, the red and black oaks are too porous for cooperage, but their unique character can be explored by making extracts from them.

Including the heartwood and sapwood, Stratton has experimented with 14 different oaks. Stratton uses several of the extracts to achieve different characteristics in his wines, but he relies most on two species, *Quercus rober* and *Quercus garryana* (the native Northwest variety more commonly known as Oregon white oak).

Stratton describes Mount Baker Vineyards as research oriented, a good thing, since all of Washington's winegrowing research funds are directed east of the Cascades, to the state's agribusiness heartland. At this stage of western Washington winegrowing, combining research with a commercial enterprise is almost a necessity. Well equipped for the task, Mount Baker Vineyards is broadening the scope of the Washington wine industry, and expanding the horizons of wine appreciation with unique grape varieties and wine styles.

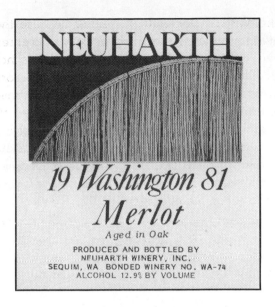

NEUHARTH

19 *Washington* 81
Merlot
Aged in Oak

PRODUCED AND BOTTLED BY
NEUHARTH WINERY, INC.
SEQUIM, WA BONDED WINERY NO. WA-74
ALCOHOL 12.9% BY VOLUME

NEUHARTH WINERY

148 Still Road
Sequim, Washington 98382
(206) 683-9652 or 683-3706

Wine Production
2,200 cases

Vineyards
½ acre

Year First Planted
1979

First Vintage
1979

Leading Wines
Chardonnay, Cabernet Sauvignon

A retired grape grower from California's northern San Joaquin Valley, Eugene Neuharth and his wife Maria moved to Sequim, on Washington's Olympic Peninsula, in 1973. In 1979, the Neuharths planted 33 different grape varieties, mostly French-American hybrids, in two small experimental vineyards. The Olympic Peninsula is Washington's rainiest region, but Sequim's unusual climate, situated in highly localized rain shadow, is one of the driest in the western part of the state.

Born on his mother's and father's vineyard in the Lodi area of California, and living and working on that same vineyard all his life until his move to Washington, grape growing is a fundamental part of Neuharth's fabric. If Neuharth finds premium grapes ideally suited to to the Sequim growing climate, he will expand his experimental vineyards.

In the meantime, grapes from Neuharth's experimental vineyards are used in his less expensive proprietary blends. Premium vinifera wines from Columbia Valley grapes grown east of the Cascade Mountains are Neuharth's principal focus. All Neuharth's premium wines are made in a dry style to go with food.

PACIFIC CREST WINE CELLARS

1326 Sixth Street
Marysville, Washington 98270
(206) 653-3925

Wine Production
1,500 cases

Vineyards
none

First Vintage
1985

Leading Wines
Riesling

Most Washington wineries regard Riesling as a grape for cash-flow wine, a grape that can quickly be made into wine and released to the market. Gary Graves, Pacific Crest's owner and winemaker, releases his own Riesling soon after the vintage as well, but he regards the grape differently. Riesling is his only wine. Says Graves, "Most Washington wineries are not putting in the time and care to make the best possible Riesling. Other wines get a lot of attention, but because Riesling can be sold almost immediately after the vintage, it is regarded as a money maker, a wine to make cheaply and sell quickly."

Although his winery is small, Graves chose not to economize on his grape press. "I could have bought twice as big a plate press for half the cost of the bladder press I did get, but the plate press crushes seeds and extracts more of the astringent phenolics." With the bladder press, Graves presses for a moderate yield of just under 150 gallons a ton. Some wineries use pectic enzymes to get more juice from the grapes. Graves thinks that the enzymes are fine with some grape varieties, but not Riesling. In his view, the enzymes cause a phenolic astringency in the Riesling.

When the grapes come in, Graves crushes and presses the grapes, then chills the juice for about five days to let the grape solids settle out. The Riesling is fermented with an Alsatian yeast noted for producing highly fruity qualities in the wine. With his floating lid tanks, air space can be adjusted to almost zero, so less sulfur dioxide is needed for protection.

Graves planned to make twice as much wine for his first vintage, but the grapes from one of the growers were poor quality, and Graves rejected the shipment. Now, Graves relies solely on Roza Vineyard grapes from the Yakima Valley.

Graves plans to expand to a few other grape varieties in the coming years. For now, he is content to focus his efforts on quality Riesling.

1984
WHITE RIESLING
YAKIMA VALLEY
WASHINGTON

ALCOHOL 9.5% BY VOLUME
PRODUCED FOR PONTIN DEL ROZA, PROSSER, WASHINGTON.
BOTTLED BY PONTIN DEL ROZA, LTD.,
GRANDVIEW, WASHINGTON. BW WA 99.

PONTIN DEL ROZA

Route 1, Box 1129
Prosser, Washington 99350
(509) 786-4449

Wine Production
5,000 cases

Vineyards
15 acres

Year First Planted
1979

First Vintage
1984

Leading Wines
Riesling, Chenin Blanc

In the 1920s, an Italian immigrant, Angelo Pontin, planted grapes in the Cottonwood Canyon area west of Yakima. In the 1950s, Angelo's son, Nesto, and daughter-in-law, Delores, started a farm in the Yakima Valley near the community of Prosser. In the 1980s, Nesto and Delores opened a winery, Pontin del Roza. Son Scott is general manager.

The winery and vineyards are located along the Roza Canal, a major irrigation system that opened up much of the Yakima Valley to farming. They are the Pontins of the Roza—in Italian, Pontin del Roza, the winery name.

Supplementing their own small Riesling vineyard, the Pontins buy grapes from other growers along the Roza. The wine is made at Coventry Vale, a custom crushing facility in the Yakima Valley. Kay Simon, formerly winemaker at Chateau Ste. Michelle, is consulting enologist. Increasingly, Scott Pontin will assume a greater role in the winemaking.

The Pontins specialize in white wines, principally Riesling, Chenin Blanc, and Chardonnay. The wines for wood aging are kept at the Pontins' tasting room. Eventually, the tasting room will be expanded to include winemaking facilities.

In 1975, the Pontin family returned to northern Italy and visited the original family vineyards that Scott's grandfather, Angelo, knew as a child. The Pontins of the Roza are carrying on a long family tradition—growing grapes and making wine.

PRESTON WINE CELLARS

502 East Vineyard Drive
Pasco, Washington 99301
(509) 545-1990

Wine Production
65,000 cases

Vineyards
181 acres

Year First Planted
1972

First Vintage
1976

Leading Wines
Fume Blanc, Riesling, Chenin Blanc,
Chardonnay, Desert Gold

The Snake and Columbia Rivers converge in the southern Columbia Valley forming a broad V-shaped section of land, geographically defining one of the Columbia Valley's major grape growing areas. In the southern center of this V-shaped area of land, just five miles north of the city of Pasco, is Preston Wine Cellars, the Northwest's largest family-owned winery. Just off Highway 395, a large 48 foot sign marks the entrance to the winery estate. And Preston is a winery estate in the fullest sense, with the winery and family home set amidst the vines.

A moderately large winery, Preston Wine Cellars retains a family-owned flavor. Preston's son Brent designed and built the tasting room bar and furniture. Daughter Cathy is public relations manager. Winemaker since 1984, non-family member Thomas Sans Souci first joined Preston Wine Cellars in 1980 as assistant winemaker, but most of the other key operations are run by the family.

For those accustomed to the dramatic grandeur of lushly green mountains and snowcapped peaks, the southern Columbia Valley looks stark, empty, and desolate. But the vastness of the desert flatlands and rolling hills commands its own grandeur. In the more lushly green areas of the Northwest, so much visual stimuli continuously bombard the viewer that sometimes nothing really stands out—nothing is really seen. In the southern Columbia Valley, every sensory happening stands forth and commands attention. The furrowed desert fields are, to some, like a Zen garden on a vast scale.

But Bill Preston's cultural base is quite different. A native of the area, Preston is a self-made man in the American tradition. Preston retired from his irrigation and farm implement business to plant one of Washington's first commercial premium grape vineyards in the modern era, followed soon after by the Preston winery. Preston's vineyard estate is planted to 11 varieties: Chardonnay, Riesling, Cabernet Sauvignon, Pinot Noir, Sauvignon Blanc, Chenin Blanc, Gewurztraminer, Merlot, Gamay Beaujolais, Muscat of Alexandria, and Royalty.

The southern Columbia Valley is one of the warmer growing areas in the state. Preston is convinced that this area produces the finest wines in the Northwest. He characterizes the area as a huge natural greenhouse. The desert soil is too dry and sandy to support much natural vegetation, yet as a viticultural medium, it is highly receptive to the means and ends of winegrowing technology. Precise moisture control is achieved through irrigation; desired nutrient balance is maintained by adding fertilizers to the neutral

Ready for the hectic harvest.

After the grapes are crushed, the stems are carried away for disposal.

sandy soil; and the warm sunny climate means there is little chance rain will fall at inopportune times.

This is not to say the area is without problems. Unlike a greenhouse, Preston's vineyards, as others in the Columbia Valley, have been subjected to frosts and winter freezing that severely damage the vines. A good portion of Preston's first plantings was destroyed the following winter. The cold is a problem most winters, but even in this context, Preston sees the advantages of the region. The growing climate fosters vigorous growth for replanted vines, and rapid recovery for those that are damaged.

The climate is well suited to a broad range of grape varieties, and individual sections of Preston's vineyard can be cooled by a computerized overhead sprinkler system. *Botrytis cinerea*, the mold responsible for special sweet wines, is naturally occurring, and is encouraged when desirable, and prevented when not. Vineyard yield can be restricted for varietal intensity, or increased to levels rivaling California's Central Valley while maintaining adequate sugar-acid balance and varietal profile.

Chardonnay and Fume Blanc, both fermented in stainless steel and aged in French oak, are Preston's leading wines. Gewurztraminer and Riesling predominate in Desert Gold, a popular, moderately sweet, proprietary blend. Preston also makes a limited release of a bottle fermented sparkling wine. In addition to the winery's premium Preston Wine Cellars label, Preston releases a second, inexpensive line of wines, Columbia River Cellars.

The Preston tasting room is directly over the winery. Its large windows and an open deck provide a panoramic view of the estate vineyard, small picnic park, amphitheater for outdoor performances, and the expansive desert countryside. The tasting room has seating for 60 visitors, and a gift shop for wine related items. Some of Preston's specialty wines such as botrytised Riesling and botrytised Sauvignon Blanc are available only at the tasting room. A self-guided tour allows visitors to look at various parts of the winery through viewing areas that overlook winery operations below.

QUARRY LAKE

2505 Commercial Ave., Suite C
Pasco, Washington 99301
(509) 547-2724

Wine Production
18,500 cases

Vineyards
110 acres

Year First Planted
1971

First Vintage
1985

Leading Wines
Sauvignon Blanc, Chardonnay, Cabernet Sauvignon

In 1927, the Balcom family of Grandview and the Moe family of Ellensburg formed a farming partnership. More than half a century and several generations later, the partnership, now a corporation, continues to prosper. In 1965, Balcom and Moe pioneered farming just north of Pasco, in of one of the last segments of the vast Columbia Basin Irrigation Project. Lush agricultural crops replaced the sagebrush. Balcom and Moe grow many crops on their 3,000 acre farm, including potatoes, cherries, apples—and wine grapes.

Maurice Balcom, one of the original founding partners, believed that Balcom and Moe could produce fine premium wine grapes. In 1971, Balcom and Moe planted the first commercial vinifera vineyard in the area. Maurice's son, Maury, went to Fresno State in California to study enology and viticulture. Maury received a degree in enology, and almost a degree in viticulture, save for the required courses on raisin and table grapes which he decided to forego.

Today it seems difficult to believe, but scarcely more than a decade ago, the viability of Washington's wine industry was far from proven, only a few wineries existed, and few or none were interested in buying more grapes. For the first few years, Balcom and Moe had difficulty selling their grapes. The first grape crops were finally purchased by Oregon wineries.

Change came rapidly for Washington's wine industry, and Balcom and Moe's grapes were soon in much demand. From the beginning, Balcom and Moe had planned to open a winery. In 1985, the company fulfilled the original intent, and crushed Balcom and Moe's first commercial vintage. The Quarry Lake name is taken from a lake formed in a depleted gravel quarry located along highway 395, just north of Pasco. Balcom and Moe purchased the lake and property, and eventually plan to plant more vineyards and build a new winery on the site.

Maury Balcom is currently making Quarry Lake's wines at the superbly equipped Langguth winery in Mattawa. The wines are field crushed in the vineyard, fermented at Mattawa, transported to Quarry Lake's winery in Pasco for barrel aging, and shipped back to Mattawa for bottling. Balcom travels to Mattawa twice a week throughout the year to oversee his wines.

Balcom believes that their vineyard produces especially good Chardonnay, Cabernet Sauvignon, and Merlot, and he is focusing his efforts accordingly. Unusual in the Northwest, in part because of their expense, Quarry Lake's red wines are fermented in special rotary fermentation tanks.

When red wine is fermented, a cap of pulp and skins floats to the surface, and must be resubmerged and mixed back into the fermenting wine. The fermenting wine is usually pumped back over the cap, or else the cap is punched down into the wine. With the rotary fermenters, the entire tank turns continuously like a cement mixer, and a central auger further helps mix and macerate the pulp and skins. So far, Balcom is very pleased with the results.

.Balcom and Moe recently planted a new, small, Cabernet Sauvignon vineyard. The vine rows are planted on a conventional ten foot spacing, but only three feet apart between each vine within the row, instead of the usual six or more foot spacing. With 1,450 vines per acre, double or more the usual number of vines, each vine does not need to produce as much fruit to achieve the same yield per acre. With a denser vine spacing, Balcom hopes to achieve lower pH, more intensely flavored, better quality fruit—and better wines.

For a decade and a half, Balcom and Moe has been waiting for the "right" time to start a winery. Other wineries have been been making fine wines from Balcom and Moe's grapes. Now Maury Balcom has his turn.

QUILCEDA CREEK VINTNERS

5226 Machias Road
Snohomish, Washington 98290
(206) 568-2389

Wine Production
1,000 cases

Vineyards
none

First Vintage
1979

Leading Wines
Cabernet Sauvignon

Consulting enologist for the tiny Quilceda Creek Vintners is none other than Andre Tchelistcheff, the legendary California winemaker. It so happens that Alex Golitzin, Quilceda Creek's owner and winemaker, is Tchelistcheff's nephew. Since 1946, when Golitzin came came to America from France, he remembers frequent visits with his uncle, and afternoons playing in the Beaulieu vineyards. A chemical engineering graduate from the University of California at Berkeley, in 1972 Golitzin moved to Snohomish, a small community not far from Seattle. At about that time,

Alex Golitzin.

Tchelistcheff was consulting regularly with nearby Chateau Ste. Michelle. At Tchelistcheff's encouragement, Golitzin experimented with winemaking, and ultimately, started a small commercial winery of his own.

The association with Tchelistcheff is notable, but Golitzin is an exceptional winemaker in his own right. After a decade of aging, Golitzin's early experimental Cabernets have developed exceptionally well, showing fine breed and complexity — and the capacity for further aging. Employed full time as a chemical engineer, and without a large volume of wine to market, Golitzin is not tied to the necessities of immediate cash flow and pushing product. "We are a bit perfectionist here," says Golitzin, "but if you start letting go of a small detail here and there, soon those small concessions add up and you find that a measure of quality has been lost."

Fermented in the low 80s, the Cabernet is punched down by hand two to three times a day. Prior to completion of fermentation, the wine is pulled off the skins and put into barrels. To insure that none of the wine's character is stripped away, the Cabernet is never filtered, rarely fined, and then only with egg whites. Quilceda Creek Cabernet is not released until four years after the vintage.

Golitzin's Cabernet style is gradually evolving. The first Cabernets were made from grapes grown at Otis Vineyards in the Yakima Valley, one of the state's oldest commercial Cabernet Sauvignon vineyards. After several vintages of buying grapes from Kiona Vineyards as well as Otis, Golitzin made the switch to the Kiona grapes. Located at the warmer far eastern end of the Yakima Valley, grapes from the Kiona Vineyard ripen sooner and yield wines with a fuller, less angular texture, though sometimes without the pronounced aromatics associated with the Otis grapes. The first Cabernets were aged primarily in very old American oak barrels, but Golitzin began fazing in French Nevers oak barrels with the '81 vintage.

Production from the first commercial vintage was a mere 150 cases, and still remains at no more than 1,000 cases a year. Quilceda Creek is open to the public by appointment only.

REDFORD CELLARS

H.C. 74, Box 401
Prosser, Washington 99350
(509) 894-4741

Seattle Office:
4035 8th N.E.
Seattle, Washington 98105
(206) 633-2249

Wine Production
800 cases

Vineyards
none

First Vintage
1978

Leading Wines
Cabernet Sauvignon, Merlot

Steve Redford has been making Cabernet Sauvignon and Merlot under his Redford Cellars label since 1978. Redford first made his wines at his brother's winery in Oregon. There Redford worked as Amity's lab technician and cellarman. Like his brother Myron, Steve Redford is ardently dedicated to Northwest red wines. Complementing his brother's focus on the Burgundian variety, Pinot Noir, Steve directs his focus toward the Bordeaux varieties, Cabernet Sauvignon and Merlot.

In spite of having inconsistent access to quality grapes, Redford has earned an excellent reputation for his craftsmanship with Cabernet Sauvignon and Merlot. While at Amity, Redford made wines from both Oregon and Washington grapes. Redford's 1979 Cabernet Sauvignon and Merlot from Oregon grapes remain benchmarks for what can be produced from Willamette Valley fruit in a warm vintage—but Oregon's Willamette Valley is not the place to go to make consistently fine Cabernet Sauvignon and Merlot year after year.

Most vintages in Oregon's Willamette Valley are too cool for the best quality wines from the Bordeaux varieties. For consistently good Cabernet Sauvignon and Merlot grapes, Redford turned to Washington's Columbia Valley. Now winemaker for Washington's Mercer Ranch Vineyards, Redford continues to release Cabernet and Merlot under his own label.

Redford's wines are aged mostly in older, neutral American oak barrels, with a few newer French oak barrels for a touch of oak character. The emphasis is on the flavors of the wine, not the taste of the oak.

Redford's Cabernet Sauvignon and Merlot each have some of the other grape in the blend. Says Redford, "I really like Bordeauxs. I don't blend Merlot into the Cabernet Sauvignon just to soften the wine. I don't like that concept. I blend to make a more complex wine."

1978
Salishan Vineyards
Washington
Pinot Noir

PRODUCED & BOTTLED BY PONZI VINEYARDS,
BEAVERTON, OREGON BW-OR-56

ALCOHOL by VOLUME 12%

SALISHAN VINEYARDS

Route 2, Box 8
La Center, Washington 98629
(206) 263-2713

Wine Production
2,000 cases

Vineyards
12 acres

Year First Planted
1971

First Vintage
1976

Leading Wines
Pinot Noir, Dry Riesling, Chardonnay

In 1971, Joan and Lincoln Wolverton planted 11 acres of grapes near the town of La Center in southwest Washington, and became the first winegrowers in western Washington to focus on vinifera grapes. The first wines were released in 1976, but until 1982, when Joan Wolverton assumed winemaking duties, the wines were made for Salishan by other northwest wineries.

The first years were not easy. The Wolvertons now live at the vineyard site, and Joan devotes full time to the vineyard and winery, but at first, the Wolvertons both had full-time jobs in Seattle, commuting to the vineyard on weekends for the back breaking pleasure of tending 9,000 vines. In the first six years, a third of the vines were lost to deer and rabbit. Closer to Mt. St. Helens than any other winery, one of the 1980

eruptions dropped ash on Salishan's vineyard, scouring away the pollen. Bloom and berry set were poor, reducing the 1980 grape crop, but making the wines more concentrated. In 1981, the destructive form of botrytis destroyed nearly all the crop.

Experience has brought accommodation and innovation. The Wolvertons put plastic mesh rabbit guards around the young vines, simultaneously protecting the vines and eliminating the need for stakes to keep them growing straight. The soil, a Hessom clay loam, retains more moisture than sandier soils, delaying growth in the spring, but to compensate, the Wolvertons cover the new vine rows with black plastic film. The black plastic absorbs heat, keeps down weeds, and controls water evaporation. The space between the vine rows is left exposed, and the clay loam soil lets the moisture from rain disperse laterally underneath the black plastic. Irrigation for the young vines, otherwise a necessity, is rarely needed. According to the Wolvertons, new vines pro-

Joan Wolverton — plastic mesh supports the young vines and protects them from rabbits.

184

duce a good grape crop after only two years, instead of the usual four or five years.

The Salishan climate is neither like the hot, dry, Columbia Valley growing climate east of the Cascade Mountains, nor like the wetter, cooler, western Washington growing climates situated further north. Salishan's climate is most like that of Oregon's northern Willamette Valley, and like the Willamette Valley, Pinot Noir is the leading grape variety. Slightly cooler than the northern Willamette, the Pinot Noir typically ripens a week later at Salishan, a disadvantage in cooler years, but a qualitative advantage in warmer years. The climate is excellent for Pinot Noir, and Salishan is virtually the only Washington winery producing consistently successful wines from this difficult varietal.

Nearly two decades ago, Lincoln Wolverton extensively researched meteorological data from Burgundy and Bordeaux, and with the assistance of a computer, generated climatic correlations with potential grape growing sites in the northwest. Salishan Vineyards is the result of his research. The Wolverton's pioneering effort is succeeding. Others are planting grapes, and Clark County now has more than a hundred acres in vine.

SALMON BAY WINERY

430-3 South 96th Street
Seattle, Washington 98108
(206) 763 3633

Wine Production
6,500 cases

Vineyards
none

First Vintage
1982

Leading Wines
Sauvignon Blanc, Chardonnay

Located in the Seattle metropolitan area, the Salmon Bay Winery came into being out of the conversations of Bruce Crabtree, then sommelier at Rosellini's Four-10, a prominent Seattle restaurant, and patrons of the restaurant, Kenneth Rogstad and Bobby Capps.

Formerly known as Vernier Wines, the new Salmon Bay name emerged from a realignment in the winery's focus and approach. Crabtree's family has long been associated with the restaurant industry. At one time, the family owned 26 restaurants in the Pacific Northwest. Drawing upon Crabtree's association with the restaurant trade, Salmon Bay plans to sell much of of their wines through restaurants. Plans also call for a new location in the Seattle metropolitan area, and, eventually, a restaurant in the winery. A new, full-time winemaker will free Crabtree to market the wines.

The close association with food influences Salmon Bay's approach to winemaking. Salmon Bay makes Cabernet Blanc and Riesling with some residual sweetness, but most of the wines are dry, barrel aged whites and reds. French oak is used for aging, but the oak component is not emphasized. The white wines are fermented at a moderately high temperatures to reduce the immediate fruitiness of the grape in favor of restrained complexities.

The Chardonnay begins fermentation in a stainless steel tank at about 65 degrees, then is racked into small stainless steel barrels where the fermentation temperature drops to about 45 to 50 degrees. The Chardonnay is aged in oak puncheons, a slightly larger sized barrel holding about 100 gallons.

Sauvignon Blanc is treated in the same manner. Fermenting the Sauvignon Blanc for a time at a higher temperature moderates the herbaceous character that typifies most Washington renditions of the grape. Before bottling, the Sauvignon Blanc is blended with Semillon, as is done in Bordeaux.

Crabtree says of the name change and shift in focus, "We want to become 'Seattle's winery,' and we wanted a name that was identified with western Washington, with Seattle, and with our local and regional cuisine. Salmon Bay captures that for us."

SNOQUALMIE WINERY

1000 Winery Road
Snoqualmie, Washington 98065
(206) 888-4000 or 392-4000 (Seattle)

Wine Production
40,000 cases

Vineyards
none

First Vintage
1983

Leading Wines
Riesling, Chenin Blanc, Semillon

Winemaker at Chateau Ste. Michelle from 1974 to 1982, Joel Klein left the Northwest's largest winery to start a winery of his own. Klein formed Snoqualmie Winery in 1983. While the Snoqualmie winery was being built, Klein made the first wines at Coventry Vale, a bonded winemaking facility in the Yakima Valley.

Search for a winery site led Klein to a picturesque setting just outside the small city of Snoqualmie, about a half hour drive from Seattle. The winery offers an impressive view of the Snoqualmie Valley, Mount Si, and the Cascade Foothills. One hundred and thirty-five acres of lawn and natural vegetation surround the winery, inviting picnicking and enjoyment of the view. Deer and occasional elk roam the nearby woods.

Impacted by the decline in the lumber industry, the city of Snoqualmie is very supportive of Klein's venture. Bearing the city's name on the label, Snoqualmie Winery draws attention to Snoqualmie's cultural and tourism interests. Snoqualmie sees the winery as another, and important, attraction to the city.

Snoqualmie's historic train depot and the nearby Snoqualmie Falls are two other visitor attractions to the area. The train depot, Snoqualmie Falls, and Snoqualmie Winery can all be reached by taking eastbound exit 27 off I-90. The train depot is on the National Register of Historic Places. Built in 1890, restoration began in 1979, and the depot is again open to the public. A steam locomotive carries passengers on a picturesque ten mile round trip between North Bend, Snoqualmie Falls, and back again to the depot in Snoqualmie.

Organizing and financing the three million dollar winery was a new venturesome step for Klein, but designing the winery was not. Before coming to the Northwest in 1974, Klein helped design and equip California's Geyser Peak Winery. Later, Klein helped design the winemaking facilities at Chateau Ste. Michelle's Woodinville and Paterson wineries.

Klein began his career in chemical engineering, but a project developing specialty chemicals for the wine industry led Klein to change his profession. Klein returned to school at U. C. Davis to study grape growing and wine making. After leaving Davis, Klein worked on the Research and Development Group for Inglenook and Italian Swiss Colony before moving on to Geyser Peak and Chateau Ste. Michelle.

The picturesque Snoqualmie Winery was designed with the tastes and interests of the consumer in mind—and Klein's wines are similarly styled. The white wines are made in the highly popular fresh, fruity style. Most are finished with slight residual sweetness to balance the piquancy of the Washington fruit.

Klein thinks that tastes are gradually changing. Says Klein, "It's my opinion that America's taste for wine is drying out." As tastes change, Snoqualmie Winery will shift its emphasis and style to meet them. Semillon, Chardonnay, Cabernet Sauvignon, and Merlot are Klein's personal favorites, and they are destined to play an increasing role at Snoqualmie in the coming years.

Joel Klein at Snoqualmie's grand opening ceremony.

STATON HILLS
VINEYARD AND WINERY

2290 Gangl Road
Wapato, Washington 98951
(509) 877-2112

1910 Post Alley
Pike Place Market
Seattle, Washington 98101
(206) 443-8084

Wine Production
20,000 cases

Vineyards
16 acres

Year First Planted
1982

First Vintage
1984

Leading Wines
Chenin Blanc, Riesling, Sauvignon Blanc

Leaving the city of Yakima and traveling south and east on I-82, the road and the Yakima River immediately funnel through a narrow constriction formed by the convergence of the Rattlesnake Hills and the Ahtanum Ridge, emerging into the northeasternmost end of the Yakima Valley. The valley immediately opens broadly to the south and west, but the river and highway hug the lower slopes of the Rattlesnake Hills.

On this route, less than ten minutes from Yakima, is one of the Yakima Valley's showcase wineries. Surrounded by the estate vineyard, the winery looks out upon a distant snowcapped Mt. Adams, a dormant volcanic dome just east of Mt. St. Helens.

An attorney, owner David Staton grew tired of Wall Street and New York and moved to San Francisco to become president of a large energy company. Weekend trips to the nearby Napa and Sonoma Valleys spurred Staton's interest in wine. In the early 1970s, seeing an article about the potential of premium wine in Washington state, Staton corresponded with Dr. Walter Clore, the dean of Washington viticulture.

Proceeding cautiously, Staton and his family purchased an apple orchard in the Yakima Valley, and moved to Washington in 1974. The Washington wine industry and Staton's own grape test plots were proving highly successful, and in 1982, Staton purchased the land for his winery and vineyard.

Appointed by two state administrations to the Tree Fruit Research Commission, Staton helped oversee extensive research programs. Staton's interest in research and innovation carry through to his own 16 acre vineyard which features three uncommon trellising systems.

Virtually all Washington grape vines are trained vertically along a single plane. With the traditional method, the upper foliage droops over the lower foliage, shading the grapes and lower leaves from the sun. With all three of Staton's trellising systems, Gable, Tartura, and a modified Double-Guyot, two trunks are trained into an open vertical V-shape with the lateral arms of the vines running along the wires in the vine row. With these systems, the grapes and vine canopy are better and more uniformly exposed to the sun.

All three systems have similarities to the Open Lyre system developed by Carbonneau, in the early 1970s, at the Viticultural Research Station in Bordeaux. Among the theoretical advantages, these systems should produce better quality grapes at higher and more consistent crop levels. Their advantages and disadvantages will emerge more clearly with succeeding vintages.

Staton's vines are planted relatively densely, at more than 1,000 vines per acre, reducing the load that each vine must produce. The closer spacing also crowds the root systems longitudinally, forcing the roots deeper into the soil, adding increased protection for the vine's winter survival. The irrigation pattern is also controlled to force the roots deeper. Yakima Valley soils are usually shallow, but Staton's site, probably a turn in the Yakima River at one time, has soil 35 feet deep.

Staton's vineyard provides the opportunity to evaluate the trellising methods on a commercial scale instead of the few vines and five gallon lots normally associated with such research. The majority of Staton's grapes, however, are purchased from growers throughout the state. Experimentation continues through agreements with other growers, including pruning portions of a vineyard to crop levels above and below the norm to evaluate it's effects on wine quality.

Rob Stuart, formerly with Oregon's Valley View winery, is Staton's winemaker. Charles Ortman, friend and associate of Staton, is consulting enologist. Ortman operates his own winery in California, and has earned a reputation as consultant for many of California's highly regarded premium wineries. In addition to the Staton Hills label, the winery offers a second label, Ridgemont, which often bears an "American" viticultural designation. The Ridgemont wines are made from grapes grown in Oregon, Idaho, and California, as well as Washington.

Chenin Blanc in a Vouvray style is one of Staton Hills' first specialties. Washington Chenin Blanc far exceeds the reputation the grape has in California. Most Washington Chenin Blanc is made similar to Riesling, in a fruity semi-sweet style. Staton Hills' Chenin Blanc harks back to the grape's origins in the Loire Valley of France, and is made in an off-dry style with some oak aging. The balance of sugar, acidity, and oak complement the grape's character, and create a wine that is good within a year of the vintage, but also capable of developing in the bottle.

Most Yakima Valley wineries are not immediately visible from the main highway through the valley. But now, at the head of the valley, a few minutes from the city of Yakima, the prominence of the elegant Staton Hills winery, the estate vineyards, terraced landscape, and gabled trellises clearly announce that the traveler is entering the premium wine country of the Yakima Valley.

For those in the Seattle metropolitan area, Staton Hills has a satellite winery and tasting room in the city's historic Pike Place Market. Director of the winery is noted artist, Sebastian Titus, designer of more than 175 wine labels for American and European wineries. Titus's art is on display in the winery's tasting room.

Rob Stuart explains Staton Hills' special trellising systems.

189

Estate Bottled Washington Wine

STEWART VINEYARDS
1985

COLUMBIA VALLEY

Johannisberg Riesling

WAHLUKE SLOPE

grown, produced and bottled by
Stewart Vineyards, Granger, Washington
Alcohol by volume, 12.0%

STEWART VINEYARDS

Route 3, Box 3578
Sunnyside, Washington 98944
(509) 854-1882

Wine Production
6,500 cases

Vineyards
50 acres

Year First Planted
1968

First Vintage
1983

Leading Wines
Riesling, Chardonnay, Cabernet Sauvignon

A vinifera grape grower since the late 1960s, Dr. George Stewart planted his first vineyard in the Yakima Valley on Harrison Hill near Sunnyside. The Harrison Hill site was once a part of the vineyards owned by William Bridgman, a pioneering vinifera winegrower of the 1930s and 1940s. The old vineyard was planted to less than desirable varieties, so Stewart tore out the old vines and planted the site to Cabernet Sauvignon and other premium grapes.

Stewart was the first grower to plant grapes on the Wahluke Slope of the Columbia River near Priest Rapids Dam. A warm, cold-protected growing site, the Wahluke Slope is one of the Columbia Valley's more promising winegrowing areas. Muscat Canelli, a grape that is easily damaged by cold, thrives on the Wahluke. In vintages

following cold damage, Stewart is sometimes one of the few wineries able to produce Muscat Canelli wine. Stewart has 40 acres planted on the Wahluke, but he owns a total of 150 acres on the slope suitable for vineyards.

Winemaker Mike Januik came to the Stewart winery after completing a Masters degree program in enology from U. C. Davis. According to Januik, grapes from the Wahluke and Yakima Valley are quite similar with relatively subtle differences. In his view, Riesling from the Wahluke has more citrusy/peachy qualities, Yakima Riesling having more floral and apricot characteristics.

Many Washington winemakers release Riesling and other semi-sweet white wines with dissolved carbon dioxide in the wine, a natural occurrence if the wine is bottled cool, and nothing further is done to the wines after a cool fermentation. The carbon dioxide gives the wine a slight refreshing spritziness (bubbles), altering the character of the wine even when the bubbles are scarcely visible. Januik thinks this practice can add to the quality of wines made with some residual sweetness, but only if excessive amounts of carbon dioxide are not left in the wine. His Gewurz-

Winemaker, Mike Januik.

190

traminer and Muscat Canelli are bottled with a tiny amount of dissolved carbon dioxide.

Januik's wine style emphasizes the fruit of the grape. All the white wines are fermented primarily in stainless steel at temperatures no higher than 55 degrees. "You hear talk of the art of making wine," says Januik, "but to me, the art of making wine is deciding the style of wine I want to make, then using my technical skills to achieve it."

PAUL THOMAS WINES

1717 136th Place N.E.
Bellevue, Washington 98005
(206) 747-1008

Grape Wine Production
7,000 cases

Fruit And Berry Wine Production
15,000 cases

Vineyards
none

First Vintage
1979

Leading Wines
Crimson, Riesling, Chenin Blanc

On a wall in the Paul Thomas winery, in elegant calligraphy, is a poster with a quote by John Stuart Mill from "On Liberty." The quote reads, "Eccentricity has always abounded when and where strength of character has abounded. And the amount of eccentricity in a society has generally been proportional to the amount of genius, mental vigor, and moral courage it contained. That too few dare to be eccentric marks the chief danger of our time."

The quotation is no less than a rallying cry for Paul Thomas, a vinous call to arms. Something of a dichotomy has evolved, wherein serious wine drinkers always drink vinifera grape wines, and these wines are almost always dry. Nonserious wine drinkers drink fruit and berry wines, and these are always sweet. Paul Thomas wines militate against this dichotomy. Most Paul Thomas fruit wines have only moderate residual sweetness. They are wines meant to accompany food, wines, in Paul Thomas's view, for the serious wine drinker.

Paul Thomas's winemaker, Brian Carter, makes table wines from vinifera grapes as well as from fruit. The grape wines include Riesling, Chenin Blanc, Muscat Canelli, Sauvignon Blanc, and Cabernet Sauvignon.

Although most makers of premium grape wines would not think of defiling their product line with fruit wines, Thomas sees no inconsistency in his combined approach. Most grape wineries rely on wines with some residual sweetness, such as Riesling and Chenin Blanc, for a major portion of their production. Paul Thomas's fruit wines are finished in a similar style, with slight residual sweetness balanced by crisp acidity.

Crimson, a rhubarb blush wine, accounts for 40 percent of the winery's production. Although it has some residual sugar, the taste is relatively dry, and the wine goes well with food. In appearance and taste, it is not totally unlike the currently popular blush wines from red grapes, scoring well against these wines in competitions.

Thomas makes a distinction between berry wines and other fruit wines. Raspberry is Paul Thomas's only berry wine. Made in small quantities, it has become a traditional release for the holidays. As Thomas explains, berries are high in acid, and they lend themselves better to somewhat sweeter wines. Still, with crisp acidity and only two percent residual sugar, Thomas's Raspberry wine is far from cloyingly sweet. Nonberry fruit wines have the appropriate balance of sugar and acid for drier wines, and these are the focus of Thomas's efforts. The "fruit" wines include Dry Bartlett Pear, and Crimson. Apricot, nectarine, and cherry wine are made as time and production facilities permit.

Federal regulations prohibit vintage dating of fruit and berry wines, but the lot numbers on Paul

Paul Thomas.

Thomas wines tell the story. Lot 786, for example, means that the fruit was crushed and fermented in July of 1986.

Paul Thomas became interested in wine on a trip to Paris in 1960, and has been studying and drinking wine ever since. He began making vinifera grape wine at home in 1968. A Wenatchee native, some of his friends from the area suggested he make wine from Bing cherries, and so began his interest in table wines made from fruits.

When the time came to open a commercial winery, Thomas decided it would be better to enter the market with a unique product, nearly dry, premium fruit wines, rather than trying to improve on and compete with the vinifera grape wines already on the market. Thomas is increasingly shifting more of his emphasis to grape wines, but the popularity of Crimson has proven the success of his original thesis—and there has been little competition.

TUCKER CELLARS

Route 1, Box 1696
Sunnyside, Washington 98944
(509) 837-8701

Wine Production
6,000 cases

Vineyards
55 acres

Year First Planted
1979

First Vintage
1981

Leading Wines
Riesling, Muscat Canelli, Gewurztraminer

In the heart of the Yakima Valley, the small agricultural community of Sunnyside is moving apace with the rest of the world. Local motels host small fraternal conventions. A well-known fast food restaurant chain and other modern day artifacts affirm the certainty of change, yet some of the changes echo and reaffirm the community's unchanging historical roots. Founded in the 1980s amidst Washington state's winegrowing boom, Tucker Cellars traces its own roots to the very beginnings of Washington's vinifera wine industry.

Born in 1930, Dean Tucker has lived all his life on the family farmlands near Sunnyside.

Dean's father, M. F. Tucker, was one of the original growers supplying grapes to Washington's first vinifera grape winery, the Upland Winery at Sunnyside. William B. Bridgman founded the Upland Winery shortly after repeal of Prohibition and brought in a winemaker from Europe to make the wines. The Tucker family's first vineyard included Malvoisie, Muscat, Riesling, and Semillon grapes. A large photograph of Dean Tucker as a boy in the family vineyards now hangs in the Tucker Cellar's tasting room.

In his authoratative book *The Wines of America,* Leon Adams reports tasting some of the Upland wines in the 1940s and finding them poorly made. The wines were withdrawn from sale, and Upland went into a decline leading to its eventual demise. With little market for the grapes, the Tuckers moved off their vineyard property, and shortly thereafter, the vineyards were pulled up, and the land planted to sugar beets.

Dean Tucker has seen crops come and go as interests and needs wax and wane. After sugar beets came orchards, then concord grapes and

Dean Tucker.

row crops, then sugar beets again. Then in 1980, on 22 acres of the Tucker family's 500 acre farm, the Tuckers again planted wine grapes. This time, the Tuckers opened a winery of their own, adjacent to the family fruit and vegetable market on the outskirts of Sunnyside.

After several generations, the Tucker farm is still very much a family business. All of Tucker's four children help operate various aspects of the enterprise. The farm includes an 80 acre orchard, hay, and a variety of row crops. The diversification provides a steady year-round work cycle for the Tucker family and their employees. After the apples are picked, the grapes are ready for harvest and crush. Late fall and winter allow time for work in the winery. Spring brings on furious planting, and the main asparagus harvest.

Begun as a secondary element in the family's farm operations, the Tucker winery is emerging as an important focal point and flagship for the family business. Kay Simon was retained as consulting winemaker, and son Randy returned to the family business to manage winery operations. In addition to traditional Yakima Valley grape varieties, the Tuckers are experimenting with Pinot Noir grown on cooler, north-sloping growing sites.

The muted background mosaic for Tucker's redesigned wine label features symbols for some of the family's other food products, including honeycomb, peaches, cherries, and popcorn, echoing a growing line of Gourmet food items under the Tucker label. Besides wines, a winery visit offers the opportunity to purchase the specialty food items, and fresh fruits and vegetables from the Tucker farm.

MANFRED VIERTHALER WINERY

17136 Highway 410
Sumner, Washington 98390
(206) 863-1633

Wine Production
6,000 cases

Vineyards
6 acres

Year First Planted
1976

First Vintage
1976

Leading Wines
Riesling, Gewurztraminer

Built in a Bavarian architectural style, the Manfred Vierthaler winery and restaurant is located on El-Hi Hill overlooking the Puyallup River Valley. One of the few wineries making wine from western Washington grapes, Vierthaler's own vineyard is planted on the steep slope surrounding the winery, but most of the acreage is under contract with growers on Vashon Island, and in the Puyallup and Carbon River Valleys near Orting. Gutedel, Muller-Thurgau, and Riesling are the principal varieties.

Although Vierthaler produces wine from western Washington grapes, most of the wine is made from California grape juice. The wines from the California juice have the word "American" included on the label. Some of Vierthaler's generic wine names are unique and fanciful. They include Moselle, American Rhine Rose, Late Harvest American Burgundy, and Late Harvest Rose of Pinot Noir.

Though he has lived most of his life in America, Vierthaler was born in Germany, and, as described in the winery's literature, is a direct descendant of the Emperor Charlemagne, as well as some of the royal families of Bavaria. In discussing the criteria for labeling a wine "Late Harvest," Vierthaler refers to German wine laws, and speaks of sugar levels in terms of the German Oechsle scale. From Vierthaler's perspective, "Late Harvest" wines should be designated as such based solely on the sugar content of the grapes—or grape juice. From this point of view, most of the wines from California's hot Central Valley would be considered "Late Harvest"—or better.

In the same building as the winery and tasting room is the Roofgarden restaurant, overlooking the Puyallup River Valley. Included on the menu are vineyard snails in herb butter, breaded wild boar filets, and hippopotamus roast, as well as more conventional German and American dishes.

WATERBROOK WINERY

Route 1, Box 46
McDonald Road
Lowden, Washington 99360
(509) 529-4770

Wine Production
4,500 cases

Vineyards
none

First Vintage
1984

Leading Wines
Sauvignon Blanc, Merlot, Chardonnay

Eric and Janet Rindal worked at the nearby L'Ecole 41 winery during its first crush. Inspired by the experience, the Rindals decided to start a winery of their own. Janet Rindal is a Walla Walla Valley native. A building on one of her family's farms houses the winery.

Most Washington wineries produce Riesling, Chenin Blanc, or other varieties typically finished with some residual sweetness. Preferring "food wines" in a European style, the Rindals shun the grape varieties that are usually finished slightly sweet, in favor of grape varieties that traditionally make the best dry wines—Sauvignon Blanc, Chardonnay, Semillon, Cabernet Sauvignon, and Merlot.

Waterbrook's white wines strike a balance between a highly fruity style and a style that sacrifices the fruit of the grape for richer flavors and textures. Part of the Chardonnay is fermented in oak barrels, part in stainless steel. The portion in the barrel is left on the lees (the sediment of yeast and grape solids) following the completion of fermentation. The Chardonnays are put through a malolactic fermentation and blended together prior to bottling.

Rindal does not put his Sauvignon Blanc through a malolactic fermentation, letting the grape's more angular profile and herbaceous character assert itself. If the Sauvignon Blanc needs any toning down, Rindal blends in a companion grape, Semillon.

To cut down on the grassy element typical of many Columbia Valley grapes, the juice for Rindal's white wines is left in contact with the skins only briefly prior to fermentation. If possible, Rindal avoids adding sulfur dioxide at crush which he believes causes the wine to pick up astringency and bitterness from the skins.

Waterbrook white wines were the first on the market, but Cabernet Sauvignon and Merlot are a major focus for the winery. Rindal believes in keeping the red wines a little "dirty" in the earlier stages of winemaking, not filtering the wine before it goes into the aging barrels, and letting the wine rest on the sediment longer before racking. Such practices tend to produce more complex flavors in the finished wine.

One of the Northwest's earliest winegrowing regions, the Walla Walla Valley is one of the newer regions to join the Washington wine renaissance. The small band of Walla Walla winemakers is a cohesive group, and the Rindals share its perspective in their dedication to traditional French grape varieties made into dry wines to complement food.

WOODWARD CANYON WINERY

Route 1, Box 387
Lowden, Washington 99360
(509) 525-4129

Wine Production
2,000 cases

Vineyards
10 acres

Year First Planted
1977

First Vintage
1981

Leading Wines
Chardonnay, Cabernet Sauvignon

The Walla Walla Valley is one of three Washington viticultural areas recognized by the Bureau of Alcohol, Tobacco, and Firearms (BATF). Darcey Fugman-Small, a land use planner for Walla Walla County, and wife of winemaker Rick Small, prepared the BATF petition for the Walla Walla Valley viticultural area.

The Walla Walla Valley, extending across the state boundary into Oregon, does not have many acres in vines, but it is one of the Northwest's oldest grape growing areas. The Smalls' Woodward Canyon Winery is part of a resurgent interest in Walla Walla Valley grape growing and winemaking.

The Walla Walla area is relatively cooler and moister than most of Washington's major grape growing areas. Woodward Canyon's small, terraced, Chardonnay vineyard is equipped for drip irrigation, but is usually dry-farmed.

Most Washington Chardonnays are made in a fresh, fruity style. Wines in this style are immediately appealing, but typically lack dimension. Small's Chardonnays are very Burgundian in style. They are barrel fermented in French oak, put through a malolactic fermentation, and left in contact with the lees. Small's Chardonnays are less fruity, but rich with complex flavors and textures.

For those who prefer a rich, Burgundian-style Chardonnay, and have wondered if Washington was capable of producing such a wine, Small's Chardonnays answer emphatically in the affirmative. His more recent Chardonnays set new benchmarks for Washington Chardonnay.

Because so few Walla Walla grapes were available, most of Woodward Canyon's earlier wines were made from grapes grown outside the Walla Walla Valley. In 1983, Small's Cabernet Sauvignon, his best to that date, was made partially from Walla Walla grapes. One of his 1984 Cabernet Sauvignons, made entirely from Walla Walla Valley grapes, from the Seven Hills Vineyard, on the Oregon side of the border, was even better. The Walla Walla Valley may become one of the state's prime Cabernet Sauvignon growing areas. Small's excellent Cabernets only reinforce that prospect.

WORDEN'S WASHINGTON WINERY

7217 West 15th
Spokane, Washington 99204
(509) 455-7835

Wine Production
15,000 cases

Vineyards
none

First Vintage
1980

Leading Wines
Riesling, Gamay Beaujolais Rose, Chenin Blanc

A native of the Columbia Valley, Jack Worden was looking to expand his apple orchards when he got caught up in the enthusiasm of Washington's wine boom. A transition from growing apples to growing grapes seemed like a logical course of action, but at the time, Washington had more than ample vineyard acreage but too few wineries, so Worden set aside the idea of grape growing to open Spokane's first commercial winery in the modern era.

Ninety percent of Worden's grapes come from the 80 acre Moreman Vineyard near Pasco. The Moreman grapes display a distinctive style, and have shown well in comparison with grapes from other growers in the area. The vineyard's Sauvignon Blanc has been particularly good.

Worden had produced very little red wine, focusing primarily on white wine varieties usually finished with some residual sweetness, such as Riesling, Chenin Blanc, and Gewurztraminer. Consumer demand dictated his choice, but increasing consumer interest in red and the drier white wines from Washington is prompting Worden to adjust his emphasis. Nearly half of Worden's production is in Riesling, but production of red wines and Chardonnay will increase in the coming years.

Worden's Sauvignon Blanc is finished with a trace of residual sweetness, a currently popular style for Washington Sauvignon Blanc. The Sauvignon Blanc and Chardonnay are aged in small French oak barrels. Cabernet Sauvignon and Merlot are aged in American oak. In some vintages, Cabernet Sauvignon is blended with up to 50 percent Merlot for texture, and for the grape's inherent softening effect.

A specialty of the winery, Worden produces a Gamay Beaujolais Rose from the Gamay clone of Pinot Noir. The wine is made in a fresh, fruity style with slight residual sweetness.

When conditions are right, Worden's produces special late harvest dessert wines. Riesling and Gewurztraminer are the major varieties for these rich sweet wines. The grapes for late harvest wines are often picked up to two months or more after the regular harvest. Some of Worden's late harvest wines, produced in small quantities, are available only at the winery.

A long-time fruit grower, Jack Worden is still considering a vineyard of his own, a decision that will be made in the next few years as the variables of grape supply, wine production, and consumer demand sort themselves out.

Worden's tasting room.

YAKIMA RIVER WINERY

North River Road
Route 1, Box 1657
Prosser, Washington 99350
(509) 786-2805

Wine Production
25,000 cases

Vineyards
none

First Vintage
1979

Leading Wines
Late Harvest Rieslings, Chardonnay, Chenin Blanc

A pipefitter by profession and a resident of New York, John Rauner and his wife, Louise, first encountered Washington grapes on a vacation trip through the state in 1974. A home winemaker for many years, Rauner purchased a few grapes and made two gallons of wine in their travel trailer. Rauner was impressed by the fruit. Even under the primitive conditions of the travel trailer, the wine was far superior to what he had made in New York. The following year, the Rauners moved to the Yakima Valley and began preparations for their winery.

Unlike most Washington wineries located on the east side of the Cascades, the Yakima River Winery, with only three acres of vines, relies almost totally on grapes purchased from independent growers. Arguments abound both for and against this arrangement. From his perspective, Rauner believes he could not do justice to both grape growing and winemaking—both highly demanding and time consuming activities. Rauner develops a close working relationship with his growers, and provides additional quality incentives by frequently displaying vineyard names on Yakima River's labels.

Rauner believes that by not owning any vineyards, he can select the best available grapes. If he had his own vineyard, Rauner reasons, he would be committed to his own grapes whether or not his vineyard site proved good or bad. "Some people ask," says Rauner, "if I don't feel at a disadvantage in not having my own vineyard. I say no—I would feel at a disadvantage if I did have my own vineyard."

Nearly all of Yakima River's grapes come from the Yakima Valley, and most come from smaller vineyards. Many come from the Ceil du Cheval Vineyard at the far eastern end of the

John Rauner.

valley. The vineyard, on the lower slopes of Red Mountain, ripens early and is nearly free of damaging spring and fall frosts. Though cooler than much of the Columbia Basin to the east, the vineyards are among the warmest in the Yakima Valley.

For Riesling and Chenin Blanc, Rauner strives for a moderate 11 percent alcohol, a practice, that along with cool fermentation temperatures, preserves the delicate fruit flavors of these wines. Chardonnay is fermented in French oak barrels, a practice that often lends a suppleness to the wine. Somewhat unusually, Rauner's Merlot and Cabernet Sauvignon are also partially fermented in oak barrels. Pursuing a softer, more readily accessible red wine style, Rauner begins fermentation in stainless steel tanks, then at about 8 degrees Brix, takes the must off the pulp and tannic skins, and completes the fermentation in small French and American oak barrels. Made in a soft, early drinking style, restaurants are the principal target market for Rauner's red wines.

Ice wine, although produced infrequently, is one of Yakima River's specialties. In 1980, Rauner produced his first ice wine. Gewurztraminer grapes were harvested December 5, frozen on the vine at 18 degrees Fahrenheit. At pressing, the grapes yielded highly concentrated juice, measuring 40.4 Brix sugar. The wine was finished at 17 percent residual sugar and .88 acid. The second opportunity did not come until 1984, when Rauner brought in botrytised Riesling grapes frozen on the vine at two degrees above zero. The must analysis measured 44.3 Brix with a good balancing acidity reading of 1.2. Availability is limited, and the ice wines, not surprisingly, are very expensive.

IDAHO

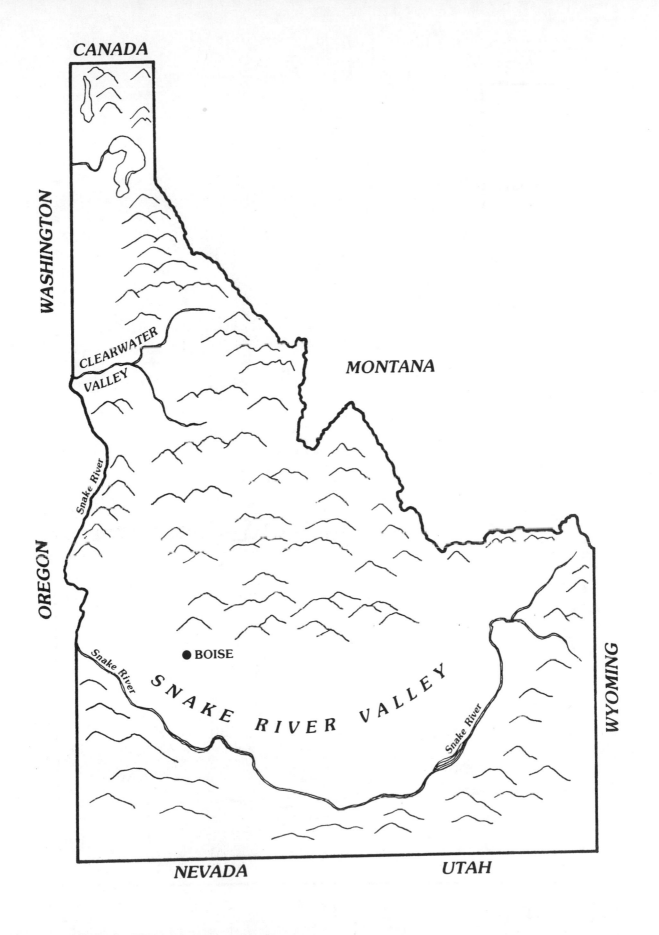

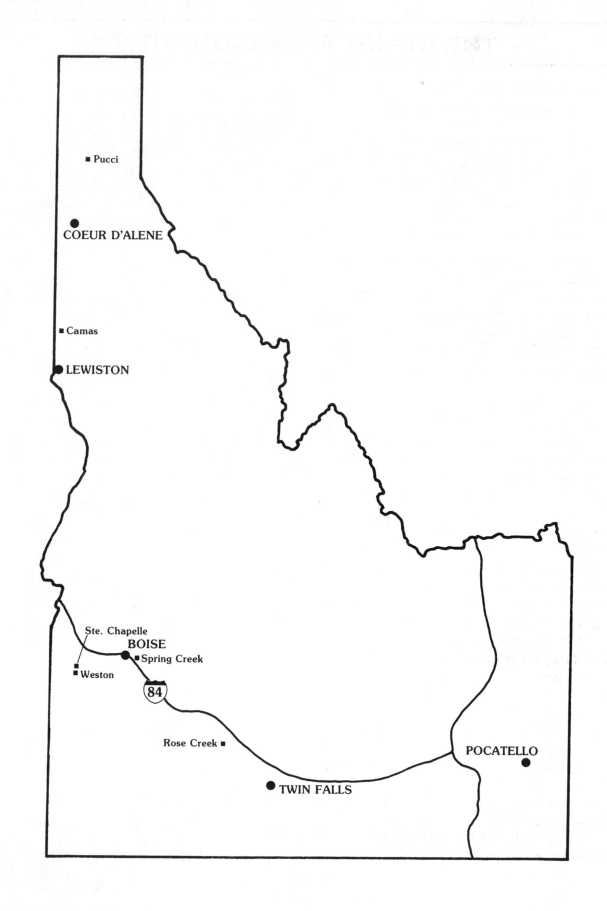

Pucci

● COEUR D'ALENE

■ Camas

● LEWISTON

Ste. Chapelle
BOISE
●■ Spring Creek
■ Weston

84

Rose Creek ■

POCATELLO
●

● TWIN FALLS

THE IDAHO WINE INDUSTRY

WINE GROWING ACREAGE
1,000 acres
WINEGROWING REGIONS
Snake River Valley, Clearwater Valley
MAJOR GRAPE VARIETIES
Riesling, Chardonnay
LEADING WINES
Chardonnary, Riesling, Gewurztraminer, Chenin Blanc

Idaho's modern day wine industry is scarcely a decade old, but its winegrowing roots are traceable to the last century, to the Clearwater River Valley, near the northwestern Idaho town of Lewiston. Winegrowing in the Clearwater Valley dates back to the 1860s. The last Clearwater Valley winery finally closed its doors in 1945.

After a long dormancy, Idaho's wine industry began anew in the 1970s. A winery in northwestern Idaho opened in 1971, making wine from hybrid grapes, but soon folded. About the same time, however, Robert Wing, a weatherman and climate researcher, planted premium vinifera grape varieties in an experimental vineyard in the Clearwater Valley. And in 1976, in the Snake River Valley in southwestern Idaho, Bill Broich crushed the first commercial vintage for Ste. Chapelle, then a tiny Snake River Valley winery that would soon become the second largest in the Northwest.

Wine aficionados outside the state did not immediately accept the idea that Idaho could have a good growing climate for premium vinifera grape wines. Idaho is usually perceived as mountainous, with a climate as rugged as the landscape, but parts of the state have a warm, relatively temperate climate. Doubts about Idaho winegrowing were rapidly dispelled in Ste. Chapelle's first few vintages. The winery's first Riesling release established Idaho as a viable winegrowing region.

It may not have been too difficult to accept that Idaho could make good Riesling. After all,

it could be reasoned, German Rieslings are grown in very cool growing regions, and it was not too farfetched that Idaho might succeed with the grape. Other grape varieties, most thought, would not fair nearly as well. Ste. Chapelle's first Chardonnay release shattered most of the remaining misconceptions. The wine was not an austere, French Chablis style of Chardonnay, but a rich, buttery, high alcohol wine, not too far removed from the prevalent California style of the day. Idaho is capable of a range of Chardonnay styles, including the leaner, crisper renditions, but that first Chardonnay proved a point—many common conceptions about Idaho winegrowing did not apply.

Unlike some earlier Idaho winegrowing efforts, all of Ste. Chapelle's wines are made from *Vitis vinifera* grape varieties. Today, virtually all of Idaho's grape wines are made from vinifera grapes. Until the 1980s, Ste. Chapelle remained Idaho's only winery. Ste. Chapelle still dominates the state's wine industry, but each new Idaho winery broadens the scope of the industry, adding its own focus and style.

Frosts, winter cold, and a relatively short growing season are Idaho's only major limitations, but within those limits, the shorter or cooler season grape varieties do well. Gewurztraminer, Chenin Blanc, and Pinot Noir have since joined the list of Idaho wines, and other varieties, in smaller quantities, have been planted to vine. So far, Pinot Noir is the most likely candidate for an Idaho red wine. Unlike Chardonnay, however, Pinot Noir is not a very flexible variety. Pinot Noir produces fine wines only if conditions are just right, and it may be some time before Idaho winegrowers know if the climate and the grape are well matched.

The Oregon and Washington wine industries have had the support of their state governments. Located in a section of the state where anti-alcohol sentiments are common, Idaho's wine industry is not as fortunate. The agribusiness environment of the Snake River Valley, however, offers a source of land and financial resources for the Idaho wine industry. Idaho's largest wineries are backed by local orchard and farming interests.

Like Oregon in the early years of its wine industry, Idaho, with more winery capacity than grapes, has turned to Washington's Columbia Valley (and now, to Oregon as well) for much of its grape supply. As Idaho's vineyard acreage increases and the vines mature, Washington grapes will play a decreasing role. Idaho's place in America's world of wine is firmly established.

IDAHO WINEGROWING REGIONS

Idaho is usually associated with mountains, forests, snow, and potatoes. Wine, made from grapes grown in Idaho, shakes our usual vision of the state. More startling still, Idaho's wines are not made from native American varieties or hybrids, but from premium *Vitis vinifera* grape varieties such as Chardonnay and Riesling. The state is separated from the moderating marine influences of the Pacific Ocean by 300 miles and two mountain ranges. How can delicate vinifera grapes grow in such a northerly inland region?

Parts of Idaho are still directly affected by the Pacific marine air. Idaho's climate is linked to the Pacific Ocean by the Columbia River and its major tributary, the Snake River. Cutting through the mountain ranges, the Columbia River carves a climatic pathway through the Northwest landscape. Marine air travels through the Columbia River Gorge and into the Columbia Valley in Washington and Oregon. The Snake River merges with the Columbia in southwest Washington, and the marine air flows further inland up the Snake River, into the tributary river valleys that feed the Snake, through the narrow and rugged Snake River Canyon on the Oregon and Idaho border, and into the broad Snake River Valley in southwest Idaho.

After such a great distance along a convoluted path, the effect of the marine air is greatly reduced, but the remaining marine influence, and the sheltered, low elevation (for Idaho) valleys make winegrowing possible. The first fall frost is delayed, and winter temperatures are not as extreme as areas more separated from the marine influence. Because of the Pacific Ocean, the Columbia River and its tributaries, and the shape of the landscape, parts of Idaho have a growing season long enough for premium wine grapes, and winters mild enough not to kill the vines.

Several areas in Idaho are suitable for winegrowing, including the Clearwater Valley near the Washington border, site of some of Idaho's earliest vineyards. Robert Wing, an independent grape researcher with a 15 year old experimental vineyard at Lewiston, has recorded 2,475 average yearly heat units with 177 frost free growing days. Further up the valley, Wing estimates that heat units exceed 2,600 with more than 180 growing days—conditions suited to a wide range of premium vinifera grape varieties. Wing estimates that some 1,000 acres in the Clearwater Valley are suitable for growing premium wine grapes. As yet, however, only the Snake River Valley in southwest Idaho has been developed in any major way.

SNAKE RIVER VALLEY

The Snake River Valley cuts a broad crescent through southern Idaho. The eastern half is a very broad, flat, nearly featureless lava plain, bordered by mountains to the north, south, and east. Toward the west, the Snake River River Valley narrows, and the landscape is featured with new and old lakebeds, terraces, small canyons, and open valleys created by the Boise River and other streams that feed into the Snake. Nearly all of Idaho's wine grapes are grown on the south facing slopes at the far western end of the Snake River Valley. Traditional orchard land, vineyards now share the choice slopes with apples, peaches, and other tree fruits.

Most Northwest vineyards are planted at elevations of less than 1,000 feet. All Snake River Valley vineyards are planted above the 2,000 foot elevation mark, and partly because of this, the valley's growing season is one of the shortest in the Northwest. In many respects, the climate is very similar to the climate of Washington's Columbia Valley. During the growing season, the days are sunny, dry, and hot. The nights are cool, and progressively more so during the final ripening of the grapes, as fall approaches and the growing season comes to a close. Like the Columbia Valley, Idaho grapes can achieve high sugar levels while retaining crisp acidity. The cool nights and moderating climate during the final ripening of the grapes preserves the acidity and the grape's delicate flavor nuances.

As might be expected, frosts and winter cold can damage the vines and reduce the grape crop in difficult years. Sun scalding is a greater threat in the Snake River Valley than in the Columbia Valley. Dominated by an interior high pressure cell in the winter, courtesy of the climatic influence of the northern Sierra Nevada Mountains to the southwest, the days are intensely bright and sunny, and the nights are cold. Bright sunlight reflecting off the snow cover can cause sun scalding as parts of the vines are warmed during the daytime, followed by a rapid temperature drop at nightfall. Any agricultural crop anywhere faces difficulties. Frosts, cold, and sun scalding are Idaho's blessings. These may be a threat to a year's grape harvest—but not Idaho's winegrowing industry.

Although the Snake River Valley climate is very similar to the Columbia Valley climate, the Snake's shorter growing season limits its range of grape varieties. Cabernet Sauvignon, for example, a variety requiring a long, warm growing season, is a major Columbia Valley variety, but little is planted in Idaho. On the other hand, in terms of the usual perception of the Idaho climate, the Snake River Valley is quite versatile. Winegrowing is not limited to Riesling or other very cool climate varieties.

Chardonnay and Gewurztraminer, both short season varieties, do exceptionally well, and Chenin Blanc, though susceptible to the winter cold, produces wines that far exceed the American reputation for the grape. Other varieties show promise as well. Ironically, Riesling is a long season grape, but it yields distinctive wines under a wide range of conditions, from very low sugars in an underripe state, to high sugars with a riper, more muscat-like character. Idaho is capable of the latter style, but as in Washington, some winegrowers are beginning to tend toward a less ripe, more delicate, refined style.

So new are the Northwest's winegrowing regions, their potential is scarcely known. Historical winegrowing efforts notwithstanding, Idaho's Snake River Valley winegrowing region is by far the youngest in the Northwest. In its first decade, each new successful variety brought new surprises, broadening the Snake River Valley's winegrowing horizons still further. It seems safe to say that the future promises more surprises and continued extensions of the Snake River Valley's winegrowing horizons.

IDAHO GRAPE VARIETIES

SNAKE RIVER VALLEY GRAPE VARIETIES

The Idaho wine industry is based solely on *Vitis vinifera* grape varieties. Occasionally a few odd plantings of non-vinifera grapes are made into wine and released for sale, but only as a novelty. Nearly all the grapes are white. Pinot Noir is the only red variety of any significant acreage, and so far its most prominent role has been in Pinot Noir Blanc and sparkling wine. Riesling and Chardonnay, by far, are the state's major varieties.

Experimental plots and small vineyards are scattered among several western Idaho river valleys, but virtually all the state's wine grapes come from Snake River Valley vineyards at the far southwestern corner of the state.

At first, many viewed Idaho as a viticulturally limited region, a region that might do acceptably well with one or two varieties, but a marginal grape growing area of limited scope. This is not the case. Idaho is not only a quality grape growing region, it is a fairly flexible one as well. Grape varieties that need long growing seasons, and grape varieties highly sensitive to winter cold do not fair as well as other varieties, but these are the only major limitations.

Because of the utter newness of Idaho's wine industry, an adequate assessment of grape varieties is scarcely feasible. Many vineyards on new growing sites, or with grape varieties new to Idaho, are only beginning to bear fruit. Idaho has few wineries, and separating a winemaker's own style from the characteristics of the region is an uncertain proposition. In experimental plots and small commercial plantings, nearly every major vinifera grape variety is grown in Idaho. As new vineyards and new varieties begin to bear fruit, new wineries come on stream, and grape growing expands to other Idaho growing areas, more will be known of the depth and breadth of the Idaho region.

CHARDONNAY put Idaho firmly on the wine map. With the first release of Chardonnay, Idaho wine could no longer be dismissed as a vinous quirk. Those expecting Idaho Chardonnays to be, at best, austere and Chablis-like were in for a surprise. The grapes ripen well while maintaining good acidity, and the wines range in style from ripe, round, and viscous to crisp, flavorful, and elegant.

An early ripening variety, Chardonnay works well in Idaho's very warm but short growing season. Although full-bodied, moderately high alcohol still wines have been the norm, Chardonnay grapes picked less ripe, at lower sugar levels, are ideally suited for production of quality sparkling wine. Chardonnay is an excellent Idaho grape.

CHENIN BLANC has a reputation for producing large quantities of mediocre wine. The reputation stems largely from the Chenin Blanc grown in some of California's warmest growing regions, where the grape is often a constituent in inexpensive jug wines. In Europe, Chenin Blanc is regarded differently. Although the grape is not as distinguished as Chardonnay, in cooler growing climates, Chenin Blanc produces far better wines than its American reputation would suggest.

Made in a fruity style with crisp acidity and some residual sweetness, Idaho Chenin Blanc shows distinctive flavors with a slightly grassy finish. The vine is susceptible to frosts and winter cold, so careful site selection and vineyard practices are important.

GEWURZTRAMINER, one of the more recent Idaho varietals, makes fine wine. The spicy character for which the variety is known comes through in Idaho Gewurztraminers. It is an early season variety that is at its flavorful best with sunny daytime heat, but moderate heat accumulations during the growing season and cool night temperatures to protect its moderate acidity, conditions that exist in its native Alsace in France, and in Idaho's Snake River Valley.

Very little Gewurztraminer is produced in Idaho, however. The variety has relatively low yields and is sometimes difficult to grow and prune. Gewurztraminer is not a fashionable wine. A difficult variety to grow economically and market on a major scale, Gewurztraminer attracts only limited interest from winegrowers and consumers.

PINOT NOIR, an early ripening grape variety, will be an important wine grape in Idaho's emerging sparkling wine industry. Destined, as well, to be the state's principal red wine grape, Idaho Pinot Noirs should be fairly ripe and full bodied. No grape variety is more sensitive to growing climate than Pinot Noir, and the Snake River Valley's growing season may be too warm and too short for the very best Pinot Noir red wines.

The grape is not easily predictable, however, and with careful site selection, Pinot Noir may make an excellent Idaho red wine. A fickle grape, winegrowers will need a succession of vintages at several growing sites before Pinot Noir's potential is better known. As a sparkling wine, Pinot

Noir has already established its place.

RIESLING, also called Johannisberg Riesling and White Riesling, is the grape that ushered in Idaho's wine industry. Still the industry's mainstay, Idaho Rieslings are fairly ripe and full flavored, yet complemented by good acidity. As in Washington, some grapes are left on the vine late in the season to become very ripe, then made into a rich wine with high residual sugar.

Ironically for a variety that does best in some of the world's coolest growing sites, principally Germany, Riesling requires a long growing season to fully ripen. With its strong varietal character, Riesling makes fine wine at a wide range of sugar levels and degrees physiological ripeness, so Idaho's short, warm, growing season with cool acid-protecting nights suit the grape well. One of the most winter hardy of all vinifera grape varieties, Riesling readily withstands Idaho's winter cold. Riesling is also a mainstay of Idaho's emerging sparkling wine industry, made into sparkling wine by the tank fermented Charmat process, the usual method for producing the German sparkling wine, Sekt.

IDAHO WINE NOTES

Ste. Chapelle, the Northwest's second largest winery, dominates the Idaho wine scene. Until recently, Ste. Chapelle was the only Idaho winery, Ste. Chapelle the only Idaho wine. Separating the stylistic signature of Ste. Chapelle from the inherent characteristics of the winegrowing region is not a certain proposition. Several new Idaho wineries have come into being, but many of their first wines have been made from Washington grapes.

Some aspects of Idaho winegrowing have emerged quite clearly. Contrary to initial speculation, the wines from Idaho's Snake River Valley are not thin, barely ripe, low in alcohol, or ethereal in nature. Because the growing season is too compact for grape varieties that require a long season, not all varieties ripen well. Those

varieties that do not require an extended growing season, however, ripen with ease, often with high sugars. The usually ample sugar levels and accompanying crisp acidity yield wines that are quite similar to those of Washington's Columbia Valley.

The wines from Idaho's two principal grape varieties, Riesling and Chardonnay, typically have a ripe quality to them. Idaho Rieslings are more like richer German Rheingaus than the more delicate wines from the Mosel, Saar, or Ruwer regions. Idaho Chardonnays are more like the fuller-bodied white Burgundies of the Cote d'Or than they are like the traditional steely wines of Chablis. These are only relative comparisons, of course. The taste and style of Idaho Rieslings and Chardonnays are distinctively their own.

Idaho winegrowers want a red wine grape. Pinot Noir, a relatively short season grape, is the most likely candidate. Unlike its Burgundian companion, Chardonnay, however, Pinot Noir is a highly fickle grape. Pinot Noir does not like hot climates. Heat burns away the grape's textural flavor complexities, leaving in their stead simple, and not always entirely pleasant, flavors.

The intense heat of Idaho summer days may be too much for the grape, yet Idaho's Snake River Valley is quite different from a typical hot climate region. The nights are very cool, and temperatures moderate rapidly during the critical ripening period. Initial results have been inconclusive, and only moderately encouraging. The real possibility for a quality Pinot Noir red wine still remains, however, and Idaho winegrowers are continuing their efforts with the grape.

Sparkling wine offers a good fallback strategy, in case the Pinot Noir proves less than satisfactory for red wine. Or, for that matter, sparkling wine is another excellent use for Pinot Noir, even if it does prove out for red wine.

IDAHO WINERIES

CAMAS WINERY

521 North Moore Street
Moscow, Idaho 83843
(208) 882-0214

Wine Production
1,200 cases

Vineyards
none

First Vintage
1983

Leading Wines
Blanc de Noir, Cabernet Sauvignon

In the mid 1970s, Stuart Scott worked in a retail wine shop, and lived within a short distance of more than a half a dozen wineries in California's Santa Clara Valley. Talking with the winemakers and helping out with cellar work spurred his interest in home winemaking. Camas Winery is an outgrowth of his hobbiest winemaking interests. A small family operation, Camas Winery is located at the family home in a residential neighborhood of Moscow, Idaho. The winery is open to the public by appointment only.

Since so few grapes are available from the nearby Clearwater Valley, Scott makes most of his wine from grapes grown in Washington's Columbia Valley. Scott likes his wines in a smoother, slightly lower acid style than the Northwest norm, and he makes his wines to fit this preference.

To achieve this style in his Chardonnay, Scott looks for amply ripe grapes. Riper grapes have lower acidity. Riper grapes also have higher sugar levels. Higher sugars mean more alcohol in the finished wine, and alcohol decreases the perception of acidity. Scott's Chardonnay, in the 13 percent alcohol range, is also finished with very slight residual sugar, not for sweetness, but for the perception of smoothness and body.

Because of limited space, Scott cannot store red wines for long aging. Scott makes his Cabernet Sauvignon in a less tannic, more delicate style, ready for drinking within two years of the vintage. Both his Cabernet and Chardonnay are aged in American oak cooperage.

A Camas specialty, Scott makes small quantities of a wine called Hog Heaven Red, a proprietary blend of grape wine and cherry wine. Scott's small winery can handle only very small quantities of fruit at a time. Since cherries ripen well before grapes, Scott can finish making the cherry wine before he makes the grape wines. Hog Heaven Red is slightly sweet, but does not taste strongly of cherries. Scott likens its character to Lambrusco.

PUCCI WINERY

1055 Garfield Bay Road
Sandpoint, Idaho 83864
(208) 263-5807

Wine Production
2,000 cases

Vineyards
none

First Vintage
1982

Leading Wines
Cabernet Sauvignon, Chardonnay

Skip Pucci's grandfather emigrated from Italy to California's Sacramento Valley and began making Zinfandel for the family table. Skip Pucci and his children continue the family tradition, making Zinfandel, and other wines, for the home— and now for commercial release. The Northwest's growing seasons are generally too short and too cool for Zinfandel, so Pucci brings in Zinfandel grapes from California and makes red, rose, and white Zinfandel wine. Pucci also makes Cabernet Sauvignon, Riesling, and Chardonnay from Washington grapes.

All Pucci's wines are fermented dry, and all are fermented and aged in oak. Pucci buys old whiskey barrels, scrapes away the char, and treats the barrels with citric acid and soda ash to remove the whiskey taste. Says Pucci, "Its taken some practice, but I've gotten so I can take a barrel com-pletely apart and reassemble it in seven minutes." Pucci's oak grape crusher is patterned after his father's.

For red wines, Pucci removes the end of a barrel, and stands it on end, for an open-topped fermenter. When the wine is almost fermented dry, Pucci transfers it to oak barrels to finish fermentation and begin the aging process. Even all the white wines, including Riesling, are fermented in oak barrels. Made in this way, the wines are less fruity than the Northwest norm, but offer an alternate set of flavors, and a touch of oak.

A construction superintendent by occupation, Pucci operates the winery in his spare time. Complete with picnic grounds, the winery overlooks Pend Oreille Lake, and the view on into Montana.

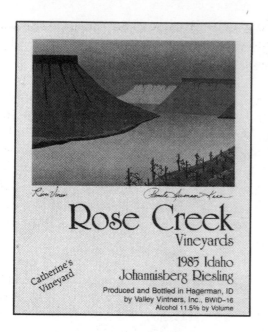

ROSE CREEK VINEYARDS

P.O. Box 356
Hagerman, Idaho 83332
(208) 837-6430

Wine Production
2,500 cases

Vineyards
6 acres

Year First Planted
1980

First Vintage
1984

Leading Wines
Riesling, Chardonnay

Idaho's major grape growing region is centered in the Snake River Valley, at the far southwestern corner of Idaho. The Hagerman area is located more than 100 miles further up the valley, almost half way across the width of the state. The Hagerman area vineyards are situated along the valley floor and at the base of the surrounding rimrocks.

Jamie and Susan Martin sold the grapes from their own small vineyard to other Idaho wineries. As acreage in the area increased, the Martins decided to open their own winery, and make wine from Hagerman grapes. The Hagerman area now has about 40 acres of grapes in several small vineyards of two to ten acres each. Riesling and Chardonnay, the two grapes that have become the Idaho standards, are proving best for the Hagerman area as well. The Martins also buy Pinot Noir from Oregon to supplement their grape supply, and add a red wine to their list.

A the high elevation of 2,700 to 3,000 feet above sea level, frosts are a risk and the growing season is usually shortened, but the proximity of the Snake River, the shelter of the Snake's canyon walls, and their heat reflectance tempers the climate. Overhead sprinkler systems also help control frosts.

Known as the melon belt for its warm climate and large melon crop, Hagerman is proving advantageous for premium wine grapes as well. In some vintages, the grapes ripen earlier than they do further down the valley, in Idaho's main vineyard region. A sandy loam soil is typical of the Hagerman area.

For their winery, the Martins refurbished a 100 year old, historic, stone building, digging out some of the earth for their cooperage area. Built in 1887, with three foot thick walls from native lava stone, the building effectively resists the heat of a southern Idaho summer, and air conditioning is unnecessary. When outside summer temperatures reach over 100 degrees, the winery cellar remains at a cool 55 degrees.

STE. CHAPELLE WINERY

Route 4, Box 775
Caldwell, Idaho 83605
(208) 459-7222

Wine Production
130,000 cases

Vineyards
260 acres

Year First Planted
1971

First Vintage
1976

Leading Wines
Chardonnay, Gewurztraminer, Riesling, Chenin Blanc

Ste. Chapelle Vineyards is a remarkable success story. The first winery in a virtually untested new winegrowing region, Ste. Chapelle almost instantly became the Northwest's second largest winery, and one of its best known wineries.

Marketed in 35 states and two foreign countries, Ste. Chapelle wines have garnered an excellent track record in regional, national, and international wine judgings—all this from a winery and wine industry that was literally non-existent barely more than a decade ago. Several Idaho wineries have since started operation, but to most people, Ste. Chapelle and Idaho wine are still virtually synonymous. Because of Ste. Chapelle's growth, Idaho winegrowing developed faster than it had in any other Northwest state.

Ste. Chapelle was founded by Bill Broich. Broich made his first wines, then formed a corporation with the Symms family, prominent fruit growers in Idaho's Snake River Valley. The Symms family provided necessary land and capital for Ste. Chapelle's meteoric growth. The Ste. Chapelle winery and estate vineyards are located on the Symms' property, in the Sunnyslope area near the Idaho communities of Nampa and Caldwell.

Ste. Chapelle crushed its first commercial vintage in 1976, from vines planted in the early 1970's. Bill Broich was Ste. Chapelle's winemaker until he left the corporation in 1985. Geoff Fischer, Broich's successor, was formerly winemaker at California's Bargetto winery. After receiving a Masters degree in enology from U.C. Davis, Fischer worked for several years as a research associate at Davis before moving on to United Vintners, and then Bargetto.

Ste. Chapelle began its existence in, what must have seemed to most, a financial and meteorological climate of great uncertainty. Many outside the state have the conception that potatoes and snow are Idaho's only viable crops, yet the Snake River Valley has long been noted for its orchards of cherries, pears, apples, peaches, and other fruits.

It is a viticultural rule of thumb that any area that can grow peaches can also grow premium vinifera wine grapes. The overwhelming success of Ste. Chapelle's vineyards and wines do not contradict this maxim. At an elevation of 2,500 feet, the area is the highest major growing region in the Northwest.

Ste. Chapelle's winegrowing climate is more similar to Washington's Columbia Valley than the climate of Oregon's major grape growing areas. Like the Columbia Valley, warm, dry, sunny days, cool nights, and cold winters characterize the climate. The growing season, however, is shorter than most of the grape growing areas in the Columbia Valley.

In cooler Oregon, vines are cane pruned, but

The old windmill presides over the winery and vineyards.

Oregon is gradually phasing out the use of Washington grapes, but Ste. Chapelle continues to look to Washington for enough grapes to satisfy its capacity, and as a source for varieties such as Cabernet Sauvignon that are better suited to the Washington climate.

Not unexpectedly, Riesling was Ste. Chapelle's first wine from Idaho grapes, soon followed by Chardonnay, Chenin Blanc, Gewurztraminer, and Pinot Noir. In 1986, Ste. Chapelle added another variety to its list of grapes, with a 25 acre planting of Sauvignon Blanc.

Many could accept the idea that Idaho was capable of producing Riesling, a cool climate grape that shows well even when underripe, but when Ste. Chapelle released a successful Chardonnay, it was a revelation, a confirmation that Idaho is not just a winegrowing curiosity, but a broadly based winegrowing climate, a stellar new wine region.

Getting the grapes to ripen is not a problem. Ste. Chapelle's Chardonnays have been the most consistently successful wines in Northwest competitions, and have received considerable national acclaim. The Chardonnays are made in a ripe, full-bodied, relatively high alcohol style—quite the opposite of high acid, austere, Chablis style that many thought would be the nature of Idaho Chardonnays. The Chardonnays clearly demonstrate that Idaho has no difficulty ripening grapes, at least those that do not demand a long growing season.

Ste. Chapelle produces excellent Gewurztraminer. In some grape growing areas, Gewurztraminer makes wines with low acidity, some bitterness in the finish, and a bubble gum character. Ste. Chapelle's Gewurztraminers show off the grape at its best, with the spiciness typical of the variety. Unfortunately, Gewurztraminer is not in high demand with the consumer, and most of Ste. Chapelle's Gewurztraminer goes into a proprietary blend with Riesling.

As with the other major Idaho varieties, Ste. Chapelle was the first to make Chenin Blanc from Idaho grapes. In America, Chenin Blanc has earned a reputation as a grape for making indifferent jug wines in large quantities. Its reputation

like Washington, Idaho vines can be cordon pruned, a less troublesome and less time consuming method that trains two permanent canes into lateral arms called cordons. From these cordons, new growth sprouts each spring. After the harvest, the seasonal canes are pruned away, leaving the lateral cordons and the vine trunk to form a stylized "T." Grape yields have been good with this method, six tons an acre for Chardonnay and Riesling.

Winter cold and spring and fall frosts can threaten the vines. Low winter temperatures are themselves a danger, made all the more threatening by sun scalding. Idaho's sunny winter days cause rapid temperature fluctuations. Bright sunlight reflecting off the snow cover can cause parts of the vines to be warmed to fifty or sixty degrees during the daytime, followed by a rapid temperature drop to zero degrees at nightfall.

Like many Oregon wineries, Ste. Chapelle made some of their first wines from Washington grapes while waiting for its own vines to mature.

is largely a consequence of the Chenin Blanc jug wines made from grapes grown in California's warmest growing regions. Chenin Blanc may not be the world's greatest wine grape, but it deserves a much better reputation.

In northern European growing climates, and in Washington and Idaho, Chenin Blanc makes wines of some distinction. Ste. Chapelle's is made in the Northwest style—fresh and fruity, with crisp acidity and some residual sweetness. Unfortunately, Chenin Blanc is susceptible to winter damage, especially when the vines are allowed to produce large grape crops, a characteristic of the variety. Idaho growers are showing reluctance to plant more of the variety because of this danger. Ste. Chapelle also makes a Chenin Blanc from Washington grapes.

Ste. Chapelle produces far more sparkling wine than any other Northwest winery, some 25,000 cases a year. Ste. Chapelle is taking an unusual approach to sparkling wine. Most wineries make premium varietal sparkling wines by the bottle fermented process. Wines made by the Charmat process, fermenting sparkling wine in pressurized tanks, are usually made from inexpensive, nondescript grape varieties and are sold at cheap prices. There are some notable exceptions. German Sekt is one. Even the very best Sekts, made from Riesling grapes, are still made in tanks by the Charmat process.

Ste. Chapelle makes small quantities of bottle fermented sparkling wine, but most of its sparkling wines are made by the Charmat process, and all are made from premium grape varieties, Riesling, Chardonnay, and Pinot Noir. The Pinot Noir sparkling wine is made from Oregon, Washington, and Idaho grapes. The Riesling and Chardonnay are made from Idaho grapes.

The three sparkling wines emphasize the fruit of the varietals rather than a yeasty character. The Riesling is moderately sweet with pronounced Riesling flavors. The Chardonnay is much drier, with a fresh, fruity character—different than most sparkling Chardonnays, but very successful. The wines are moderately priced, selling for less than bottle fermented wines made from the same varieties.

Ste. Chapelle continues to explore and expand Idaho's winegrowing horizons. Some of Ste. Chapelle's new Pinot Noir vineyards are destined for a red wine. In 1985, for the first time, Ste. Chapelle had botrytis in some of their Riesling grapes, and Ste. Chapelle produced its first botrytised wine.

In 1983, county laws changed, allowing sales of alcoholic beverages on Sundays. For eleven Sundays a year, during the summer months, Ste. Chapelle holds afternoon jazz concerts in an amphitheater adjacent to their winery and vineyards. Nationally known jazz greats are featured at some of the concerts.

Ste. Chapelle's winery is distinctive and striking. Designed by architect Nat Adams from photographs of the Ste. Chapelle chapel in Paris, its octagonal roof reaches a peak 52 feet above the winery floor. Multiple windows, 24 feet high, allow a panoramic view of the vineyards and the broad, gently sloping valley below. The tasting room and reception area are finished in oak, and contribute to the winery's warm atmosphere. By right and example, Ste. Chapelle is a showcase for Idaho's new wine industry.

Ste. Chapelle.

"THE RIVER RUNNER"
1985
IDAHO
WHITE RIESLING

Produced and Bottled by Weston Winery
Sunnyslope, Caldwell, Idaho BWID 13
Alcohol 11% by Volume
Residual Sugar 2.0% by Weight

WESTON WINERY

Route 4, Box 759
Caldwell, Idaho 83605
(208) 454-1682

Wine Production
4,000 cases

Vineyards
12 acres

Year First Planted
1981

First Vintage
1982

Leading Wines
Riesling, Chardonnay

During his student days, Cheyne Weston worked with the now defunct Charles Coury winery in Oregon, then with California's Sebastiani winery. Not long after graduating from college, Weston left Sebastiani to pursue his career as a cinematographer. After six years of extensive traveling and absences from his family in Idaho, Weston gave up his career, returned full-time to his wife and children, and returned full-time to winemaking, in Idaho's Snake River Valley.

Formerly vineyard manager for Bill Brioch's Dakota Vineyard, and crush foreman for the Ste.

Chapelle winery, Weston formed a partnership with his father and brother and founded Weston Winery in 1982. Weston's main vineyard, located near Brioch's Dakota Vineyard where Idaho's modern day wine rennaisance began, is at more than 2,500 feet above sea level, one of the highest elevations of any vineyard in the northwest. The Weston Winery, not far from the much larger Ste. Chapelle, is situated in the Sunnyslope area of the Snake River Valley in the southwest corner of the state, the heart of Idaho's wine country. Weston works with grapes from several other Snake River Valley vineyards, including the Weston/Brown Vineyard just across the state boundary, on the Oregon side of the valley near the town of Adrian, one of the easternmost vineyards in Oregon.

Not content with only Riesling and Chardonnay, Idaho's traditional grape varieties, Weston is experimenting with Gewurztraminer and Pinot Noir, and more unique still, Muscat Canelli, Sauvignon Blanc, and Zinfandel. A white wine grape, Gewurztraminer berries are actually a pinkish-brown. To carry a hint of the color into the wine, Weston leaves the skins in contact with the juice for more than the usual period, giving the wine a slight blush quality now popular with consumers. For full-bodied red wines, Zinfandel requires a very warm growing climate and long growing season. The Snake River Valley's growing season is too short for full-bodied red Zinfandels, but Weston makes a white Zinfandel, a style requiring less ripeness in the grapes.

The Weston winery.

The Chardonnays are fermented and aged in French Limousin oak barrels. Weston prefers the Limousin oak fermentation over stainless steel fermentation for the lemony, buttery qualities it imparts to the wine. Riesling, comprising 60 percent of the winery's production, is made in a variety of styles ranging from off-dry to intensely sweet.

Weston's best wines from the Idaho grapes are released with labels painted by Cheyne Weston's brother, Jeff, an Idaho artist. The ongoing label series depicts a lifestyle typifying Idaho high-country living.

THE WINERY AT SPRING CREEK

9600 Brookside
Boise Idaho 83703
(208) 939-4200

Wine Production
80,000 cases

Vineyards
260 acres

Year First Planted
1982

First Vintage
1985

Leading Wines
Chardonnay, Riesling

The virtual founder of Idaho's modern wine industry, Bill Broich left the Ste. Chapelle winery in 1985 to start a winery of his own. A minority stockholder in Ste. Chapelle, the Northwest's second largest winery, Broich wanted more control over his wines, and a winery for his children.

Broich's winery consists of two separate winemaking facilities. The ownership structure is complex, courtesy of the tax laws. Broich and his associates, Pete Eliopulos, and Jerry Bookwalter of Washington's Bookwalter Winery, bought the

Louis Facelli Winery in Wilder, Idaho. The Wilder winery is now a wine production facility only, and is not open to the public, but Broich's Boise winery, The Winery at Spring Creek, is a showcase for the Idaho wine industry. The winery building is an 8,000 square foot rock house heated by geothermal water. The grounds feature ponds, bridges, waterfalls, and viewing decks.

Wines are released under both the Broich and Spring Creek labels. The grapes come from the Sunnyslope area, at the western end of the Snake River Valley, the site of nearly all of Idaho's vineyards. A few wines for the Spring Creek label will be made from Washington grapes until the contracts established by the prior owners expire. Wines with the Broich label are made solely from Chardonnay and Riesling from Broich's own Sunnyslope vineyards.

Says Broich, "If I'm remembered for one thing when I'm gone, I hope its for selecting the best vineyard sites. I've always been very careful with site selection. I haven't accepted just any available farmland. In Burgundy, the site, the vineyard, is everything. You don't remember, or even know the winemaker of a Montrachet, but you remember Montrachet, you remember the vineyard."

Broich is radically committed to exploring the differences in vineyards. He is standardizing his winemaking procedures and methods, making separate batches of wine from each vineyard, keeping the batches separate, and bottling them separately. The differences that emerge will be the differences in the character of the vineyards.

"I'm among the first of the new winegrowers in the Northwest," says Broich. "I'm almost 40 now and I've been at this for a decade and a half. The Burgundians have been growing grapes and making wine for 2,000 years. In my time, and the time of my peers, we will have just barely begun to open a few doors for those that will follow."

Broich has a special affection for the wines of Burgundy—and for their regard of unique vineyard climates. From the beginning of his pioneering winegrowing efforts, Broich has worked with Chardonnay, the white wine of Burgundy. Broich loves Pinot Noir, the red wine of Burgundy, and would like to produce it alongside his Chardonnay.

At the present, Idaho has few Pinot Noir wine grapes, and the vines are susceptible to winter damage. Pinot Noir is an extraordinary fickle grape. It is greatly rewarding if the climate is just right, and usually disappointing if the climate is not quite perfect. Broich hopes to work with Idaho Pinot Noir, but if the climate does not prove out, he will look to Oregon for grapes.

Idaho is well proven for Riesling and Chardonnay. Broich makes his Riesling in a low alcohol, sweet style. His Chardonnay reflects the character of the Idaho fruit, and also his winemaking methods. The Chardonnay is fermented in new French oak and put through a malolactic fermentation. Before racking, the Chardonnay rests on the lees (the sediment of dead yeast cells and grape pulp) for six months or more.

Broich's Chardonnays are big, full-bodied wines, relatively high in both acidity and alcohol. The flavors are oaky and textural—and quite different from the predominant Washington and Idaho style which favors a leaner, crisper character, with fruitier, but more restrained flavors.

In discussions of winemaking, however, Broich always returns to the importance of the vineyards. He calls one of his vineyards, the W.F. Dakotah Ranch, the best in Idaho. In the Sunnyslope area, at one of the highest points in the county, the 67 acre Dakotah vineyard has a 360 degree drainage, and overlooks the famous Snake River and the Snake River Valley.

Broich takes great exception with what he feels is the prevailing attitude toward winegrowing in the Northwest. In his view, the young industry has little respect for the vineyard land, little respect for the uniqueness of individual and special vineyard growing sites. Says Broich, "The Northwest wine industry is acting as if winegrowing is nothing more than bringing in an agricultural crop and processing it into wine. Winegrowing is not just grape processing. I intend to bring the personality of the vineyard into the wines."

MISSION MOUNTAIN WINERY

P.O. Box 185
Dayton, Montana 59914
(406) 849-5524

Wine Production
7,500 cases

Vineyards
12 acres

Year First Planted
1979

First Vintage
1984

Leading Wines
Riesling, Pale Ruby Champagne

A Montana native, Tom Campbell graduated from the University of Montana in the mid 1970s with a degree in Zoology. A decade later, Campbell and his family bonded two wineries in two states, Horizon's Edge in Washington, and Mission Mountain in Montana, the state's first winery.

At the time of his graduation, career opportunities in zoology were limited. Interested in agricultural enterprises, Campbell went to the University of California at Davis for more training. The subjects in the department of enology and viticulture sounded appealing. A year later, Campbell left, having completed the course work in enology and viticulture.

In 1979, while working for a California winery, Campbell returned briefly to his native Montana to plant an experimental vineyard on his parents' property near Flathead Lake, in the western part of the state. A large inland body of water, Flathead Lake moderates the climate surrounding the lake. Among the resorts and retirement homes, flourishes a cottage fruit growing industry. Cherries are the principal crop.

Encouraged by the success of fruit growers, Campbell planted Riesling, Cabernet Sauvignon, Gewurztraminer, Pinot Noir, and Chardonnay. The Riesling failed to ripen in the short growing season, and the Cabernet Sauvignon was killed by winter cold. Gewurztraminer could be grown successfully, but in Campbell's view, the variety lacked adequate consumer appeal. Chardonnay and Pinot Noir proved promising. Both are winter hardy, relatively early season grapes, and both have considerable consumer appeal. Campbell ripped out the three other vinifera varieties and replaced them with more Pinot Noir and Chardonnay.

The growing conditions more closely resemble those of the eastern United States than any other region in the northwest. For more routine and reliable grape production, Campbell is looking to native American varieties and French-American hybrids, planting Pink Catawba for sparkling wine. A few small grape vineyards already exist along the lake, and Campbell is purchasing Captivator and Fredonia from these growers for sparkling wine.

At the present, most of Mission Mountain's wines are made in Washington from Washington grapes. Later, Campbell will ship the fresh juice from Washington grapes to Montana to ferment, and make more of the wines from Montana grapes. The Flathead Lake cherry crop suffers unreliable harvests and poor market conditions, and Campbell hopes to encourage other fruit growers on the lake to plant wine grapes.

INDUSTRY ORGANIZATIONS

Oregon Wine Advisory Board, 1324 S.W. 21st Avenue, Portland, Oregon 97201, (503) 224-8167, a promotion and public relations organization of the Oregon wine industry. The Oregon Wine Advisory Board publishes a touring guide that includes road maps of winery areas, and maps and visiting hours for individual wineries. The board acts as a clearing house for media information on the Oregon winegrowing scene.

Washington Wine Institute, 1932 First Avenue, Room 510, Seattle, Washington 98101, (206) 441-1892, a promotion and public relations organization of the Washington wine industry. The Washington Wine Institute publishes a state wine map with winery visiting hours, and informational booklets on Washington wine. The institute acts as a clearing house for media information on the Washington winegrowing scene.

BIBLIOGRAPHY AND CREDITS

Adams, Leon D. *The Wines of America*. Third Edition. New York: McGraw-Hill, 1985.

Adelsheim, David, *"Recent Developments in the Wine Industry: Pacific Northwest, West of the Cascade Mountains,"* The International Symposium on Cool Climate Viticulture and Enology. Corvallis: Oregon State University, 1985.

Adelsheim, David. *"Spacing, Training, and Trellising Vinifera Grapes in Western Oregon,"* Oregon Winegrape Grower's Guide. Portland: Oregon Winegrowers Association, 1983.

Alt, David D., and Hyndman, Donald W. *Roadside Geology of Oregon*. Missoula, Montana: Mountain Press Publishing Company, 1978.

Alt, David D., and Hyndman, Donald W. *Roadside Geology of Washington*. Missoula, Montana: Mountain Press Publishing Company, 1984.

Amerine, M. A., and Joslyn, M. A. *Table Wines, The Technology of Their Production* Second Edition. Berkeley, Los Angeles, London: University of California Press, 1970.

Amerine, M. A., and Singleton, V.L. *Wine*. Berkeley and Los Angeles: University of California Press, Ltd., 1971.

Amerine, Maynard A., and Roessler, Edward B. *Wines: Their Sensory Evaluation*. San Francisco: W. H. Freeman and Company, 1976.

Becker, Helmut. *"The Muller-Thurgau Grape Variety Celebrates its Centenary (1882-1982),"* German Wine Review. West Germany: 1982.

Becker, Helmut. Personal Communication.

Benson, Robert. *Great Winemakers of California*. Santa Barbara: Capra Press, 1977.

Bourasaw, Noel V. *"History of the Northwest Grape,"* Northwest Wine Almanac. Seattle: First Noel Publishing Company, 1986.

Brown, Ken. *"Soils and Fertilization,"* Oregon Winegrape Grower's Guide. Portland: Oregon Winegrowers Association, 1983.

Cattell, Hudson, and Miller, Lee. *Wine East of the Rockies*. Lancaster, Pennsylvania: L & H Photojournalism, 1982.

Chroman, Nathan. *The Treasury of American Wines*. New York: Crown Publishers, 1973.

Clark, D. Corbet. *Great Grapes*. Tacoma, Washington: Heath Communications, 1984.

Clore, Walter. Personal communication.

Clore, Walter, and Tukey, Ronald. *"Trellising and Training Grapes for Production in Washington,"* Washington State University Extension Bulletin 637, 1973.

Crook, Lynn. *Wine and Dine. A Culinary Guide to Washington State Wines*. Washington State Department of Agriculture, 1984

Doerper, John. *Eating Well, A Guide to Foods of the Pacific Northwest*. Seattle: Pacific Search Press, 1984.

Federal Register. *Columbia Valley Viticultural Area*. 27 CFR Part 9, Volume 49, No. 220, November 13, 1984.

Federal Register. *Umpqua Valley Viticultural Area*. 27 CFR Part 9, Volume 49, No. 62, March 29, 1984.

Federal Register. *Walla Walla Valley Viticultural Area*. 27 CFR Part 9, Volume 49, No. 25, February 6, 1984.

Federal Register. *Willamette Valley Viticultural Area*. 27 CFR Part 9, Volume 48, No. 232, December 1, 1983.

Federal Register. *Yakima Valley Viticultural Area*. 27 CFR Part 9, Volume 48, No. 65, April 4, 1983.

Fegan, Patrick W. *Vineyards and Wineries of America*. Brattleboro, Vermont: The Stephen Greene Press, 1982.

Ford, Gene. *Ford's ABC's of Wines, Brews, and Spirits*. Seattle: Murray Publishing, 1984.

Ford, Gene. *Ford's Illustrated Guide to Wines, Brews, and Spirits*. Dubuque, Iowa: Wm. C. Brown Publishers, 1983.

Folwell, Raymond J. *"Environment Surrounding Wine Grape Vineyard Development in Washington,"* Washington State University Department of Agricultural Economics Publication 85-4, 1985.

Folwell, Raymond J., and Castaldi, Mark A. *"Impacts of Input and Product Prices of Winery Returns,"* Washington State University Department of Agricultural Economics Publication 85-3, 1985.

Galet, Pierre. *A Practical Ampelography*. Ithaca and London: Cornell University Press, 1979.

Harris, Stephen L. *Fire and Ice. The Cascade Volcanoes*. Seattle: The Mountaineers, 1980.

Highsmith, Richard M.; Kimerling, A. Jon; et. al. *Atlas of the Pacific Northwest*. Corvallis: Oregon State University Press, 1979.

Holden, Ronald, and Holden, Glenda. *Touring the Wine Country of Oregon*. Seattle: Holden Pacific, 1984.

Holden, Ronald, and Holden, Glenda. *Touring the Wine Country of Washington*. Seattle: Holden Pacific, 1983.

Hutchinson, Ralph E.; Figiel, Richard; and Meredith, Ted Jordan. *A Dictionary of American Wines*. New York: William Morrow, 1985.

Jackish, Philip. *Modern Winemaking*. Ithaca and London: Cornell University Press, 1985.

Jackson, David, and Schuster, Danny. *Grape Growing and Winemaking, A Handbook For Cool Climates*. Orinda, California: Altarinda Books, 1981.

Johnson, Hugh. *The World Atlas of Wine*. New York: Simon and Schuster, 1971.

Klein, Joel. *"Wine Production in Washington State," Wine Production Technology in the United States*. Washington, D.C.: American Chemical Society, 1981.

Kleingartner, L.G. *"Data on Weather from 1924 to 1976, Irrigated Agriculture Research and Extension Center Near Prosser, Washington," Washington State University Extension Bulletin 858*, 1977.

Kliewer, Mark. *"Management Practices for Maximizing Photosynthesis and Cluster Formation in Vineyards," Proceedings of the 1984 Umpqua Grape Day*. Sutherlin, Oregon, 1984.

Lett, David R. *"Grape Variety and Site Selection with an Emphasis on the Willamette Valley," Oregon Winegrape Grower's Guide*. Portland: Oregon Winegrowers Association, 1983.

Lichine, Alexis. *New Encyclopedia of Wines and Spirits*. New York: Alfred A. Knopf, 1974.

Lichine, Alexis. *Wines of France*. Fifth Edition. New York: Alfred A. Knopf, 1973.

Loomis, Susan Herrmann. *Vineyard to Vintage: The Washington State Wine Guide*. Seattle: Washington Wine Institute, 1986.

McKee, Bates. *Cascadia. The Geologic Evolution of the Pacific Northwest*. New York: McGraw-Hill Book Company, 1972.

Meredith, Ted. *Northwest Wine*. Second Edition. Kirkland, Washington: Nexus Press, 1983.

Middleton, J. E.; Pruitt, W.P.; and Jensen, M. C. *"Climatic Data, Lower Yakima Valley, 1954-1962," Washington State University Agricultural Extension Station Circular 446*, 1965.

Morton, Lucie T. *Winegrowing in Eastern America*. Ithaca and London: Cornell University Press, 1985.

Nichol, Alexander E. *Wines and Vines of British Columbia*. Vancouver, B. C.: Bottesini Press, 1983.

Norton, R. A. *"Growing Grapes for Wine and Table in the Puget Sound Region," Washington State University Extension Bulletin 0775*, 1981.

Norton, Robert A. *"'New' Wine Grape Varieties with Potential for Western Washington," and "Grape Notes—1984."* Mount Vernon, Washington: Northwest Washington Research Unit, 1984.

Pearkes, Gillian. *Vinegrowing in Britain*. London and Melbourne: J. M. Dent & Sons Ltd., 1982.

Penning-Rowsell, Edmund. *The Wines of Bordeaux*. New York: Stein and Day, 1971.

Peppercorn, David. *Bordeaux*. London: Faber and Faber, 1982

Peterson-Nedry, Judy. *Showcase Oregon Wineries*. Portland, Oregon: H. Dieter Rickford, 1981.

Phillips, Earl L. *"Washington Climate for the counties Asotin, Benton, Columbia, Franklin, Garfield, and Walla Walla," Washington State University EM 3127*, 1970.

Purser, Elizabeth J., and Allen, Lawrence J. *The Winemakers of the Pacific Northwest*. Vashon Island, Washington: Harbor House Publishing Ltd.,1977.

Schoonmaker, Frank. *Encyclopedia of Wine*. New York: Hastings House, 1974.

Schreiner, John. *The World of Canadian Wine*. Vancouver, B. C.: Douglas and McIntyre Ltd., 1984.

Stockley, Tom. *Winery Tours in Oregon, Washington, Idaho, and British Columbia*. Mercer Island, Washington: The Writing Works, Inc., 1978.

Trenhaile, Jack, and Casteel, Terry. *"Vineyard Economics," Oregon Winegrape Grower's Guide*. Portland: Oregon Winegrowers Association, 1983.

Watson, Barney. Personal communication.

Watson, Barney. *"Promising New Varieties and Clones," Proceedings of the 1984 Umpqua Grape Day*. Sutherlin, Oregon, 1984.

Wagner, Philip M. *Grapes Into Wine*. New York: Alfred A. Knopf, 1979.

Wing, Robert N. Personal communication.

Winkler, A. J.; Cook, James A.; Kliewer, W. M.; and Lider, Lloyd A. *General Viticulture*. Berkeley, Los Angeles, and London: University of California Press, 1974.

Wolfe, Wade H., and Hirschfelt, Donna J. *"Recent Developments in the Wine Industry: East of the Cascade Mountains, Pacific Northwest, U.S.A.," The International Symposium on Cool Climate Viticulture and Enology*. Corvallis: Oregon State University, 1985.

Yoxall, H. W. *The Wines of Burgundy*. New York: Stein and Day, 1968.

MAPS AND PHOTOS

Map drawings by Cynthia Lenz, map pasteup by Linda Wilson. All photographs by author except The Hogue Cellars, Mercer Vineyards, Mount Baker Vineyards, and Snoqualmie Winery by photographer Chris Bennion, 5234 36th Avenue N. E., Seattle, Washington 98105.